*Manhattan*GMAT
the new standard

July 1st, 2010

Dear Student,

Thank you for picking up this study guide for the GMAT—we hope that it refreshes your memory of the junior-high math that you haven't used in a long time.

This book got its start a couple of years ago with one of our Los Angeles Instructors, Mike Kim. Mike had a number of private students who had not seen many of the ground-level math concepts in quite a while. Mike, being a very productive guy, took it upon himself to create a set of presentations that would give his students the runway they needed to get back up to speed on algebra, geometry, and all of the other topics tested on the GMAT. The Foundations of Math Workshops were such a success that we decided to turn Mike's work into this book.

Many people contributed to the Foundations of GMAT Math book. First is David Mahler, who tirelessly found new and better ways to explain and present various concepts. Next is Robert Wilburn, who lent a hand with several chapters. Chris Ryan, the Company's Lead Instructor and Director of Curriculum Development, provided an editorial eye to the proceedings. And last, Dan McNaney made sure that all of the words, figures and drawings were translated properly to the printed page.

At Manhattan GMAT, we continually aspire to provide the best Instructors and resources possible. We hope that you'll find our dedication manifest in this book. If you have any comments or questions, please e-mail me at andrew.yang@manhattangmat.com. I'll be sure that your comments reach the rest of the team —and I'll read them too.

Best of luck in preparing for the GMAT!

Sincerely,

Andrew Yang
President
Manhattan GMAT

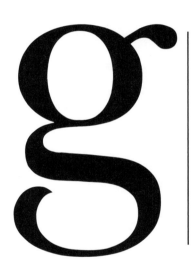

FOUNDATIONS
OF GMAT MATH

Math Strategy Guide

This supplemental guide provides in-depth and
easy-to-follow explanations of the fundamental
math skills necessary for a strong performance
on the GMAT.

Foundations GMAT of Math Strategy Guide, Fourth Edition

10-digit International Standard Book Number: 0-9841780-0-7
13-digit International Standard Book Number: 978-0-9841780-0-1

This Foundations of GMAT Math Guide is a supplement to our

8 GUIDE INSTRUCTIONAL SERIES

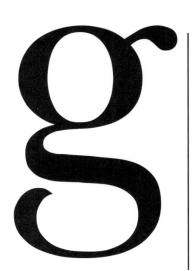

Math GMAT Strategy Guides

Number Properties (ISBN: 978-0-9824238-4-4)

Fractions, Decimals, & Percents (ISBN: 978-0-9824238-2-0)

Equations, Inequalities, & VICs (ISBN: 978-0-9824238-1-3)

Word Translations (ISBN: 978-0-9824238-7-5)

Geometry (ISBN: 978-0-9824238-3-7)

Verbal GMAT Strategy Guides

Critical Reasoning (ISBN: 978-0-9824238-0-6)

Reading Comprehension (ISBN: 978-0-9824238-5-1)

Sentence Correction (ISBN: 978-0-9824238-6-8)

HOW TO ACCESS YOUR ONLINE RESOURCES

If you...

⊳ ### are a registered Manhattan GMAT student

and have received this book as part of your course materials, you have AUTOMATIC access to ALL of our online resources. This includes all practice exams, question banks, and online updates to this book. To access these resources, follow the instructions in the Welcome Guide provided to you at the start of your program. Do NOT follow the instructions below.

⊳ ### purchased this book from the Manhattan GMAT Online store or at one of our Centers

1. Go to: http://www.manhattangmat.com/practicecenter.cfm

2. Log in using the username and password used when your account was set up.

⊳ ### purchased this book at a retail location

1. Go to: http://www.manhattangmat.com/access.cfm

2. Log in or create an account.

3. Follow the instructions on the screen.

Your one year of online access begins on the day that you register your book at the above URL.

You only need to register your product ONCE at the above URL. To use your online resources any time AFTER you have completed the registration process, login to the following URL: http://www.manhattangmat.com/practicecenter.cfm

Please note that online access is non-transferable. This means that only NEW and UNREGISTERED copies of the book will grant you online access. Previously used books will not provide any online resources.

⊳ ### purchased an e-book version of this book

Email a copy of your purchase receipt to books@manhattangmat.com to activate your resources.

For any technical issues, email books@manhattangmat.com or call 800-576-4628.

Please refer to the following page for a description of the online resources that come with this book.

YOUR ONLINE RESOURCES

Your purchase includes ONLINE ACCESS to the following:

➤ *Foundations of GMAT Math* Online Question Bank

The Bonus Online Drill Sets for FOUNDATIONS OF GMAT MATH consist of 400+ extra practice questions (with detailed explanations) that test the variety of Foundational Math concepts and skills covered in this book. These questions provide you with extra practice beyond the problem sets contained in this book. You may use our online timer to practice your pacing by setting time limits for each question in the bank.

➤ Online Updates to the Contents in this Book

The content presented in this book is updated periodically to ensure that it reflects the GMAT's most current trends. You may view all updates, including any known errors or changes, upon registering for online access.

ManhattanGMAT*Prep
the new standard

TABLE OF CONTENTS

g

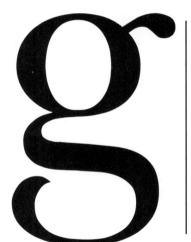

Introduction
to
FOUNDATIONS OF GMAT MATH

INTRODUCTION

Welcome to Manhattan GMAT's Foundations of GMAT Math guide!

If you've decided to take the GMAT, but are feeling a little overwhelmed by the quantitative section, you are not alone! It's likely been a while since you've seen some (or most) of these concepts. The purpose of this book is to help you relearn basic GMAT math and become proficient with a number of core math skills that are necessary to score well on the GMAT.

We'll cover a variety of topics, including
- Order of operations
- Equations with variables in them
- Combining equations
- Translating word problems into equations
- Inequalities and absolute values
- Divisibility and exponents
- Fractions, decimals, and percents
- Geometry

Perhaps you're not familiar with all of the terms above. Don't worry—you'll be quite comfortable with them by the end of this book.

Helpful Hints for Using This Book

Notes Used in this Book

Time Saving Tips suggest ways that you can speed up your work.

Safety Tips warn you about common traps and errors.

Nerd Notes give you some extra facts that you might find interesting as you learn more about mathematics.

Also, if there's a word we use that you don't understand, flip back to the glossary—you'll likely find a definition there.

Drill Sets

Our goal is not only to introduce and review fundamental math skills, but also to provide a means for you to practice applying these skills.

Toward this end, we have included a number of drill sets throughout the book. After each important topic there is a set of questions entitled "Check Your Skills". **If you find these questions challenging, it's probably a sign that you need to re-read the section you just finished.**

At the end of each chapter, you'll find drill sets that cover everything you learned in the entire chapter. These drills offer a great way to reinforce the content and make sure that you really understand how to apply the material.

How Does this Book Relate to the Other Manhattan GMAT Strategy Guides?

Manhattan GMAT publishes eight Strategy Guides that form the core of its curriculum. This Foundations of GMAT Math Guide is intended to complement Manhattan GMAT's 5 math Strategy Guides by providing a resource for more in-depth instruction in a few foundational areas throughout the curriculum.

5 Math Strategy Guides
1. Number Properties
2. Fractions, Decimals, & Percents
3. Equations, Inequalities, & VICs
4. Word Translations
5. Geometry

Foundations of GMAT Math
In-depth explanation of fundamental math topics and skills

As you work through this book, many of the concepts and techniques may be familiar to you. Feel free to skim the topics that you feel comfortable with and spend more time on other chapters. One good way to determine if you understand a chapter is to see if you can quickly perform the Check Your Skills problems distributed throughout.

Chapter 1
of
FOUNDATIONS OF GMAT MATH

EQUATIONS:
SOLVING FOR VARIABLES

In This Chapter . . .

EQUATIONS: SOLVING FOR VARIABLES

In This Chapter:

- Simplifying expressions, using the order of operations
- Solving an equation with a variable in it
- Combining multiple equations to solve for a variable (or variables)

Equations are the heart and soul of GMAT math. For almost every GMAT math problem, you will have to solve an equation. If you haven't faced equations since you were last in school, this can be intimidating. In this chapter, our objective is to help you become comfortable setting up and solving equations. We'll start with some basic equations (we'll even take out the variables at first), and then work our way up to some pretty tricky problems. Let's dive in.

The Order of Operations (PEMDAS)

$$3 + 4(5 - 1) - 3^2 \times 2 = ?$$

Before we start dealing with variables, let's spend a moment looking at expressions that are made up of only numbers, such as the example above. It's a string of numbers, with mathematical symbols in between them. Which part of the expression should you focus on first?

Intuitively, most of us think of going in the direction we read, from left to right. When we read a book, moving left to right is a wise move (unless you're reading a language like Chinese or Hebrew). However, when we perform basic arithmetic, there is an order that is of greater importance: **the order of operations**.

The order in which you perform the mathematical functions should primarily be determined by the functions themselves. In the correct order, the six operations are **P**arentheses, **E**xponents, **M**ultiplication/**D**ivision, and **A**ddition/**S**ubtraction (or **PEMDAS**).

Before we solve a problem that requires PEMDAS, here's a quick review of the basic operations.

Parentheses can be written as ( ) or [ ] or even { }.

Exponents are 5^2 ← these numbers. 5^2 ("five squared") can be expressed as 5×5. In other words it is 5 times itself twice, or 2 times.

Likewise, 4^3 ("four cubed," or "four to the third power") can be expressed as $4 \times 4 \times 4$ (4 times itself 3 times).

Roots are very closely related to exponents. $\sqrt[3]{64}$ is the third root of 64 (commonly called the cube root). $\sqrt[3]{64}$ is basically asking the question "What multiplied by itself 3 times equals 64?" $4 \times 4 \times 4 = 64$, so $\sqrt[3]{64} = 4$. The plain old square root $\sqrt{9}$ can be thought of as $\sqrt[2]{9}$. What times itself equals 9? $3 \times 3 = 9$ so $\sqrt{9} = 3$.

> **Nerd Note:** Technically, an *equation* must have an equals sign. When there are variables and/or numbers, but no equals sign, you are looking at an *expression*.

> **Safety Tip:** We will be discussing exponents and roots in more detail in Chapter 5.

Exponents and roots can also undo each other. $\sqrt{5^2}=5$ and $(\sqrt[3]{7^3})=7$.

Multiplication and Division can also undo each other. $2\times3\div3=2$ and $10\div5\times5=10$.

> **Nerd Note:** All of these rules apply to variables as well as numbers (i.e. $y\times3\div3=y$).

Multiplication can be expressed with parentheses: $(5)(4)=5\times4=20$. Division can be expressed with a division sign ($\div$), a slash (/) or a fraction bar(—): $20\div5=20/5=\dfrac{20}{5}=4$. Also remember that multiplying or dividing by a negative number flips the sign:

$$4\times(-2)=-8 \qquad -8\div(-2)=4$$

To review how to multiply larger numbers and to do long division, see the Appendix to this chapter on page 45.

Addition and Subtraction can also undo each other. $8+7-7=8$ and $15-6+6=15$

PEMDAS is a useful acronym you can use to remember the order in which operations should be performed. Some people find it useful to write PEMDAS like this:

$$PE^M/_D{}^A/_S$$

The reason that Multiplication and Division are at the same level of importance is that any Multiplication can be expressed as Division, and vice-versa. $7\div2$ is equivalent to $7\times1/2$. In a sense, Multiplication and Division are two sides of the same coin.

Addition and Subtraction have this same relationship. $3-4$ is equivalent to $3+(-4)$. The correct order of steps to simplify this expression is as follows:

Parentheses $\quad 3+4(5-1)-3^2\times2$

$3+4(4)-3^2\times2$

Exponents $\quad 3+4(4)-9\times2$

Multiplication or Division $\quad 3+16-18$

Addition or Subtraction $\quad 3+16-18=19-18=1$

Safety Tip: With the two pairs, Multiplication/Division and Addition/Subtraction, do not first solve all the additions and then all the subtractions. Instead, consider them simultaneously as you move from inside parentheses to outside and from **left to right**.

Remember: If you have two operations of equal importance, you should do them in left-to-right order: $3-2+3=1+3=4$. The only instance in which you would override this order is when the operations are in parentheses: $3-(2+3)=3-(5)=-2$.

Let's do two problems together. Try it first on your own, then we'll go through it together:

$$5 - 3 \times 4^3 \div (7 - 1)$$

P

E

M/D

A/S

> **Safety Tip:** Re-write the expression as you simplify it. It might take a bit longer but you're much less likely to make errors that require you to do the whole problem again.

Your work should have looked like this:

$$5 - 3 \times 4^3 \div (7 - 1)$$

$$5 - 3 \times 4^3 \div 6 \longrightarrow 4^3 = 4 \times 4 \times 4 = 64 \longrightarrow$$

$$\begin{array}{r} {}^{2} \\ 16 \\ \times\ 4 \\ \hline 64 \end{array}$$

$$5 - 3 \times 64 \div 6$$

$$\begin{array}{r} {}^{1} \\ 64 \\ \times\ 3 \\ \hline 192 \end{array}$$

$$5 - 192 \div 6$$

$$5 - 32$$

$$-27$$

$$\begin{array}{r} 32 \\ 6\overline{)192} \\ -18 \\ \hline 12 \\ -12 \\ \hline 0 \end{array}$$

> **Safety Tip:** If you had trouble with the last step (5 − 32), you may want to review integer addition and subtraction. This guide will assume that you are comfortable with basic arithmetic operations.

Let's try one more:

$$32 \div 2^4 \times (5 - 3^2)$$

P

E

M/D

A/S

Here's the work you should have done:

$$32 \div 2^4 \times (5 - 3^2)$$

$$32 \div 2^4 \times (5 - 9)$$

$$32 \div 2^4 \times (-4)$$

$$32 \div 16 \times (-4)$$

$$2 \times (-4)$$

$$-8$$

> **Safety Tip:** Order of operations also applies inside the parentheses.

Check Your Skills

Evaluate the following expressions.

1. $-4 + 12/3 =$
2. $(5 - 8) \times 10 - 7 =$
3. $-3 \times 12 \div 4 \times 8 + (4 - 6) =$
4. $2^4 \times (8 \div 2 - 1)/(9 - 3) =$

Answers can be found on page 29.

Solving for a Variable With One Equation

Expressions vs. Equations

So far, we've been dealing only with expressions. Now we're going to be dealing with equations. The big difference between expressions and equations is that, while expressions only have numbers and/or variables on one side of the equals sign, equations have numbers and/or variables on *both* sides of the equals sign.

Pretty much everything we will be doing with equations is related to one basic principle: we can do anything we want to one side of the equation, *as long as we also do the same thing to the other side of the equation.* Take the equation $3 + 5 = 8$. I want to subtract 5 from the left side of my equation, but I still want my equation to be true. All I have to do is subtract 5 from the right side as well, and I can be confident that my new equation will still be valid.

$$\begin{array}{rcl} 3 + 5 &=& 8 \\ -5 && -5 \\ \hline 3 &=& 3 \end{array}$$

Note that this would also work if I had variables in my equation:

$$\begin{array}{rcl} x + 5 &=& 8 \\ -5 && -5 \\ \hline x &=& 3 \end{array}$$

Next we're going to see some of the many ways we can apply this principle to solving algebra problems.

Solving Equations

But first, what does it mean to solve an equation? What are we really doing when we manipulate algebraic equations?

A solution to an equation is a number that, when substituted in for the value of a variable, makes the equation *true*.

Take the equation $2x + 7 = 15$. We are looking for the value of x that will make this equation true. What if we plugged in 3 for x? If we replaced x with the number 3, we would get $2(3) + 7 = 15$. This equation can be simplified to $6 + 7 = 15$, which further simplifies to $13 = 15$. 13 definitely does NOT equal 15, so when $x = 3$, the equation is NOT true. So $x = 3$ is NOT a solution to the equation.

Now, if we replaced x with the number 4, we would get $2(4) + 7 = 15$. This equation can be simplified to $8 + 7 = 15$. Simplify it further, and you get $15 = 15$, which is a true statement.

That means that when $x = 4$, the equation is true. So $x = 4$ is a solution to the equation.

Now the question becomes, what is the best way to find these solutions? What is an efficient way to determine what value or values of a variable will make an equation true? If we had to use trial and error, or guessing, the process could take a very long time. The following sections will talk about the ways in which we can efficiently and accurately manipulate equations so that solutions become easier to find.

Isolating a Variable

Now that we know that we're allowed to change one side of an equation, as long as we make the same change to the other side, let's look at the different kinds of changes we can make. We'll discuss these changes as we try to solve the following problem.

If $5(x - 1)^3 - 30 = 10$, then $x = ?$

To solve for a variable, we need to get it by itself on one side of the equals sign. To do that, we'll need to make a number of changes to the equation that will change its appearance, but not its value. The good news is, all of the changes we will need to make to this equation to solve for x will actually be very familiar to you—they're the PEMDAS operations!

To get x by itself, we want to move everything that isn't the variable to the other side of the equation. The easiest thing to move at this stage is the 30, so let's start there. If 30 is being subtracted on the left side of the equation, and we want to move it to the other side, then we need to do the opposite operation in order to cancel it out. So we're going to **add** 30 to both sides, like this:

$$5(x - 1)^3 - 30 = 10$$
$$+30\ \ +30$$
$$5(x - 1)^3 = 40$$

Now we've only got one term on the left side of the equation. x is still inside the parentheses, and the parentheses is being multiplied by 5, so the next step will be to move that 5 over to the other side of the equation. Once again, we want to perform the opposite operation, so we'll **divide** both sides of the equation by 5.

$$\frac{\cancel{5}(x-1)^3}{\cancel{5}} = \frac{40}{5}$$ ← These horizontal lines mean division.

$$(x - 1)^3 = 8$$

> **Safety Tip:** Whenever you are making these kinds of changes to equations, make sure that you perform an operation on the entire side of the equation, and not on specific terms.

Now at this point we could cube $(x - 1)$, but that is going to involve a whole lot of multiplication. Instead, we can get rid of the exponent by performing the opposite operation. The opposite of exponents is roots. So if the left side of the equation is raised to the third power, we can undo that by taking the third root of both sides, also known as the cube root.

$$\sqrt[3]{(x-1)^3} = \sqrt[3]{8}$$

$$(x - 1) = 2$$

> **Safety Tip:** The GMAT often uses numbers that make calculations easy. $\sqrt[3]{8}$, for instance, is 2 because $2 \times 2 \times 2 = 8$.

Now that nothing else is being done to the parentheses, we can just get rid of them, so really, the equation is:

$$x - 1 = 2$$

After that, we add 1 to both sides, and we get $x = 3$. This would have been hard to guess!

Now, take a look at the steps that we took in order to isolate x. Notice anything? We **added** 30, then we **divided** by 5, then we got rid of the **exponent** and then we simplified our **parentheses**. We did PEMDAS backwards! And in fact, when you're isolating a variable, it turns out that the simplest way to do so is to reverse the order of PEMDAS when deciding what order you will perform your operations. Start with addition/subtraction, then multiplication/division, then exponents, and finish with terms in parentheses.

Now that you know the best way to isolate a variable, let's go through one more example. Try it on your own first, then we'll go through it together.

If $4\sqrt{(x-6)} + 7 = 19$, then $x = ?$

A/S

M/D

E

P

Let's get started. The equation we're simplifying is $4\sqrt{(x-6)} + 7 = 19$. If there's anything to add or subtract, that will be the easiest first step. There is, so the first thing we want to do is get rid of the 7 by subtracting 7 from both sides.

$$4\sqrt{(x-6)}+7=19$$
$$\underline{\phantom{4\sqrt{(x-6)}}-7-7}$$
$$=12$$

Now we want to see if there's anything being multiplied or divided by the term containing an x. The square root that contains the x is being multiplied by 4, so our next step will be to get rid of the 4. We can do that by dividing both sides of the equation by 4.

$$\frac{\cancel{4}\sqrt{(x-6)}}{\cancel{4}}=\frac{12}{4}$$
$$\sqrt{(x-6)}=3$$

Now that we've taken care of multiplication and division, it's time to check for exponents. And that really means we need to check for exponents and roots, because they're so intimately related. There are no exponents in the equation, but the x is inside a square root, so that's the next thing we need to deal with. In order to cancel out a root, we can use an exponent. Squaring a square root will cancel it out, so our next step is to square both sides.

$$\sqrt{(x-6)}=3$$
$$(\sqrt{(x-6)})^2=(3)^2$$
$$x-6=9$$

> **Safety Tip:** If there are multiple terms inside a square root (e.g. $x-6$), there may not be parentheses around them, but you should treat them as if there are parentheses when dealing with order of operations.

The final step is to add 6 to both sides, and we end up with $x=15$.

Check Your Skills
Solve for x in the following equations:

5. $3(x+4)^3-5=19$

6. $\dfrac{3x-7}{2}+20=6$

7. $\sqrt[3]{(x+5)}-7=-8$

Answers can be found on page 29.

Equation Clean-Up Moves

We've covered the basic operations that we'll be dealing with when solving equations. But what would you do if you were asked to solve for x in the following equation?

$$\frac{5x-3(4-x)}{2x}=10$$

Now x appears in multiple parts of the equation, and our job has become more complicated. In addition to our PEMDAS operations, we also need to be able to simplify, or clean up, our equation. Let's see the different ways we can clean up this equation. First, notice how we have an x in the denominator (the bottom of the fraction) on the left side of the equation.

*Manhattan*GMAT*Prep
the new standard

We're trying to find the value of x, not of some number divided by x. So our first clean-up move is to **always get variables out of denominators**. The way to do that is to multiply both sides of the equation by the *entire* denominator. Watch what happens:

$$2x \times \frac{5x - 3(4 - x)}{2x} = 10 \times 2x$$

> **Safety Tip:** There's a lot more on fractions in Chapters 6 and 7.

If you multiply a fraction by its denominator, you can cancel out the entire denominator. Now we're left with

$$5x - 3(4 - x) = 20x$$

No more fractions! What should we do next? At some point, if we want the value of x, we're going to have to get all the terms that contain an x together. But right now, that x sitting inside the parentheses seems pretty tough to get to. To make that x more accessible, we should **simplify grouped terms within the equation**. That 3 on the outside of the parentheses wants to multiply the terms inside, so we need to **distribute** it. What that means is we're going to multiply the 3 by the terms inside, one at a time. 3 times 4 is 12, and 3 times $-x$ is $-3x$, so our equation becomes

$$5x - (12 - 3x) = 20x$$

Now, if we subtract what's in the parentheses from $5x$, we can get rid of the parentheses altogether. Just as we multiplied the 3 by *both* terms inside the parentheses, we also have to subtract both terms.

$$5x - (12) - (-3x) = 20x$$
$$5x - 12 + 3x = 20x$$

> **Safety Tip:** Don't forget to distribute the negative sign when subtracting multiple terms inside a parentheses.

Remember, subtracting a negative number is the same as adding a positive number; the negative signs cancel out!

Now we're very close. We're ready to make use of our final clean up move—**combine like terms.** "Like terms" are terms that can be combined into one term. For example, "$3x$" and "$5x$" are like terms because they can be combined into "$8x$." Ultimately, all the PEMDAS operations and clean up moves have one goal—to get a variable by itself so we can determine its value. At this point, we have 4 terms in the equation: $5x$, -12, $3x$ and $20x$. What we want to do is to get all the terms with an x on one side of the equation, and all the terms that only contain numbers on the other side.

First, let's combine $5x$ and $3x$, because they're on the same side of the equation. That gives us:

$$8x - 12 = 20x$$

Now we want to get the $8x$ together with the $20x$. But which one should we move? The best move to make here is to move the $8x$ to the right side of the equation, because that way, one side of the equation will have terms that contain only numbers (-12) and the right side will have terms that contain variables ($8x$ and $20x$). So now it's time for our PEMDAS operations again. Let's find x.

$$8x - 12 = 20x$$
$$\underline{-8x \qquad\quad -8x}$$
$$-12 = 12x$$
$$\frac{-12}{12} = \frac{12x}{12}$$
$$-1 = x$$

Before moving on to the next topic, let's review what we've learned.

1. You can do whatever you want to one side of the equation, as long as you do the same to the other side at the same time.

2. To isolate a variable, you should perform the PEMDAS operations in reverse order:

   a) Addition/Subtraction
   b) Multiplication/Division
   c) Exponents/Roots
   d) Parentheses

3. To clean up an equation:

   a) Get variables out of denominators   Example: $(x+2) \times \dfrac{3x-7}{x+2} = 7 \times (x+2)$
       by multiplying both sides

   b) Simplify grouped terms by   Example: $4x - 6(x-6) \rightarrow 4x - 6x + 36$
       multiplying or distributing

   c) Combine similar or like terms   Example: $2x - 7 - 6x = 8 \rightarrow -4x - 7 = 8$

Check Your Skills

Solve for x in the following equations.

8. $\dfrac{11 + 3(x+4)}{x-3} = 7$

9. $\dfrac{-6 - 5(3-x)}{2-x} = 6$

10. $\dfrac{2x + 6(9-2x)}{x-4} = -3$

Answers can be found on page 30.

Solving for Variables with Two Equations

Many GMAT problems, including word problems, give you two equations, each of which has two variables. To solve such problems, you'll need to solve for one or each of those variables. At first glance, this problem may seem quite daunting:

If $3x + y = 10$ and $y = x - 2$, what is the value of y?

Maybe you've gotten pretty good at solving for one variable, but now you face two variables and two equations!

> **Nerd Note:** As you get into harder GMAT problems, you'll be asked to solve for combinations of variables, for instance, "What is the value of $x + y$?"

You might be tempted to test numbers, and indeed you could actually solve the above problem that way. Could you do that in under two minutes? Maybe not. Fortunately, there is a much faster way.

Substitution

One method for combining equations is called substitution. In substitution, we insert one equation into the other. The goal is to end up with one equation with one variable, because once you get a problem to that point, you know you can solve it!

There are four basic steps to substitution. We'll go through them one by one with this sample question. If $3x + y = 10$, and $y = x - 2$, then $y = ?$

> **Nerd Note:** In general, you need two different equations to solve for two variables, three different equations for three variables, etc.

Step One is to isolate one of the variables in one of the equations. For this example, y is already isolated in the second equation. $y = x - 2$

For Step Two, it is important to understand that the left and right sides of the equation are equivalent. This may sound obvious, but it has some interesting implications. If y equals $x - 2$, then that means we could replace the variable y with the expression $(x - 2)$ and the equation would have the same value. And in fact, that's exactly what we're going to do. Step Two will be to go to the first equation, and substitute (hence the name) the variable y with its equivalent, $(x - 2)$. So:

$$3x + y = 10 \rightarrow 3x + (x - 2) = 10$$

Now for Step Three, we have one equation and one variable, so the next step is to solve for x.

$$3x + x - 2 = 10$$
$$4x = 12$$
$$x = 3$$

> **Safety Tip:** Whenever you substitute one value for another, put parentheses around the new value.

Now that we have a value for x, Step Four is to use that value to solve for our second variable, y.

$$y = x - 2 \rightarrow y = (3) - 2 = 1$$

So the answer to our question is $y = 1$. It should be noted that Step Four will only be necessary if the variable you solve for in Step Three is not the variable the question asks for. The question asked for y, but we found x, so Step Four was needed to answer the question.

Now that you've gotten the hang of substitution, let's try a new problem:

If $2x + 4y = 14$ and $x - y = -8$, what is the value of x?

As we learned, the first step is to isolate our variable. Because the question asks for x, the simplest way to do this is in this problem is to manipulate the second equation to isolate y. Taking this approach will make Step Four unnecessary and save us time.

$x - y = -8$ becomes $x = -8 + y$, which becomes
$x + 8 = y$

> **Time Saving Tip:** If the question asks for the value of one variable (x) then you should isolate the other variable (ex. y) in step one.

Then for Step Two we can substitute for y in the first equation.

$2x + 4y = 14$
$2x + 4(x + 8) = 14$

> **Nerd Note:** Solving for a variable (or both) when given two equations is called *solving a system of equations.*

Now for Step Three we isolate x.

$2x + 4x + 32 = 14$
$6x = -18$
$x = -3$

So the answer to our question is $x = -3$.

Check Your Skills

Solve for x and y in the following equations.

11. $x = 10$
    $x + 2y = 26$

12. $x + 4y = 10$
    $y - x = -5$

13. $6y + 15 = 3x$
    $x + y = 14$

Answers can be found on pages 30–31.

Check Your Skills Answer Key:

1. $-4 + 12/3 =$ Divide first
    $-4 + 4 = 0$ Then add the two numbers
    Answer: 0

2. $(5 - 8) \times 10 - 7 =$
    $(-3) \times 10 - 7 =$ First, combine what is inside the parentheses
    $-30 - 7 =$ Then multiply -3 and 10
    $-30 - 7 = -37$ Subtract the two numbers
    Answer: -37

3. $-3 \times 12 \div 4 \times 8 + (4 - 6)$
    $-3 \times 12 \div 4 \times 8 + (-2)$ First, combine what's in the parentheses
    $-36 \div 4 \times 8 + (-2)$ Multiply -3 and 12
    $-9 \times 8 - 2$ Divide -36 by 4
    $-72 + (-2) = -74$ Multiply -9 by 8 and subtract 2
    Answer: -74

4. $2^4 \times (8 \div 2 - 1) / (9 - 3) =$
    $2^4 \times (4 - 1) / (6) =$ $8/2 = 4$ and $9 - 3 = 6$
    $16 \times (3) / (6) =$ $4 - 1 = 3$ and $2^4 = 16$
    $48/6 =$ Multiply 16 by 3
    $48/6 = 8$ Divide 48 by 6
    Answer: 8

5. $3(x + 4)^3 - 5 = 19$
    $3(x + 4)^3 = 24$ Add 5 to both sides
    $(x + 4)^3 = 8$ Divide both sides by 3
    $(x + 4) = 2$ Take the cube root of both sides
    $x = -2$ Remove the parentheses, subtract 4 from both sides
    Answer: $x = -2$

6. $\dfrac{3x - 7}{2} + 20 = 6$

    $\dfrac{3x - 7}{2} = -14$ Subtract 20 from both sides

    $3x - 7 = -28$ Multiply both sides by 2
    $3x = -21$ Add 7 to both sides
    $x = -7$ Divide both sides by 3
    Answer: $x = -7$

7. $\sqrt[3]{(x + 5)} - 7 = -8$

    $\sqrt[3]{(x + 5)} = -1$ Add 7 to both sides
    $x + 5 = -1$ Cube both sides, remove parentheses
    $x = -6$ Subtract 5 from both sides
    Answer: $x = -6$

8. $\dfrac{11 + 3(x + 4)}{x - 3} = 7$

$11 + 3(x + 4) = 7(x - 3)$	Multiply both sides by the denominator $(x - 3)$
$11 + 3x + 12 = 7x - 21$	Simplify grouped terms by distributing
$23 + 3x = 7x - 21$	Combine like terms (11 and 12)
$23 = 4x - 21$	Subtract $3x$ from both sides
$44 = 4x$	Add 21 to both sides
$11 = x$	Divide both sides by 4

Answer: $x = 11$

9. $\dfrac{-6 - 5(3 - x)}{2 - x} = 6$

$-6 - 5(3 - x) = 6(2 - x)$	Multiply both sides by the denominator $(2 - x)$
$-6 - 15 + 5x = 12 - 6x$	Simplify grouped terms by distributing
$-21 + 5x = 12 - 6x$	Combine like terms (-6 and -15)
$-21 + 11x = 12$	Add $6x$ to both sides
$11x = 33$	Add 21 to both sides
$x = 3$	Divide both sides by 11

Answer: $x = 3$

10. $\dfrac{2x + 6(9 - 2x)}{x - 4} = -3$

$2x + 6(9 - 2x) = -3(x - 4)$	Multiply by the denominator $(x - 4)$
$2x + 54 - 12x = -3x + 12$	Simplify grouped terms by distributing
$-10x + 54 = -3x + 12$	Combine like terms ($2x$ and $-12x$)
$54 = 7x + 12$	Add $10x$ to both sides
$42 = 7x$	Subtract 12 from both sides
$6 = x$	Divide both sides by 7

Answer: $x = 6$

11. $x = 10$
         $x + 2y = 26$

$(10) + 2y = 26$	Substitute 10 for x in the second equation
$2y = 16$	Subtract 10 from both sides
$y = 8$	Divide both sides by 2

Answer: $x = 10$, $y = 8$

12. $x + 4y = 10$
     $y - x = -5$

$y = x - 5$	Isolate y in the second equation
$x + 4(x - 5) = 10$	Substitute $(x - 5)$ for y in the first equation
$x + 4x - 20 = 10$	Simplify grouped terms within the equation
$5x - 20 = 10$	Combine like terms (x and $4x$)
$5x = 30$	Add 20 to both sides
$x = 6$	Divide both sides by 5
$y - (6) = -5$	Substitute 6 for x in the second equation to solve for y
$y = 1$	Add 6 to both sides
Answer: $x = 6$, $y = 1$	

13. $6y + 15 = 3x$
     $x + y = 14$

$2y + 5 = x$	Divide the first equation by 3
$(2y + 5) + y = 14$	Substitute $(2y + 5)$ for x in the second equation
$3y + 5 = 14$	Combine like terms ($2y$ and y)
$3y = 9$	Subtract 5 from both sides
$y = 3$	Divide both sides by 3
$x + (3) = 14$	Substitute (3) for y in the second equation to solve for x
$x = 11$	
Answer: $x = 11$, $y = 3$	

Chapter Review: Drill Sets

DRILL SET 1:

Drill 1: Evaluate the following expressions.

1. $19 \times 5 =$
2. $39 - (25 - 17) =$
3. $17(6) + 3(6) =$
4. $3(4 - 2) \div 2 =$
5. $15 \times 3 \div 9 =$
6. $(9 - 5) - (4 - 2) =$
7. $14 - 3(4 - 6) =$
8. $6/3 + 12/3 =$
9. $-5 \times 1 \div 5 =$
10. $\dfrac{-3 + 7}{-4} =$

Drill 2: Evaluate the following expressions.

1. $(4)(-3)(2)(-1) =$
2. $5 - (4 - (3 - (2 - 1))) =$
3. $7 - (6 + 2) =$
4. $7 - (6 - 2) =$
5. $-4(5) - 12/(2 + 4) =$
6. $-3(-2) + 6/3 - (-5) =$
7. $-12 \times 2/(-3) + 5 =$
8. $(6 \times 5) + 14/7 =$
9. $32/(4 + 6 \times 2) =$
10. $-10 - (-3)^2 =$

Drill 3: Evaluate the following expressions.

1. $-5^2 =$
2. $2^3/2 =$
3. $-2^3/2 =$
4. $(3^2 \times 24) / (2^3) =$
5. $36 / (2 + 2^2) \times 4 \times (4 + 2) =$
6. $\sqrt{6^2} + (-3^3) =$
7. $5^3 - 5^2 =$
8. $\sqrt{81} - \sqrt{9} =$
9. $[\sqrt{16} + (4 \times 2^3)] / (-2)^2 =$
10. $(3 + (-2)^3)^2 - 3^2 =$

Drill 4: Evaluate the following expressions.

1. $4^3 - 4^2 =$
2. $5^{(2+1)} + 25$

3. $(-2)^3 - 5^2 + (-4)^3$
4. $(63/3^2)^3/7$
5. $5(1) + 5(2) + 5(3) + 5(4) =$
6. $\sqrt{3^4 / 9} =$
7. $3 \times 7^2 =$
8. $4^2(3 - 1) - 19 + 4(-2) =$
9. $\dfrac{(3 + 7)(5 - 3)}{(5 - 4)(5 - 4)} =$
10. $3 \times 99 - 2 \times 99 - 1 \times 99 =$

DRILL SET 2:

Drill 1: Solve for the variable.

1. $5x - 7 = 28$
2. $14 - 3x = 2$
3. $z - 11 = 1$
4. $3(7 - x) = 4(1.5)$
5. $7x + 13 = 2x - 7$
6. $13 - (-2w) = 6 + 3(11)$
7. $6a/3 = 12 + a$
8. $13x + 2(x + 5) - 7x = -70$
9. $(z - 4)/3 = -12$
10. $y - 15/3 = 7$

Drill 2: Solve for the variable.

1. $y + 3y = 28$
2. $15z + (4z/2) = 51$
3. $3t^3 - 7 = 74$
4. $7(x - 3) + 2 = 16$
5. $z/6 = -8$
6. $1{,}200x + 6{,}000 = 13{,}200$
7. $(1{,}300x + 1{,}700)/43 = 100$
8. $90x + 160 + 5x - 30 + 5x - 30 = 900$
9. $4(x + 2)^3 - 38 = 70$
10. $4(5x + 2) + 44 = 132$

Drill 3: Solve for the variable.

1. $\sqrt{x} = 3 \times 5 - 20 \div 4$
2. $-(x)^3 = 64$
3. $x^3 = 8$
4. $4x^3 - 175 = 325$
5. $9 = y^3/3$
6. $-\sqrt{w} = -5$
7. $\dfrac{\sqrt{3x + 1}}{2} - 1 = 3$

8. $128 = 2z^3$

9. $5\sqrt[3]{x} + 6 = 51$

10. $\dfrac{\sqrt{x-2}}{5} - 20 = -17$

Drill 4: Isolate x.

1. $3x + 2(x + 2) = 2x + 16$

2. $\dfrac{3x+7}{x} = 10$

3. $4(-3x - 8) = 8(-x + 9)$

4. $3x + 7 - 4x + 8 = 2(-2x - 6)$

5. $2x(4 - 6) = -2x + 12$

6. $\dfrac{3(6-x)}{2x} = -6$

7. $\dfrac{13}{x+13} = 1$

8. $\dfrac{10(3x+4)}{10-5x} = 2$

9. $\dfrac{8 - 2(-4 + 10x)}{2 - x} = 17$

10. $\dfrac{50(10 + 3x)}{50 + 7x} = 50$

DRILL SET 3:

Solve for the value of both variables in each system of equations. Explanations will follow the four steps discussed in the chapter. Not every step will be necessary to answer every question.

Drill 1:

1. $7x - 3y = 5$
   $y = 10$
2. $2h - 4k = 0$
   $k = h - 3$
3. $64 - 2y = x$
   $y = 33$
4. $3q - 2y = 5$
   $y = 2q - 4$
5. $5r - 7s = 10$
   $r + s = 14$

Drill 2:

1. $3x + 6y = 69$
   $2x - y = 11$
2. $4w - (5 - z) = 6$
   $w - 3(z + 3) = 10$

3. $6x + 15 = 3y$
   $x + y = 14$
4. $4c + 3t = 33$
   $c + 6 = t + 2$
5. $50x + 20y = 15$
   $10x + 4y = 3$ *(watch out!)*

Drill 3: Practicing for Rates Problems

1. $5(t + 1) = d$
   $7t = d + 7$
2. $4t = d$
   $6(t - 1) = d + 4$
3. $50t = d$
   $30t = d - 40$
4. $4r + 10t = 140$
   $r + 25t = 170$
5. $7t = d$
   $5(t - 2) = d - 22$

Many Rates and Distance problems come down to setting up and solving two equations for two variables. Solving these systems of equations is good practice for when you review Rate problems for the GMAT.

Drill 4: Practicing for Other Types of Word Problems

1. $4x = 3y$
   $x - 2y = -15$

2. $12b = 2g$
   $4g - 3b = 63$

3. $y = 4x + 10$
   $y = 7x - 5$

4. $j + 10 = 2m$
   $j = m - 3$

5. $2s = t$
   $s + t = 36$

*Manhattan*GMAT*Prep
the new standard

Drill Set Answers

DRILL SET 1:

Set 1, Drill 1:

1. $19 \times 5 = 95$
Tip: 20 times 5 is 100. You have one less five. $100 - 5 = 95$

2. $39 - (25 - 17) =$
       $39 - 8 = 31$
Tip: You could distribute the minus sign $(39 - 25 + 17)$ if you prefer, but our method is less prone to error.

3. $17(6) + 3(6) =$
       $102 + 18 = 120$
Tip: If you add 3 sixes to 17 sixes, you will have 20 sixes. $20 \times 6 = 120$.

4. $3 \times (4 - 2) \div 2 =$
       $3 \times (2) \div 2 =$
       $6 \div 2 = 3$

5. $15 \times 3 \div 9 =$
       $45 \div 9 = 5$

6. $(9 - 5) - (4 - 2) =$
       $(4) - (2) = 2$

7. $14 - 3(4 - 6) =$
       $14 - 3(-2) =$
       $14 + 6 = 20$

8. $6/3 + 12/3 =$
       $2 + 4 = 6$

9. $-5 \times 1 \div 5 =$
       $-5 \div 5 = -1$

10. $\dfrac{-3 + 7}{-4} = \dfrac{4}{-4} = -1$

Set 1, Drill 2:

1. $(4)(-3)(2)(-1) = 24$
Tip: To determine whether a product will be positive or negative, count the number of positive and negative terms being multiplied. An even number of negative terms will give you a positive product; an odd number of negative terms will give you a negative product.

2. $5 - (4 - (3 - (2 - 1))) =$
       $5 - (4 - (3 - 1)) =$
       $5 - (4 - 2) =$
       $5 - (2) = 3$
Tip: Start with the inner-most parentheses and be careful about the signs!

3. $7 - (6 + 2) =$
       $7 - (8) = -1$

4. $7 - (6 - 2) =$
       $7 - (4) = 3$

5. $-4 (5) - 12/(2 + 4) =$
       $-20 - 12/(6) =$
       $-20 - 2 = -22$

6. $-3(-2) + 6/3 - (-5) =$
       $6 + 2 + 5 = 13$

7. $-12 \times 2/(-3) + 5 =$
       $-24/(-3) + 5 =$
       $8 + 5 = 13$

8. $(6 \times 5) + 14/7 =$
       $(30) + 2 = 32$

9. $32/(4 + 6 \times 2) =$
       $32/(4 + 12) =$
       $32/(16) = 2$

10. $-10 - (-3)^2 =$
       $-10 - (9) = -19$

Watch out for the signs!

Set 1, Drill 3:

1. $-5^2 =$
       $-5^2 = -25$

Note: Make sure to read this as $-(5^2)$, NOT: $(-5)^2 = 25$, which would give us 25.

2. $2^3/2$
       $8/2 = 4$

3. $-2^3/2$

$-8/2 = -4$

4. $(3^2 \times 24)/(2^3)$

$(9 \times 24)/8 = 216/8 = 27$

Note: This is a good chance to practice your long division.

5. $36/(2 + 2^2) \times 4 \times (4 + 2) =$

$36/(2 + 4) \times 4 \times (6) =$

$36/(6) \times 4 \times 6 =$

$6 \times 4 \times 6 = 144$

6. $\sqrt{6^2} + (-3^3) =$

$6 + (-27) =$

$6 - 27 = -21$

7. $5^3 - 5^2 =$

$125 - 25 = 100$

8. $\sqrt{81} - \sqrt{9} =$

$9 - 3 = 6$

9. $[\sqrt{16} + (4 \times 2^3)]/(-2)^2 =$

$[4 + (4 \times 8)]/4$

$[4 + 32]/4 = 36/4 = 9$

10. $(3 + (-2)^3)^2 - 3^2 =$

$(3 - 8)^2 - 9 =$

$(-5)^2 - 9 = 25 - 9 = 16$

Set 1, Drill 4:

1. $4^3 - (4)^2 =$

$64 - 16 = 48$

2. $5^{(2+1)} + 25$

$5^3 + 25 = 125 + 25 = 150$

3. $(-2)^3 - 5^2 + (-4)^3 =$

$(-8) - 25 + (-64) =$

$-33 - 64 = -97$

4. $(63/3^2)^3/7$

$(63/9)^3/7 = 7^3/7 = 343/7 = 49$

5. $5(1) + 5(2) + 5(3) + 5(4) =$

$5 + 10 + 15 + 20 = 50$

6. $\sqrt{(3^4/9)}$

$\sqrt{(81/9)} = \sqrt{9} = 3$

7. $3 \times 7^2 =$

$3 \times 49 =$

147

8. $4^2(3 - 1) - 19 + 4(-2) =$

$4^2(2) - 19 + (-8) =$

$16(2) - 19 - 8 =$

$32 - 27 = 5$

9. $\dfrac{(3+7)(5-3)}{(5-4)(5-4)} = \dfrac{10 \times 2}{1 \times 1} = 20$

10. $3 \times 99 - 2 \times 99 - 1 \times 99 =$

$297 - 198 - 99 =$

$99 - 99 = 0$

DRILL SET 2:

Set 2, Drill 1:

1. $5x - 7 = 28$

    $5x = 35$ Add 7

    $x = 7$ Divide by 5

2. $14 - 3x = 2$

    $-3x = -12$ Subtract 14

    $x = 4$ Divide by -3

3. $z - 11 = 1$

    $z = 12$ Add 11

4. $3(7 - x) = 4(1.5)$

    $21 - 3x = 6$ Simplify
    (Decimals: Chap 7!)

    $-3x = -15$ Subtract 21

    $x = 5$ Divide by -3

5. $7x + 13 = 2x - 7$

    $5x + 13 = -7$ Subtract $2x$

    $5x = -20$ Subtract 13

    $x = -4$ Divide by 5

6. $13 - (-2w) = 6 + 3(11)$

     $13 + 2w = 6 + 33$ Simplify

     $2w = 39 - 13$ Subtract 13

     $2w = 26$ Divide by 2

     $w = 13$

7. $6a/3 = 12 + a$

     $6a = 3 \times (12 + a)$ Multiply by 3

     $6a = 36 + 3a$ Simplify

     $3a = 36$ Subtract $3a$

     $a = 12$ Divide by 3

8. $13x + 2(x + 5) - 7x = -70$

     $13x + 2x + 10 - 7x = -70$ Simplify

     $8x + 10 = -70$ Combine terms

     $8x = -80$ Subtract 10

     $x = -10$ Divide by 8

9. $(z - 4)/3 = -12$

     $z - 4 = -36$ Multiply by 3

     $z = -32$ Add 4

10. $y - 15/3 = 7$

     $y - 5 = 7$ Simplify

     $y = 12$ Add 5

Set 2, Drill 2:

1. $y + 3y = 28$

     $4y = 28$

     $y = 7$

2. $15z + (4z/2) = 51$

     $15z + 2z = 51$

     $17z = 51$

     $z = 3$

3. $3t^3 - 7 = 74$

     $3t^3 = 81$

     $t^3 = 27$

     $t = 3$

4. $7(x - 3) + 2 = 16$

     $7(x - 3) = 14$

     $x - 3 = 2$

     $x = 5$

5. $z/6 = -8$

     $z = -48$

6. $1,200x + 6,000 = 13,200$

     $1,200x = 7,200$

     $x = 6$

7. $(1,300x + 1,700)/43 = 100$

     $1,300x + 1,700 = 4,300$

     $1,300x = 2,600$

     $x = 2$

8. $90x + 160 + 5x - 30 + 5x - 30 = 900$

     $100x + 100 = 900$

     $100x = 800$

     $x = 8$

9. $4(x + 2)^3 - 38 = 70$

     $4(x + 2)^3 = 108$

     $(x + 2)^3 = 27$

     $x + 2 = 3$

     $x = 1$

10. $4(5x + 2) + 44 = 132$

     $4(5x + 2) = 88$

     $5x + 2 = 22$

     $5x = 20$

     $x = 4$

Set 2, Drill 3:

1. $\sqrt{x} = 3 \times 5 - 20 \div 4$

     $\sqrt{x} = 15 - 5$

     $\sqrt{x} = 10$

     $x = 100$

2. $-(x)^3 = 64$

     $(x)^3 = -64$

     $x = -4$

3. $x^3 = 8$

     $x = 2$

4. $4x^3 - 175 = 325$

     $4x^3 = 500$

     $x^3 = 125$

     $x = 5$

5. $9 = y^3/3$

     $27 = y^3$

     $3 = y$

6. $-\sqrt{w} = -5$
    $\sqrt{w} = 5$
    $w = (5)^2$
    $w = 25$

7. $\dfrac{\sqrt{3x+1}}{2} - 1 = 3$
    $\dfrac{\sqrt{3x+1}}{2} = 4$
    $\sqrt{3x+1} = 8$
    $3x+1 = 64$
    $3x = 63$
    $x = 21$

8. $128 = 2z^3$
    $64 = z^3$
    $4 = z$

9. $5\sqrt[3]{x} + 6 = 51$
    $5\sqrt[3]{x} = 45$
    $\sqrt[3]{x} = 9$
    $x = 9^3 = 729$

10. $\dfrac{\sqrt{x-2}}{5} - 20 = -17$
    $\dfrac{\sqrt{x-2}}{5} = 3$
    $\sqrt{x-2} = 15$
    $x - 2 = 15^2 = 225$
    $x = 227$

Set 2, Drill 4:

1. $3x + 2(x + 2) = 2x + 16$
    $3x + 2x + 4 = 2x + 16$
    $5x + 4 = 2x + 16$
    $3x + 4 = 16$
    $3x = 12$
    $x = 4$

2. $\dfrac{3x+7}{x} = 10$
    $3x + 7 = 10x$
    $7 = 7x$
    $1 = x$

3. $4(-3x - 8) = 8(-x + 9)$
    $-12x - 32 = -8x + 72$
    $-32 = 4x + 72$
    $-104 = 4x$
    $-26 = x$

4. $3x + 7 - 4x + 8 = 2(-2x - 6)$
    $-x + 15 = -4x - 12$
    $3x + 15 = -12$
    $3x = -27$
    $x = -9$

5. $2x(4 - 6) = -2x + 12$
    $2x(-2) = -2x + 12$
    $-4x = -2x + 12$
    $-2x = 12$
    $x = -6$

6. $\dfrac{3(6-x)}{2x} = -6$
    $3(6 - x) = -6(2x)$
    $18 - 3x = -12x$
    $18 = -9x$
    $-2 = x$

7. $\dfrac{13}{x+13} = 1$
    $13 = 1(x + 13)$
    $13 = x + 13$
    $0 = x$

8. $\dfrac{10(3x+4)}{10-5x} = 2$
    $10(3x + 4) = 2(10 - 5x)$
    $30x + 40 = 20 - 10x$
    $40x + 40 = 20$
    $40x = -20$
    $x = -1/2$

9. $\dfrac{8 - 2(-4 + 10x)}{2 - x} = 17$
    $8 - 2(-4 + 10x) = 17(2 - x)$
    $8 + 8 - 20x = 34 - 17x$
    $16 - 20x = 34 - 17x$
    $16 = 34 + 3x$
    $-18 = 3x$
    $-6 = x$

10. $\dfrac{50(10+3x)}{50+7x}=50$

$50(10+3x)=50(50+7x)$

$500+150x=2{,}500+350x$

$500=2{,}500+200x$

$-2{,}000=200x$

$-10=x$

DRILL SET 3:

Set 3, Drill 1:

1.   Eq. (1): $7x-3y=5$ Eq. (2): $y=10$

$7x-3(10)=5$ (Step 2) Substitute (10) for y in Eq. (1).

$7x-30=5$ (Step 3) Solve for x. Simplify grouped terms.

$7x=35$ Add 30.

$x=5$ Divide by 7.

Answer: $x=5,\ y=10$

2.   Eq. (1): $2h-4k=0$ Eq. (2): $k=h-3$

$2h-4(h-3)=0$ (Step 2) Substitute $(h-3)$ for k in Eq. (1).

$2h-4h+12=0$ (Step 3) Solve for h. Simplify grouped terms.

$-2h=-12$ Combine like terms.

$h=6$ Divide by -2.

$k=(6)-3$ (Step 4) Substitute (6) for h in Eq. 2 and solve for k

$k=3$ Simplify.

Answer: $h=6,\ k=3$

3.   Eq. (1): $64-2y=x$ Eq. (2): $y=33$

$64-2(33)=x$ (Step 2) Substitute (33) for y in Eq. (1).

$64-66=x$ (Step 3) Solve for x. Simplify.

$-2=x$

Answer: $y=33,\ x=-2$

4.   Eq. (1): $3q-2y=5$ Eq. (2): $y=2q-4$

$3q-2(2q-4)=5$ (Step 2) Substitute $(2q-4)$ for y in Eq. (1).

$3q-4q+8=5$ (Step 3) Solve for q. Simplify grouped terms.

$-q+8=5$ Combine like terms.

$-q=-3$ Subtract 8.

$q=3$ Divide by -1.

$y=2(3)-4$ (Step 4) Substitute (3) for q in Eq. (2). Solve for y.

$y=6-4$ Simplify.

$y=2$

Answer: $q=3,\ y=2$

5.   Eq. (1): $5r - 7s = 10$ Eq. (2): $r + s = 14$

$r + s = 14$

$r = 14 - s$ (Step 1) Isolate r in Eq. (2). Subtract s.

$5(14 - s) - 7s = 10$ (Step 2) Substitute $(14 - s)$ for r in Eq. (1).

$70 - 5s - 7s = 10$ Simplify grouped terms.

$70 - 12s = 10$ Combine like terms.

$70 = 10 + 12s$ Add $12s$.

$60 = 12s$ Subtract 10.

$5 = s$ Divide by 12.

$r + (5) = 14$ (Step 4) Substitute (5) for s in Eq. (2). Solve for r.

$r = 9$ Subtract 5.

Answer: $r = 9$, $s = 5$

Set 3, Drill 2:

1.   Eq. (1): $3x + 6y = 69$ Eq. (2): $2x - y = 11$

$2x - y = 11$

$-y = -2x + 11$ (Step 1) Isolate y in Eq. (2). Subtract $2x$.

$y = 2x - 11$ Divide by -1.

$3x + 6(2x - 11) = 69$ (Step 2) Substitute $(2x - 11)$ for y in Eq. (1).

$3x + 12x - 66 = 69$ (Step 3) Solve for x. Simplify grouped terms.

$15x - 66 = 69$ Combine like terms.

$15x = 135$ Add 66.

$x = 9$ Divide by 15.

$2(9) - y = 11$ (Step 4) Substitute (9) for x in Eq. (2). Solve for y.

$18 - y = 11$ Simplify.

$18 = 11 + y$ Add y.

$7 = y$ Subtract 11.

Answer: $x = 9$, $y = 7$

2.   Eq. (1): $4w - (5 - z) = 6$ Eq. (2): $w - 3(z + 3) = 10$

$4w - (5 - z) = 6$

$4w - 5 + z = 6$ Isolate z in Eq. (1). Simplify grouped terms.

$4w + z = 11$ Add 5.

$z = 11 - 4w$ Subtract $4w$.

$w - 3(z + 3) = 10$

$w - 3z - 9 = 10$ Simplify Eq. (2). Simplify grouped terms.

$w - 3z = 19$ Add 9.

$w - 3(11 - 4w) = 19$ (Step 2) Substitute $(11 - 4w)$ for z in Eq. (2).

$w - 33 + 12w = 19$ (Step 3) Solve for w. Simplify grouped terms.

$13w - 33 = 19$ Combine like terms.

$13w = 52$ Add 33.

$w = 4$ Divide by 13.

$z = 11 - 4w$
$z = 11 - 4(4)$ Substitute (4) for w in the simplified form of Eq. (1).
$z = 11 - 16$ Simplify.
$z = -5$ Simplify.

Answer: $w = 4$, $z = -5$

3.   Eq. (1): $6x + 15 = 3y$ Eq. (2): $x + y = 14$

$x + y = 14$
$x = 14 - y$ (Step 1) Isolate x in Equation 2. Subtract y.

$6(14 - y) + 15 = 3y$ (Step 2) Substitute $(14 - y)$ for x in Eq. (1).
$84 - 6y + 15 = 3y$ (Step 3) Solve for y. Simplify grouped terms.
$99 - 6y = 3y$ Combine like terms.
$99 = 9y$ Add $6y$.
$11 = y$ Divide by 9.

$x + 11 = 14$ (Step 4) Substitute (11) for y in Eq (2). Solve for x.
$x = 3$ Subtract 11.

Answer: $x = 3$, $y = 11$

4.   Eq. (1): $4c + 3t = 33$ Eq. (2): $c + 6 = t + 2$

$c + 6 = t + 2$
$c + 4 = t$ (Step 1) Isolate t in Eq. (2). Subtract 2.

$4c + 3(c + 4) = 33$ (Step 2) Substitute $(c + 4)$ for t in Eq. (1).
$4c + 3c + 12 = 33$ (Step 3) Solve for c. Simplify grouped terms.
$7c + 12 = 33$ Combine like terms.
$7c = 21$ Subtract 12.
$c = 3$ Divide by 7.

$c + 6 = t + 2$
$(3) + 6 = t + 2$ (Step 4) Substitute (3) for c in Eq. (2). Solve for t.
$9 = t + 2$ Simplify.
$7 = t$ Subtract 2.

Answer: $c = 3$, $t = 7$

5.   Eq. (1): $50x + 20y = 15$ Eq. (2): $10x + 4y = 3$

$10x + 4y = 3$
$50x + 20y = 15$ Multiply Eq. (2) by 5

Can't solve—these are the same equations!
Tip: We can only solve two equations for two variables if the equations are different.

Set 3, Drill 3:

1.   Eq. (1): $5(t + 1) = d$ Eq. (2): $7t = d + 7$

$5(t + 1) = d$
$5t + 5 = d$ (Step 1) Isolate d in Eq. (1). Simplify Eq. (1).

$7t = (5t + 5) + 7$ (Step 2) Substitute $(5t + 5)$ for d in Eq. (2).
$7t = 5t + 12$ (Step 3) Solve for t. Simplify.
$2t = 12$ Subtract $5t$.
$t = 6$ Divide by 2.

$7(6) = d + 7$ (Step 4) Substitute (6) for t in Eq. (2). Solve for d.
$42 = d + 7$ Simplify.
$35 = d$ Subtract 7.

Answer: $t = 6$, $d = 35$

2.   Eq. (1): $4t = d$ Eq. (2): $6(t - 1) = d + 4$

$6t - 6 = d + 4$ (Step 1) Simplify grouped terms in Eq. (2).
$6t - 6 = (4t) + 4$ (Step 2) Substitute $(4t)$ for d in Eq. (2).
$6t = 4t + 10$ (Step 3) Solve for t. Add 6.
$2t = 10$ Subtract $4t$.
$t = 5$ Divide by 2.

$4(5) = d$ (Step 4) Substitute (5) for t in Eq. (1). Solve for d.
$20 = d$ Simplify.

Answer : $t = 5$, $d = 20$

3.   Eq. (1): $50t = d$ Eq. (2): $30t = d - 40$

$30t = 50t - 40$ (Step 2) Substitute $(50t)$ for d in Eq. (2).
$-20t = -40$ (Step 3) Solve for t. Subtract $50t$.
$t = 2$ Divide by -20.
$50(2) = d$ (Step 4) Substitute (2) for t in Eq. (1). Solve for d.
$100 = d$

Answer: $t = 2$, $d = 100$

4.   Eq. (1): $4r + 10t = 140$ Eq. (2): $r + 25t = 170$

$r + 25t = 170$
$r = 170 - 25t$ (Step 1) Isolate r in Eq. (2). Subtract $25t$.

$4(170 - 25t) + 10t = 140$ (Step 2) Substitute $(170 - 25t)$ for r in Eq. (1).
$680 - 100t + 10t = 140$ (Step 3) Solve for t. Simplify grouped terms.
$680 - 90t = 140$ Combine like terms.
$-90t = -540$ Subtract 680.
$t = 6$ Divide by -90.

$4r + 10(6) = 140$ (Step 4) Substitute (6) for t in Eq. (1). Solve for r.
$4r + 60 = 140$ Simplify.

$4r = 80$ Subtract 60.
$r = 20$ Divide by 4.

Answer: $t = 6$, $r = 20$

5.   Eq. (1): $7t = d$ Eq. (2): $5(t - 2) = d - 22$

$5t - 10 = (7t) - 22$ (Step 2) Substitute $(7t)$ for d in Eq. (2).
$5t + 12 = 7t$ (Step 3) Solve for t. Add 22.
$12 = 2t$ Subtract $5t$.
$6 = t$ Divide by 2.

$7(6) = d$ (Step 4) Substitute (6) for t in Eq. (1). Solve for d.
$42 = d$ Simplify.

Answer: $t = 6$, $d = 42$

Set 3, Drill 4:

1.   Eq. (1): $4x = 3y$ Eq. (2): $x - 2y = -15$

$x - 2y = -15$
$x = -15 + 2y$ (Step 1) Isolate x in Eq. (2). Add $2y$.

$4(-15 + 2y) = 3y$ (Step 2) Substitute $(-15 + 2y)$ for x in Eq. (1).
$-60 + 8y = 3y$ (Step 3) Solve for y. Simplify grouped terms.
$-60 = -5y$ Subtract $8y$.
$12 = y$ Divide by -5.

$4x = 3(12)$ (Step 4) Substitute 12 for y in Eq. (1). Solve for x.
$4x = 36$ Simplify
$x = 9$ Divide by 4.

Answer: $y = 12$, $x = 9$

2.   Eq. (1): $12b = 2g$ Eq. (2): $4g - 3b = 63$

$12b = 2g$
$6b = g$ (Step 1) Isolate g in Eq. (1). Divide by 2.

$4(6b) - 3b = 63$ (Step 2) Substitute $(6b)$ for g in Eq. (2).
$24b - 3b = 63$ (Step 3) Solve for b. Simplify.
$21b = 63$ Combine like terms.
$b = 3$ Divide by 21.

$12(3) = 2g$ (Step 4) Substitute (3) for b in Eq. (1). Solve for g.
$36 = 2g$ Simplify.
$g = 18$ Divide by 2.

Answer: $b = 3$, $g = 18$

3.   Eq. (1): $y = 4x + 10$ Eq. (2): $y = 7x - 5$

$(4x + 10) = 7x - 5$ (Step 2) Substitute $(4x + 10)$ for y in Eq. (2).

$10 = 3x - 5$ (Step 3) Solve for x. Subtract $4x$.
$15 = 3x$ Add 5.
$5 = x$ Divide by 3.

$y = 4(5) + 10$ (Step 4) Substitute (5) for x in Eq. (1). Solve for y.
$y = 30$ Simplify.

Answer: $x = 5$, $y = 30$

4.   Eq. (1): $j + 10 = 2m$ Eq. (2): $j = m - 3$

$(m - 3) + 10 = 2m$ (Step 2) Substitute $(m - 3)$ for j in Eq. (1).
$m + 7 = 2m$ (Step 3) Solve for m. Simplify.
$7 = m$ Subtract m.

$j = (7) - 3$ (Step 4) Substitute (7) for m in Eq. (2). Solve for j.
$j = 4$ Simplify.

Answer: $m = 7$, $j = 4$

5.   Eq. (1): $2s = t$ Eq. (2): $s + t = 36$

$s + (2s) = 36$ (Step 2) Substitute $(2s)$ for t in Eq. (2).
$3s = 36$ (Step 3) Solve for s. Combine like terms.
$s = 12$ Divide by 3.

$2(12) = t$ (Step 4) Substitute (12) for s in Eq. (1). Solve for t.
$24 = t$ Simplify.

Answer: $s = 12$, $t = 24$

APPENDIX

Make sure you've got these mechanics down pat. The GMAT will expect you to perform these operations quickly and accurately.

Multiplication Table

Quick, what's 8×7? What's 9×6? If you paused for a moment before answering these questions, you should probably review the multiplication table below.

	2	3	4	5	6	7	8	9	10	11	12	13
2	4											
3	6	9										
4	8	12	16									
5	10	15	20	25								
6	12	18	24	30	36							
7	14	21	28	35	42	49						
8	16	24	32	40	48	56	64					
9	18	27	36	45	54	63	72	81				
10	20	30	40	50	60	70	80	90	100			
11	22	33	44	55	66	77	88	99	110	121		
12	24	36	48	60	72	84	96	108	120	132	144	
13	26	39	52	65	78	91	104	117	130	143	156	169

Multiplying Larger Numbers

$$\begin{array}{r} 57 \\ \times\ 8 \\ \hline \end{array}$$

$7 \times 8 = 56$
Put the 6 underneath, then carry the 5.

$$\begin{array}{r} {}^{5}57 \\ \times\ 8 \\ \hline 6 \end{array}$$

$5 \times 8 = 40$, + the 5 we carried = 45. Because we're at the end, put the 45 underneath.

$$\begin{array}{r} 57 \\ \times\ 8 \\ \hline 456 \end{array}$$

An alternate approach that's equivalent is to use the distribution:

$$8(57) = 8(50 + 7)$$
$$= 8 \times 50 + 8 \times 7$$
$$= 400 + 56$$
$$= 456$$

Long Division

$$13\overline{)234}$$

13 goes into 23 one time.

$$
\begin{array}{r}
1 \\
13\overline{)234} \\
-13 \\
\hline
104
\end{array}
$$

Place a 1 on top of the digit farthest to the right in 23.

1×13 is 13, so subtract 13 from 23, and bring down the next digit (4).

What is the largest multiple of 13 less than or equal to 104?

$$
\begin{array}{r}
18 \\
13\overline{)234} \\
-13 \\
\hline
104 \\
-104 \\
\hline
0
\end{array}
$$

If necessary, list multiples of 13 or try cases until you find $13 \times 8 = 104$.

The number may not always divide evenly, in which case you will be left with a remainder. E.g. $25 \div 2 = 2$ with a remainder of 1.

Go to the next page for practice with these operations.

Multiplication and Division Drills

Drill 1: Multiplication
1. 23×7
2. 44×5
3. 67×9
4. 113×6
5. 27×53

Drill 2: Division
1. $6\overline{)96}$
2. $7\overline{)84}$
3. $12\overline{)132}$
4. $16\overline{)368}$
5. $17\overline{)476}$

Multiplication and Division Answers

Drill 1: Multiplication

1.
$$
\begin{array}{r}
^{2}23 \\
\times\ 7 \\
\hline
161
\end{array}
$$

2.
$$
\begin{array}{r}
^{2}44 \\
\times\ 5 \\
\hline
220
\end{array}
$$

3.
$$
\begin{array}{r}
^{6}67 \\
\times\ 9 \\
\hline
603
\end{array}
$$

4.
$$
\begin{array}{r}
1\!\!\!13 \\
\times\ 6 \\
\hline
678
\end{array}
$$

5.
$$
\begin{array}{r}
^{2}27 \\
\times\ 53 \\
\hline
81
\end{array}
$$
Proceed normally to multiply the 3.

$$
\begin{array}{r}
^{2}27 \\
\times\ 53 \\
\hline
^{1}81 \\
1350 \\
\hline
1431
\end{array}
$$
Because the 5 is in the tens place, we need to add a 0 before we start multiplying 27 × 5.

Drill 2: Division

1.
$$
\begin{array}{r}
16 \\
6\overline{)96} \\
-6 \\
\hline
36 \\
-36 \\
\hline
0
\end{array}
$$

3.
$$
\begin{array}{r}
11 \\
12\overline{)132} \\
-12 \\
\hline
12 \\
-12 \\
\hline
0
\end{array}
$$

5.
$$
\begin{array}{r}
28 \\
17\overline{)476} \\
-34 \\
\hline
136 \\
-136 \\
\hline
0
\end{array}
$$

2.
$$
\begin{array}{r}
12 \\
7\overline{)84} \\
-7 \\
\hline
14 \\
-14 \\
\hline
0
\end{array}
$$

4.
$$
\begin{array}{r}
23 \\
16\overline{)368} \\
-32 \\
\hline
48 \\
-48 \\
\hline
0
\end{array}
$$

Chapter 2
of
FOUNDATIONS OF GMAT MATH

QUADRATIC EQUATIONS

In This Chapter . . .

QUADRATIC EQUATIONS

In this chapter:

- Factoring basic quadratic expressions
- Distributing quadratic equations
- Using factoring to solve quadratic equations

Identifying Quadratic Equations

We'll begin this section with a question:

If $x^2 = 4$, what is x?

We know what to do here. Simply take the square root of both sides.

$$\sqrt{x^2} = \sqrt{4}$$
$$x = 2$$

So $x = 2$. The question seems to be answered. But, what if x were equal to -2? What would be the result? Let's plug -2 in for x.

$$(-2)^2 = 4 \longrightarrow 4 = 4$$

If plugging -2 in for x yields a true statement, then -2 must be a solution to the equation. But, from our initial work, we know that 2 is a solution to the equation. So which one is correct?

As it turns out, they both are. An interesting thing happens when you start raising variables to exponents. The number of possible solutions increases. When a variable is squared, as in our example above, it becomes possible that there will be 2 solutions to the equation.

What this means is that whenever you see an equation on the GMAT where one of the variables is squared, you need to
1. Recognize that the equation may have 2 solutions
2. Know how to find both solutions

Any equation in which the highest power a variable is raised to is the second power (i.e. x^2) is called a **quadratic equation**. The ability to solve quadratic equations will be critical to success on the GMAT.

For an equation like $x^2 = 25$ or $x^2 = 9$, finding both solutions shouldn't be too challenging. Take a minute to find both solutions for each equation.

You should have found that x equals either 5 or -5 in the first equation, and 3 or -3 in the second equation. But what if you are asked to solve for x in the following equation?

$$x^2 + 3x - 10 = 0$$

> **Nerd Note:** Why do we call them quadratic equations? Because the word quadratic refers to something that pertains to squares (the Latin word for square is *quadratus*)—and quadratic equations always contain a term that is squared!

Unfortunately, we don't yet have the ability to deal with equations like this, which is why the next part of this chapter will deal with some more important tools for manipulating and solving equations: **distributing & factoring**.

Distributing

We first came across distributing when we were learning how to clean up equations and isolate a variable. Essentially, distributing is applying multiplication across a sum.

To review, if we are presented with the expression $3(x + 2)$, and we want to simplify it, we have to distribute the 3 so that it is multiplied by both the x and the 2.

$$3(x + 2) \rightarrow 3 \times x + 3 \times 2 \rightarrow 3x + 6$$

But what if the first part of the multiplication is more complicated? Suppose you need to simplify $(a + b)(x + y)$?

Simplifying this expression is really an extension of the principle of distribution—every term in the first part of the expression must multiply every term in the second part of the expression. In order to do so correctly every time, we can use a handy acronym to remember the steps necessary: FOIL. The letters stand for **F**irst, **O**utside, **I**nside, **L**ast.

In this case, it looks like this:

$(\boldsymbol{a} + b)(\boldsymbol{x} + y)$	F – multiply the first term in each of the parentheses:	$a \times x = ax$
$(\boldsymbol{a} + b)(x + \boldsymbol{y})$	O – multiply the outer term in each :	$a \times y = ay$
$(a + \boldsymbol{b})(\boldsymbol{x} + y)$	I – multiply the inner term in each:	$b \times x = bx$
$(a + \boldsymbol{b})(x + \boldsymbol{y})$	L – multiply the last terms in each :	$b \times y = by$

So we have $(a + b)(x + y) = ax + ay + bx + by$.

Let's verify this system with numbers. Take the expression $(3 + 4)(10 + 20)$. This is no different than multiplying $(7)(30)$, which gives us 210. Let's see what happens when we FOIL the numbers.

$(\boldsymbol{3} + 4)(\boldsymbol{10} + 20)$	F – multiply the first term in each of the parentheses:	$3 \times 10 = 30$
$(\boldsymbol{3} + 4)(10 + \boldsymbol{20})$	O – multiply the outer term in each :	$3 \times 20 = 60$
$(3 + \boldsymbol{4})(\boldsymbol{10} + 20)$	I – multiply the inner term in each:	$4 \times 10 = 40$
$(3 + \boldsymbol{4})(10 + \boldsymbol{20})$	L – multiply the last terms in each :	$4 \times 20 = 80$

Finally, we sum the four products! $30 + 60 + 40 + 80 = 210$.

Now that we have the basics down, let's go through a more GMAT-like situation. Take the expression $(x + 2)(x + 3)$. One again, we begin by FOILing it.

$(\boldsymbol{x} + 2)(\boldsymbol{x} + 3)$	F – multiply the first term in each of the parentheses:	$x \times x = x^2$
$(\boldsymbol{x} + 2)(x + \boldsymbol{3})$	O – multiply the outer term in each :	$x \times 3 = 3x$
$(x + \boldsymbol{2})(\boldsymbol{x} + 3)$	I – multiply the inner term in each:	$2 \times x = 2x$
$(x + \boldsymbol{2})(x + \boldsymbol{3})$	L – multiply the last terms in each :	$2 \times 3 = 6$

The expression becomes $x^2 + 3x + 2x + 6$. We combine like terms, and we are left with $x^2 + 5x + 6$. In the next section we'll discuss the connection between distributing, factoring, and solving quadratic equations. But for the moment, let's practice foiling expressions.

Check Your Skills

FOIL the following expressions:

1. $(x + 4)(x + 9)$
2. $(y + 3)(y - 6)$
3. $(x + 7)(3 + x)$

Answers can be found on page 63.

Factoring

What is factoring?

Factoring is reversing multiplication. For example, when we multiply y and $(5 - y)$, we get $5y - y^2$. Reversing this, if you're given $5y - y^2$, you can "factor out" a y to transform the expression into $y(5 - y)$. Another way of thinking about factoring is that you're *pulling out* a common term and rewriting the expression as a *product*.

You can factor out many different things on the GMAT: variables, variables with exponents, numbers, and expressions with more than one term such as $(y - 2)$ or $(x + w)$. Here are some examples:

$t^2 + t$ $= t(t + 1)$	Factor out a t. Notice that a 1 remains behind when you factor a t out of a t.
$5k^3 - 15k^2$ $= 5k^2(k - 3)$	Factor out a $5k^2$
$21j + 35k$ $= 7(3j + 5k)$	Factor out a 7—since the variables are different, you can't factor out any variables

If you ever doubt whether you've factored correctly, just distribute back. For instance, $t(t + 1) = t \times t + t \times 1 = t^2 + t$, so $t(t + 1)$ is the factored form of $t^2 + t$.

You should factor expressions for several reasons. One common reason is to simplify an expression (remember, the GMAT complicates equations that are actually at the root much simpler). The other reason (which we will discuss in more detail shortly) is to find possible values for a variable or combination of variables.

Check Your Skills

Factor the following expressions.

4. $4 + 8t$
5. $5x + 25y$
6. $2x^2 + 16x^3$

Answers can be found on page 63.

How Do We Apply This to Quadratics?

If you were told that $7x = 0$, you would know that x must be 0. This is because the only way to make the product of 2 or more numbers equal 0 is to have one of those numbers equal 0. 7 does not equal 0, which means that x must be 0.

Now, what if we were told that $kj = 0$? Well, now we have two possibilities. If $k = 0$, then $0(j) = 0$, which is true, so $k = 0$ is a solution to the equation. Likewise, if $j = 0$, then $k(0) = 0$, which is also true, so $j = 0$ is also a solution.

Either of these scenarios make the equation true, and in fact are the only scenarios that make the product $kj = 0$. (If this is not clear, try plugging in other numbers for k and j, and see what happens.)

So this is why we want to rewrite quadratic equations such as $x^2 + 3x - 10 = 0$ in factored form: $(x + 5)(x - 2) = 0$. The left side of the factored equation is a *product*, so it's really the same thing as $jk = 0$. Now we know that either $x + 5$ is 0, or $x - 2$ is 0. This means either $x = -5$ or $x = 2$. Once you've factored a quadratic equation, it's straightforward to find the solutions.

Check Your Skills

List all possible solutions to the following equations.

7. $(x - 2)(x - 1) = 0$
8. $(x + 4)(x + 5) = 0$
9. $(y - 3)(y + 6) = 0$

Answers can be found on page 63.

Factoring Quadratic Equations

Okay, so now we understand *why* we want to factor a quadratic expression, but *how* do we do it? It's not easy to look at $x^2 + 3x - 10$ and see that it equals $(x - 5)(x + 2)$.

To get started, try solving the puzzle below. (Hint: It involves addition and multiplication.) We've done the first two for you:

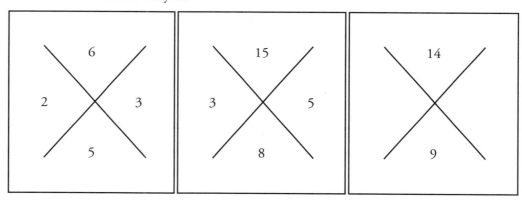

Have you figured out the trick to this puzzle? The answers are on the next page.

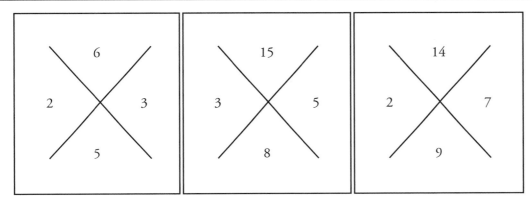

The way the diamonds work is that you multiply the two numbers on the sides to obtain the top number, and you add them to arrive at the bottom number.

Let's take another look at the connection between $(x + 2)(x + 3)$ and $x^2 + 5x + 6$.

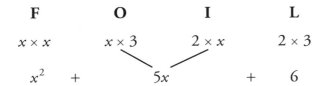

The 2 and the 3 play two important roles in building the quadratic expression:

1. They multiply together to give us 6, which is the final term in our quadratic expression.

2. Multiplying the outside terms gives us $3x$, and multiplying the inside terms gives us $2x$. We can then add those terms to give us $5x$, the middle term of our quadratic expression.

So when we are trying to factor a quadratic expression such as $x^2 + 5x + 6$, the key is to find the 2 numbers whose product equals the final term (6) and whose sum equals the coefficient of the middle term (the 5 in $5x$). In this case, the two numbers that multiply to 6 and add up to 5 are 2 and 3: $2 \times 3 = 6$ and $2 + 3 = 5$.

So the diamond puzzle is just a visual representation of this same goal. For any quadratic expression, take the final term (the **constant**) and place it in the top portion of the diamond. Take the **coefficient** of the middle term (in this case, the "5" in "$5x$") and place it in the lower portion of the diamond. For instance, if the middle term is $5x$, take the 5 and place it at the bottom of the diamond. Let's walk through the entire process with a new example: $x^2 + 7x + 12$.

The final term is 12, and the coefficient of the middle term is 7, so our diamond will look like this:

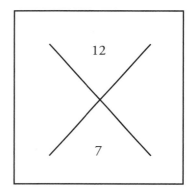

When we factor quadratics (or solve the diamond puzzle), it is better to focus first on determining which numbers could multiply to the final term. The reason is that these problems deal only with integers, and there are far fewer pairs of integers that will multiply to a certain product than will add to a certain sum. For instance, in this problem, there are literally an infinite number of integer pairs that can add to 7 (remember, negative numbers are also integers. −900,000 and 900,007 sum to 7, for instance). On the other hand, there are only a few integer pairs that multiply to 12. We can actually list them all out: 1 & 12, 2 & 6, and 3 & 4. 1 and 12 sum to 13, so they don't work. 2 and 6 sum to 8, so they don't work either. 3 and 4 sum to 7, so this pair of numbers is the one we want. So our completed diamond looks like this:

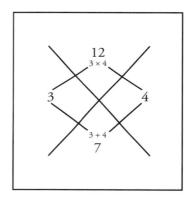

Now, because our numbers are **3** and **4**, the factored form of our quadratic expression becomes $(x + \mathbf{3})(x + \mathbf{4})$.

Note: if we are factoring $x^2 + 7x + 12 = 0$, we get $(x + 3)(x + 4) = 0$, so our solutions are MINUS 3 and MINUS 4, not 3 and 4 themselves. Remember, if we have $(x + 3)(x + 4) = 0$, then either $x + 3 = 0$ or $x + 4 = 0$.

Let's try another example with one important difference. Solve the diamond puzzle for this quadratic expression: $x^2 − 9x + 18$. Now our diamond looks like this:

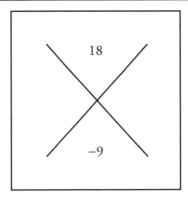

Now we need two numbers that multiply to positive 18, but sum to −9. Fortunately, two positives multiplied create a positive product, as do two negatives. So when the final term is positive and the middle term is negative, the 2 numbers we are looking for will both be negative.

Once again, it will be easier to start by figuring out what pairs of numbers can multiply to 18. In this case, three different pairs all multiply to 18: −1 & −18, −2 & −9, and −3 & −6. The pair −3 & −6, however, is the only pair of numbers that also sum to −9, so this is the pair we want. We fill in the missing numbers, and our diamond becomes:

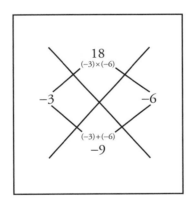

Now, if our numbers on the left and right of the diamond are **−3** and **−6**, the factored form of our quadratic expression becomes $(x - \mathbf{3})(x - \mathbf{6})$.

To recap, when the final term of the quadratic is positive, the two numbers we are looking for will either both be positive or both be negative. If the middle term is positive, as in the case of $x^2 + 7x + 12$, the numbers will both be positive (3 and 4). If the middle term is negative, as in the case of $x^2 - 9x + 18$, the numbers will both be negative (−3 and −6).

Check Your Skills

Factor the following quadratic expressions. (Explanations will include diamond puzzle.)

10. $x^2 + 14x + 33$
11. $x^2 - 14x + 45$

Answers can be found on page 64.

*Manhattan*GMAT*Prep
the new standard

In the previous section we dealt with quadratic equations in which the final term was positive. Now we need to discuss how to deal with quadratics in which the final term is negative. The basic method is the same, although there is one important twist.

Take a look at the quadratic expression $x^2 + 3x - 10$. Let's start by creating our diamond.

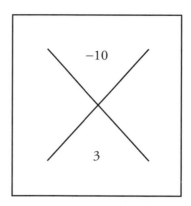

We are looking for two numbers that will multiply to -10. The only way for the product of two numbers to be negative is for one of them to be positive and one of them to be negative. That means that in addition to figuring out pairs of numbers that multiply to 10, we also need to worry about which number will be positive and which will be negative. Let's disregard the signs for the moment. There are only 2 pairs of integers that multiply to 10: 1 and 10 and 2 and 5. Let's start testing out the pair 1 and 10, and see what we can learn.

Let's try making 1 positive and 10 negative. If that were the case, our factored form of the expression would be $(x + 1)(x - 10)$. Let's FOIL it out and see what it would look like.

F	**O**	**I**	**L**
$x \times x$	$x \times -10$	$1 \times x$	1×-10
x^2	$-10x$	$1x$	-10
x^2	$-$	$9x$	$-$	10

The sum of 1 and -10 is -9, but we want 3. That's not correct, so let's try reversing the signs. Now we'll see what happens if we make 1 negative and 10 positive. Our factored form would now be $(x - 1)(x + 10)$. Once again, let's FOIL it out.

F	**O**	**I**	**L**
$x \times x$	$x \times 10$	$-1 \times x$	$(-1) \times 10$
x^2	$10x$	$-x$	-10
x^2	$+$	$9x$	$-$	10

Again, this doesn't match our target. The sum of -1 and 10 is not 3. Compare these examples to the examples in the last section. Notice that, with our examples in the last section, the two numbers summed to the coefficient of the middle term (in our example $x^2 + 7x + 12$, the two numbers we wanted, 3 and 4, summed to 7, which is the coefficient of the middle term). In these two examples, however, because one number was positive and one number was negative, it is actually the *difference* of 1 and 10 that gave us the coefficient of the middle term.

We'll discuss this further as we continue with our example. For now, to factor quadratics in which the final term is negative, we actually ignore the sign initially and look for two numbers that multiply to the coefficient of the final term (ignoring the sign) and whose *difference* is the coefficient of the middle term (ignoring the sign).

Back to our example. The pair of numbers 1 and 10 did not work, so let's look at the pair 2 and 5. Notice that the coefficient of the middle term is 3. And the difference of 2 and 5 is 3. This has to be the correct pair, now all we need to do is determine whether our factored form is $(x + 2)(x - 5)$ OR $(x - 2)(x + 5)$. Take some time now to FOIL both expressions and figure out which one is correct. We'll discuss the correct answer on the next page.

You should have come to the conclusion that $(x - 2)(x + 5)$ was the correctly factored form of the expression. That means our diamond looks like this:

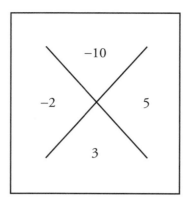

To recap, the way to factor *any* quadratic expression where the final term is negative is as follows:

1. Ignore the signs initially. Find a pair of numbers that multiply to the coefficient of the final term and whose *difference* is the coefficient of the middle term (for $x^2 + 3x - 10$, the numbers 2 and 5 multiply to 10 and $5 - 2 = 3$)

2. Now that you have the pair of numbers (2 and 5) you need to figure out which one will be positive and which one will be negative. As it turns out, this is straightforward to do. We pay attention to signs again. If the sign of the middle term is positive, then the larger of the two numbers will be positive, and the smaller will be negative. This was the case in our previous example. The middle term was +3, so our pair of numbers was +5 and −2. If the middle term is negative, the larger number will be negative, and the smaller number will be positive.

Let's work through one more example to see how this works. What is the factored form of $x^2 - 4x - 21$? Take some time to work through it for yourself, and we'll go through it together on the next page.

First let's start our diamond. It looks like this:

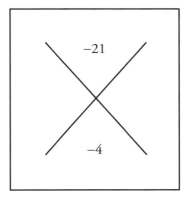

Because the coefficient of the final term (−21) is negative, we're going to ignore the signs for the moment, and focus on finding pairs of integers that will multiply to 21. The only possible pairs are 1 and 21, and 3 and 7. Next, we take the difference of both pairs. 21 − 1 = 20, and 7 − 3 = 4. Our second pair matches the −4 on the bottom of the diamond (because we are ignoring the sign of the −4 at this stage) so 3 and 7 is the correct pair of numbers.

Now all that remains is to determine the sign of each. The coefficient of the middle term (−4) is negative, so we need to assign the negative sign to the larger of the two numbers, 7. That means that the 3 will be positive. So the correctly factored form of our quadratic expression is $(x + 3)(x − 7)$.

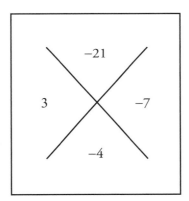

Check Your Skills

Factor the following expressions

12. $x^2 + 3x − 18$
13. $x^2 − 5x − 66$

Answers can be found on pages 64−65

Solving Quadratic Equations

Now that we know how to factor quadratic expressions, it's time to make that final jump to actually solving quadratic equations. When we first discussed factoring, we noted that when one side of the equation is equal to 0, we can make use of the rule that anything times 0 is 0. In the case of the equation $(x - 5)(x + 10) = 0$, we know that either $(x - 5) = 0$ or $(x + 10) = 0$, which means that $x = 5$ OR -10.

The whole point of factoring quadratic equations is so that we can make use of this rule. That means that, before you factor a quadratic expression, you MUST make sure that the other side of the equation equals 0.

Suppose you see an equation $x^2 + 10x = -21$, and you need to solve for x. The x^2 term in the equation should tell you that this is a quadratic equation, but it's not yet ready to be factored. Before it can be factored, you have to move everything to one side of the equation. In this equation, the easiest way to do that is to add 21 to both sides, giving you $x^2 + 10x + 21 = 0$. Now that one side equals 0, you're ready to factor.

The final term is positive, so we're looking for 2 numbers to multiply to 21 and sum to 10. 3 & 7 fit the bill, so our factored form is $(x + 3)(x + 7) = 0$. That means that $x = -3$ OR -7.

And now you know all the steps to successfully factoring and solving quadratic equations.

Check Your Skills

Solve the following quadratic equations

14. $x^2 - 3x + 2 = 0$
15. $x^2 + 2x - 35 = 0$
16. $x^2 - 15x = -26$

Answers can be found on pages 65–66.

Check Your Skills Answer Key:

1. $(x + 4)(x + 9)$

$(\boldsymbol{x} + 4)(\boldsymbol{x} + 9)$	F – multiply the first term in each parentheses: $x \times x = x^2$
$(\boldsymbol{x} + 4)(x + \boldsymbol{9})$	O – multiply the outer term in each: $x \times 9 = 9x$
$(x + \boldsymbol{4})(\boldsymbol{x} + 9)$	I – multiply the inner term in each: $4 \times x = 4x$
$(x + \boldsymbol{4})(x + \boldsymbol{9})$	L – multiply the last term in each: $4 \times 9 = 36$

$x^2 + 9x + 4x + 36 \rightarrow x^2 + 13x + 36$

2. $(y + 3)(y - 6)$

$(\boldsymbol{y} + 3)(\boldsymbol{y} - 6)$	F – multiply the first term in each parentheses: $y \times y = y^2$
$(\boldsymbol{y} + 3)(y - \boldsymbol{6})$	O – multiply the outer term in each: $y \times -6 = -6y$
$(y + \boldsymbol{3})(\boldsymbol{y} - 6)$	I – multiply the inner term in each: $3 \times y = 3y$
$(y + \boldsymbol{3})(y - \boldsymbol{6})$	L – multiply the last term in each: $3 \times -6 = -18$

$y^2 - 6y + 3y - 18 \rightarrow y^2 - 3y - 18$

3. $(x + 7)(3 + x)$

$(\boldsymbol{x} + 7)(\boldsymbol{3} + x)$	F – multiply the first term in each parentheses: $x \times 3 = 3x$
$(\boldsymbol{x} + 7)(3 + \boldsymbol{x})$	O – multiply the outer term in each: $x \times x = x^2$
$(x + \boldsymbol{7})(\boldsymbol{3} + x)$	I – multiply the inner term in each: $7 \times 3 = 21$
$(x + \boldsymbol{7})(3 + \boldsymbol{x})$	L – multiply the last term in each: $7 \times x = 7x$

$3x + x^2 + 21 + 7x \rightarrow x^2 + 10x + 21$

4. $4 + 8t$

    $4(1 + 2t)$ Factor out a 4

5. $5x + 25y$

    $5(x + 5y)$ Factor out a 5

6. $2x^2 + 16x^3$

    $2x^2(1 + 8x)$ Factor out a $2x^2$

7. $(x - 2)(x - 1) = 0$

    $(x - 2) = 0 \rightarrow x = 2$ Remove the parentheses and solve for x
    OR $(x - 1) = 0 \rightarrow x = 1$ Remove the parentheses and solve for x
    Answer: $x = 2$ OR 1

8. $(x + 4)(x + 5) = 0$

    $(x + 4) = 0 \rightarrow x = -4$ Remove the parentheses and solve for x
    OR $(x + 5) = 0 \rightarrow x = -5$ Remove the parentheses and solve for x
    Answer: $x = -4$ OR -5

9. $(y - 3)(y + 6) = 0$

    $(y - 3) = 0 \rightarrow y = 3$ Remove the parentheses and solve for y
    OR $(y + 6) = 0 \rightarrow y = -6$ Remove the parentheses and solve for y
    Answer: $y = 3$ OR -6

10. $x^2 + 14x + 33$

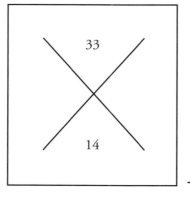

1 & 33 and 3 & 11 multiply to 33. 3 & 11 sum to 14
$(x + 3)(x + 11)$

11. $x^2 - 14x + 45$

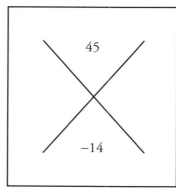 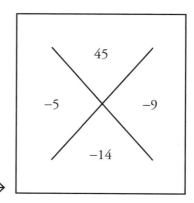

1 & 45, 3 & 15, and 5 & 9 multiply to 45. 5 & 9 sum to 14
$(x - 5)(x - 9)$

12. $x^2 + 3x - 18$

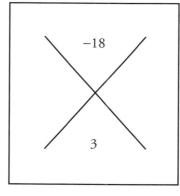 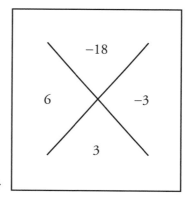

Middle term is positive, so the larger of the two numbers (6) is positive.
1 & 18, 2 & 9, and 3 & 6 multiply to 18. The difference of 3 & 6 is 3.
$(x + 6)(x - 3)$

13. $x^2 - 5x - 66$

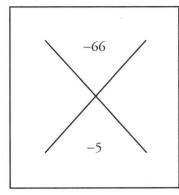   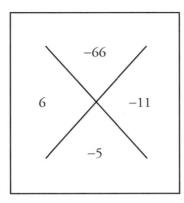

1 & 66, 2 & 33, 3 & 22, and 6 & 11 multiply to 66. The difference of 6 and 11 is 5.
$(x + 6)(x - 11)$

14. $x^2 - 3x + 2 = 0$

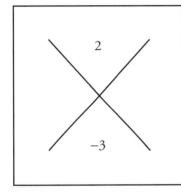   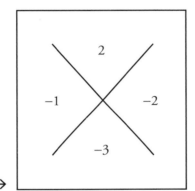

1 & 2 multiply to 2 and add to 3.
$(x - 1)(x - 2) = 0$

Answer: $x = 1$ OR 2

15. $x^2 + 2x - 35 = 0$

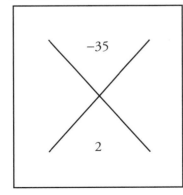   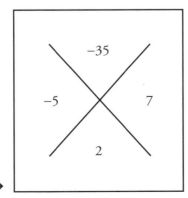

5 & 7 multiply to 35 and their difference is 2. Middle term is positive, so the larger
of the two numbers (7) is positive.

*Manhattan*GMAT*Prep
the new standard

$(x - 5)(x + 7) = 0$

Answer: $x = 5$ OR -7

16. $x^2 - 15x = -26$
     $x^2 - 15x + 26 = 0$ Add 26 to both sides so that the expression equals 0

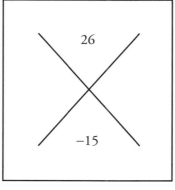 →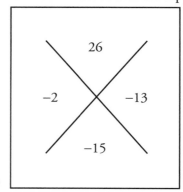

2 & 13 multiply to 26 and sum to 15
$(x - 2)(x - 13) = 0$

Answer: $x = 2$ OR 13

Chapter Review: Drill Sets

DRILL SET 1

Drill 1: Distribute the following factored forms (using FOIL).

1. $(x + 2)(x - 3) =$
2. $(2s + 1)(s + 5) =$
3. $(h - 3)(h + 6) =$
4. $(5 + a)(3 + a) =$
5. $(x + y)(x + y) =$

Drill 2: Distribute the following factored forms (using FOIL).

1. $(y + 7)(y + 13) =$
2. $(3 - z)(z + 4) =$
3. $(x + 6)(x - 6) =$
4. $(2x - y)(x + 4y) =$
5. $(x^2 + 5)(x + 2) =$

Drill 3: Factor the following expressions.

1. $18x + 24$
2. $9y - 12y^2$
3. $7x^3 + 84x$
4. $40y + 30x$
5. $5x^4 - 10x^3 + 35x$

Drill 4: Factor the following expressions.

1. $3xy^2 + 6xy$
2. $15a^2b + 30ab - 75ab^2$
3. $2xyz + 6xy - 10yz$
4. $4x^2 + 12x + 8$
5. $2y^3 - 10y^2 + 12y$

DRILL SET 2

Drill 1: Solve the following equations. List all possible solutions.

1. $x^2 - 2x = 0$
2. $y^2 + 3y = 0$
3. $z^2 = -5z$
4. $44j - 11jk = 0$
5. $4xy + 2x^2y = 0$

Drill 2: Solve the following equations. List all possible solutions.

1. $y^2 + 4y + 3 = 0$
2. $y^2 - 11y + 30 = 0$
3. $y^2 + 12y + 36 = 0$
4. $c^2 - 23c + 42 = 0$
5. $w^2 + 17w + 60 = 0$

Drill 3: Solve the following equations. List all possible solutions.

1. $a^2 - a - 12 = 0$
2. $x^2 + 8x - 20 = 0$
3. $b^2 - 4b - 32 = 0$
4. $y^2 - 4y - 45 = 0$
5. $x^2 + 9x - 90 = 0$

Drill 4: Solve the following equations. List all possible solutions.

1. $2a^2 + 6a + 4 = 0$
2. $y^2 - 7y + 4 = -6$
3. $x^3 - 3x^2 - 28x = 0$
4. $x^3 - 5x^2 + 4x = 0$
5. $-3x^3 + 6x^2 + 9x = 0$

Drill Set Answers:

Set 1, Drill 1:

1. $(x + 2)(x - 3) = x^2 - 3x + 2x - 6 = \boldsymbol{x^2 - x - 6}$

2. $(2s + 1)(s + 5) = 2s^2 + 10s + s + 5 = \boldsymbol{2s^2 + 11s + 5}$

3. $(h - 3)(h + 6) = h^2 + 6h - 3h - 18 = \boldsymbol{h^2 + 3h - 18}$

4. $(5 + a)(3 + a) = 15 + 5a + 3a + a^2 = \boldsymbol{a^2 + 8a + 15}$

5. $(x + y)(x + y) = x^2 + xy + xy + y^2 = \boldsymbol{x^2 + 2xy + y^2}$

Set 1, Drill 2

1. $(y + 7)(y + 13) = y^2 + 13y + 7y + 91 = \boldsymbol{y^2 + 20y + 91}$

2. $(3 - z)(z + 4) = 3z + 12 - z^2 - 4z = \boldsymbol{-z^2 - z + 12}$

3. $(x + 6)(x - 6) = x^2 - 6x + 6x - 36 = \boldsymbol{x^2 - 36}$

4. $(2x - y)(x + 4y) = 2x^2 + 8xy - xy - 4y^2 = \boldsymbol{2x^2 + 7xy - 4y^2}$

5. $(x^2 + 5)(2 + x) = 2x^2 + x^3 + 10 + 5x = \boldsymbol{x^3 + 2x^2 + 5x + 10}$

Set 1, Drill 3

1. $18x + 24 = \boldsymbol{6(3x + 4)}$

2. $9y - 12y^2 = \boldsymbol{3y(3 - 4y)}$

3. $7x^3 + 84x = \boldsymbol{7x(x^2 + 12)}$

4. $40y + 30x = \boldsymbol{10(4y + 3x)}$

5. $5x^4 - 10x^3 + 35x = \boldsymbol{5x(x^3 - 2x^2 + 7)}$

Set 1, Drill 4

1. $3xy^2 + 6xy = \boldsymbol{3xy(y + 2)}$

2. $15a^2b + 30ab - 75ab^2 = \boldsymbol{15ab(a + 2 - 5b)}$

3. $2xyz + 6xy - 10yz = \boldsymbol{2y(xz + 3x - 5z)}$

4. $4x^2 + 12x + 8 = 4(x^2 + 3x + 2) = \boldsymbol{4(x + 2)(x + 1)}$

5. $2y^3 - 10y^2 + 12y = 2y(y^2 - 5y + 6) = \boldsymbol{2y(y - 3)(y - 2)}$

Set 2, Drill 1

1. $x^2 - 2x = 0$

   $x(x - 2) = 0$

   $x = 0$
   OR $(x - 2) = 0 \rightarrow x = 2$ Answer: $x = 0$ OR 2

2. $y^2 + 3y = 0$

   $y(y + 3) = 0$

   $y = 0$
   OR $(y + 3) = 0 \rightarrow y = -3$ Answer: $y = 0$ OR -3

3. $z^2 = -5z$

   $z^2 + 5z = 0 \rightarrow z(z + 5) = 0$

   $z = 0$
   OR $(z + 5) = 0 \rightarrow z = -5$ Answer: $z = 0$ OR -5

4. $44j - 11jk = 0$

   $11j(4 - k) = 0$

   $11j = 0 \rightarrow j = 0$
   OR $(4 - k) = 0 \rightarrow k = 4$ Answer: $j = 0$ OR $k = 4$

5. $4xy + 2x^2y = 0$

   $2xy(2 + x) = 0$

   $2xy = 0 \rightarrow xy = 0 \rightarrow x = 0$ OR $y = 0$
   OR $(2 + x) = 0 \rightarrow x = -2$ Answer: $x = 0$ OR $y = 0$ OR $x = -2$

Set 2, Drill 2

1. $y^2 + 4y + 3 = 0$

   $(y + 1)(y + 3) = 0$

   $(y + 1) = 0 \rightarrow y = -1$

   $(y + 3) = 0 \rightarrow y = -3$ Answer: $y = -1$ OR -3

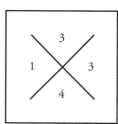

1 & 3 multiply to 3
and sum to 4.

2. $y^2 - 11y + 30 = 0$

       $(y - 5)(y - 6) = 0$

       $(y - 5) = 0$ → $y = 5$

       OR $(y - 6) = 0$ → $y = 6$ Answer: $y = 5$ OR 6

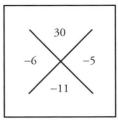

1 & 30, 2 & 15,
3 & 10, and 5 & 6
multiply to 30. 5 & 6
sum to 11.

3. $y^2 + 12y + 36 = 0$

       $(y + 6)(y + 6) = 0$

       $(y + 6) = 0$ → $y = -6$

       OR $(y + 6) = 0$ → $y = -6$ Answer: $y = -6$
                                         (same result either way)

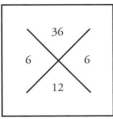

1 & 36, 2 & 18,
3 & 12, 4 & 9, and
6 & 6 multiply to 36.
6 & 6 sum to 12.

4. $c^2 - 23c + 42 = 0$

       $(c - 21)(c - 2) = 0$

       $(c - 21) = 0$ → $c = 21$

       OR $(c - 2) = 0$ → $c = 2$ Answer: $c = 21$ OR 2

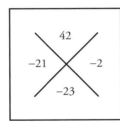

1 & 42, 2 & 21,
3 & 14, and 6 & 7
multiply to 42.
2 & 21 sum to 23.

5. $w^2 + 17w + 60 = 0$

       $(w + 12)(w + 5) = 0$

       $(w + 12) = 0 \rightarrow w = -12$

       OR $(w + 5) = 0 \rightarrow w = -5$ Answer: $w = -12$ OR -5

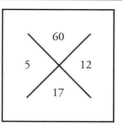

1 & 60, 2 & 30,
3 & 20, 4 & 15,
5 & 12, and 6 & 10
multiply to 60.
5 & 12 sum to 17.

Set 2, Drill 3

1. $a^2 - a - 12 = 0$

       $(a - 4)(a + 3) = 0$

       $(a - 4) = 0 \rightarrow a = 4$

       OR $(a + 3) = 0 \rightarrow a = -3$ Answer: $a = 4$ OR -3

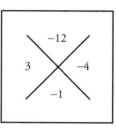

1 & 12, 2 & 6 and
3 & 4 multiply to 12.
The difference of
3 & 4 is 1.

2. $x^2 + 8x - 20 = 0$

       $(x + 10)(x - 2) = 0$

       $(x + 10) = 0 \rightarrow x = -10$

       OR $(x - 2) = 0 \rightarrow x = 2$ Answer: $x = -10$ OR 2

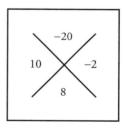

1 & 20, 2 & 10, and
4 & 5 multiply to 20.
The difference of
2 & 10 is 8.

3. $b^2 - 4b - 32 = 0$

$(b - 8)(b + 4) = 0$

$(b - 8) = 0 \rightarrow b = 8$

OR $(b + 4) = 0 \rightarrow b = -4$ Answer: $b = 8$ OR -4

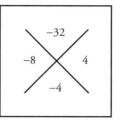

1 & 32, 2 & 16, and
4 & 8 multiply to 32.
The difference of
4 & 8 is 4.

4. $y^2 - 4y - 45 = 0$

$(y - 9)(y + 5) = 0$

$(y - 9) = 0 \rightarrow y = 9$

OR $(y + 5) = 0 \rightarrow y = -5$ Answer: $y = 9$ OR -5

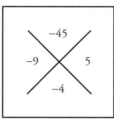

1 & 45, 3 & 15, and
5 & 9 multiply to 45.
The difference of
5 & 9 is 4.

5. $x^2 + 9x - 90 = 0$

$(x + 15)(x - 6) = 0$

$(x + 15) = 0 \rightarrow x = -15$

OR $(x - 6) = 0 \rightarrow x = 6$ Answer: $x = -15$ OR 6

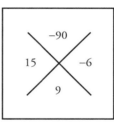

1 & 90, 2 & 45,
3 & 30, 5 & 18,
6 & 15, and 9 & 10
multiply to 90.
The difference of
6 & 15 is 9.

Set 2, Drill 4

1. $2a^2 + 6a + 4 = 0$

$2(a^2 + 3a + 2) = 0 \rightarrow 2(a + 2)(a + 1) = 0$

$(a + 2) = 0 \rightarrow a = -2$

OR $(a + 1) = 0 \rightarrow a = -1$ Answer: $a = -2$ OR -1

2. $y^2 - 7y + 4 = -6$

$y^2 - 7y + 10 = 0 \rightarrow (y - 2)(y - 5) = 0$

$(y - 2) = 0 \rightarrow y = 2$

OR $(y - 5) = 0 \rightarrow y = 5$ Answer: $y = 2$ OR 5

3. $x^3 - 3x^2 - 28x = 0$

$x(x^2 - 3x - 28) = 0 \rightarrow x(x - 7)(x + 4) = 0$

$x = 0$

OR $(x - 7) = 0 \rightarrow x = 7$

OR $(x + 4) = 0 \rightarrow x = -4$ Answer: $x = 0$ OR 7 OR -4

4. $x^3 - 5x^2 + 4x = 0$

$x(x^2 - 5x + 4) = 0 \rightarrow x(x - 1)(x - 4) = 0$

$x = 0$

OR $(x - 1) = 0 \rightarrow x = 1$

OR $(x - 4) = 0 \rightarrow x = 4$ Answer: $x = 0$ OR 1 OR 4

5. $-3x^3 + 6x^2 + 9x = 0$

$-3x(x^2 - 2x - 3) = 0 \rightarrow -3x(x - 3)(x + 1) = 0$

$-3x = 0 \rightarrow x = 0$

OR $(x - 3) = 0 \rightarrow x = 3$

OR $(x + 1) = 0 \rightarrow x = -1$ Answer: $x = 0$ OR 3 OR -1

*Manhattan*GMAT*Prep
the new standard

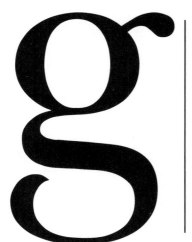

Chapter 3
of
FOUNDATIONS OF GMAT MATH

WORD PROBLEMS

In This Chapter . . .

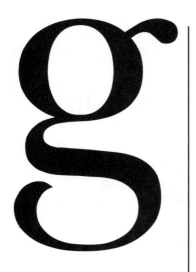

- Decoding the GMAT Word Problem

WORD PROBLEMS

In This Chapter:

- Understanding what word problems are asking
- Translating word problems into equations

Decoding the GMAT Word Problem

For many of us, solving word problems is the most difficult aspect of GMAT math. The math seems hidden beneath a confusing description of a situation (and we usually don't find ourselves in GMAT-like scenarios in our everyday lives).

Two thoughts are common to many frustrated students:

"I don't know where to get started" and "I don't know what they want me to do."

Let's attack these frustrations one at a time.

"I don't know where to get started."

A *passive thinker* takes in information, hopes that it will lead somewhere, waits for a connection to appear and then… (hopefully)… *voila!* In contrast, the *active thinker* aggressively seeks out relationships between the various elements of a problem and looks to write equations which can be solved. *You have to be an active thinker on the GMAT.*

Let's look at a sample problem:

A steel rod 50 meters long is cut into two pieces. If one piece is 14 meters longer than the other, what is the length, in meters, of the shorter piece?

The trick to word problems is to not try to do everything all at once. While it's great when the entire process is clear from the start, such clarity about your work is often not the case. That's why **we need to start by identifying unknowns and creating variables.** What quantities have we not been given specific values for? Take a moment to identify those quantities and write them down in the space provided below. Make up letters to stand for the quantities, and label these letters.

Identify Unknowns and create variables

In this question, both the length of the shorter piece and the length of the longer piece are unknown, so let's begin by assigning each of those values a variable. We could go with the traditional algebraic variables x and y, but what if we forget which is which while we're busy answering the question? Instead, let's use letters that can help us remember which variable is assigned to which value:

S = shorter piece
L = longer piece

Just like that, we've gotten started on this problem. This may seem like a minor accomplishment in terms of the entire question, but it was an important one. Often, as soon as you start translating a word problem, the path forward becomes clearer. Now it's time to deal with our second frustration.

"I don't know what they want me to do."

Even now that we've identified and labeled our variables, you might still feel confused. That's fine. Since the GMAT is computer-adaptive, everyone ends up facing a number of problems which are above his or her ability level. What distinguishes the higher performing GMAT test-takers in these moments is that they begin spelling out relationships before they know how the equations will prove useful. It's similar to untangling a ball of yarn: if you waited until you knew how the entire process would end, you might never get started. Of course, you hope to have a clear vision right from the start, but if you don't, dive in and see what you find—you'll likely make key realizations along the way. Ironically, often it's the road blocks we encounter that point the way. So our next step is to **identify relationships and create equations.**

Let's go back to our problem, look at one piece of information at a time, and start translating that information into equations. Try it first on your own, then we'll go through it together.

A steel rod 50 meters long is cut into two pieces.

The relationship expressed here is one of the two most common types of relationships found in word problems. We know the original length of the rod was 50 meters, and we know that it was cut into 2 pieces. Therefore, we know that the length of the shorter piece plus the length of the longer piece must equal 50 meters. This common relationship (one you should watch out for in other word problems) is **Parts Add to a Sum**. So a good way to express this relationship algebraically would be to write

$S + L = 50$

Now that we've translated the first part of the problem, let's move on to the next part.

If one piece is 14 meters longer than the other...

The relationship expressed here is another common type found in word problems. The longer piece of metal is 14 meters longer than the shorter piece of metal. So if we were to add 14 meters to the shorter piece, it would be the same length as the longer piece. This relationship (be on the lookout for this one too) is **One Part Can Be Made Equal to the Other**.

Either the question will say that two values are equivalent, or it will tell you exactly how they differ. This question told us how they were different, so our equation shows how we could make them equivalent. In this case, we would want to say

$$S + 14 = L$$

By the way, when constructing equations in which you are making one part equal to the other, it can be very easy to express the relationship backwards. If you mistakenly wrote down $S = L + 14$, you're not alone. A good habit to get into if you find yourself making this kind of error is to verify your equation with real, but hypothetical, numbers. To check if my equation above is correct, I'm going to start by imagining that my shorter piece of metal is 20 meters long. If the shorter piece were 20 meters long, then the longer piece would have to be 34 meters long. Now I plug those numbers into my equation. Does $(20) + 14 = (34)$? Yes, it does, so my equation is correct.

Let's move on to the final part of the question.

> …*what is the length, in meters, of the shorter piece?*

This part of the question doesn't describe a relationship that we can use to create an equation, but it does tell us something quite useful: it tells us what we're solving for! Make sure that you note in some way what value you're actually looking for as you solve a problem—it can help you stay focused on the task at hand. In this problem, we're trying to find S.

On your paper, you might even write

$$S = ?$$

So now that we've **identified** our **unknowns and created variables, identified relationships** and **created equations,** and **identified what the question is asking for,** it's time to put the pieces together and answer the question. Try it on your own first, and then when you've got an answer, turn the page and we'll go through the final steps together.

Let's recap, and then we'll complete the final steps and answer the question. After reading the question, we were able to create 2 equations:

$$S + L = 50$$
$$S + 14 = L$$

We've been in this situation before. We have 2 variables and 2 equations. It's time to solve for S.

$$S + L = 50 \;\;\rightarrow\;\; L = 50 - S$$

$$S + 14 = (50 - S)$$

$$\begin{array}{r} S + 14 = 50 - S \\ -14 \quad -14 \end{array}$$

$$\begin{array}{r} S = 36 - S \\ +S \qquad +S \end{array}$$

$$\frac{2S}{2} = \frac{36}{2}$$
$$S = 18$$

> **Time Saving Tip:** Remember first to isolate the variable you want to get rid of. In this case, we isolate L first.

If you had trouble getting the correct values for S and L, then you should probably go back and review the section on substitution on page 27. Knowing how to substitute and solve is absolutely essential if you want to do consistently well on word problems. If you're comfortable with everything we've done so far in order to answer the question, then you're ready for a tougher problem.

> Jack is 13 years older than Ben. In 8 years, he will be twice as old as Ben. How old is Jack now?

First try this problem on your own. Remember to follow the same steps we followed in the last question. After you're finished, we'll go through it together on the next page.

Ok, let's get started. The first thing we have to do is **identify** our **unknowns** and **create variables**. In this problem, the two unknowns are the ages of Jack and Ben. We can represent them like this:

J = Jack's age NOW
B = Ben's age NOW

Before we move on to the next step, it's important to understand why we want to specify that our variables represent Jack and Ben's ages NOW. As you were solving this problem by yourself, you may have noticed that there was an added wrinkle to this question. We are presented with information that describes 2 distinct points in time—now and 8 years from now. Many word problems on the GMAT provide information about 2 distinct but related situations. When you are dealing with one of those problems, specify an additional reference point for your variables. In this case, we want to say that our variables represent Jack and Ben's ages *now* as opposed to 8 years from now.

Now that we've created our variables, it's time to **identify relationships** and **create equations**. Let's go through the information presented in the question one piece at a time.

Jack is 13 years older than Ben.

Once again, we should check that we're putting this together the right way (not putting the +13 on the wrong side of the equation). Our equation should be

$J = B + 13$, NOT $J + 13 = B$

Let's move on to the next piece of information.

In 8 years, he will be twice as old as Ben.

This piece is more challenging to translate than you might otherwise suspect. Remember, our variables represent their ages now, but this statement is talking about their ages 8 years from now. So we can't just write $J = 2B$. This relationship is dependent upon Jack and Ben's ages 8 years from now. We don't want to use new variables to represent these different ages, so let's adjust the values like this:

$(J + 8)$ = Jack's age 8 years from now
$(B + 8)$ = Ben's age 8 years from now

Now we can accurately create equations related to the earlier time *and* to the later time. Plus, if we keep those values in parentheses, then we can avoid potential PEMDAS errors! So our second equation really should read

$(J + 8) = 2(B + 8)$

Only one more piece of the question to go.

How old is Jack now?

This tells us that we're looking for the value of J. In other words, $J = ?$. All the pieces are in place and we're ready to solve.

$(J + 8) = 2(B + 8) \rightarrow J + 8 = 2B + 16$ Simplify grouped terms

$J = B + 13 \rightarrow J - 13 = B$ Isolate the variable you want to eliminate

$J + 8 = 2(J - 13) + 16$ Substitute into the other equation

$J + 8 = 2J - 26 + 16$ Simplify grouped terms

$$
\begin{aligned}
J + 8 &= 2J - 10 \\
\underline{-J + 10} \quad &\quad \underline{-J + 10} \\
18 &= J
\end{aligned}
$$

The question asks for Jack's age, so we have our answer. Let's review what we know about word problems and the steps we should take to solve them.

Step 1: Identify unknowns and create variables

- Don't forget to use descriptive letters (i.e. shorter piece = S).
- Be very specific when dealing with questions that contain 2 distinct but related situations (i.e. Jack's age NOW = J vs. Jack's age in 8 years = $J + 8$).

Step 2: Identify relationships and create equations

- As a general guideline, once you have identified how many variables you have, that will give you a big clue as to how many equations you will ultimately need. If you have 2 variables, you will need 2 equations to be able to find unique values for those variables.
- Don't forget to look at one piece of the question at a time. Don't try to do everything at once!
- Use numbers to check that you have set up your equation correctly. For example, if they say that Jack is twice as old as Ben, which is correct: $J = 2B$ or $2J = B$? If Jack were 40, Ben would be 20, so $(40) = 2(20)$ or $2(40) = 20$?

Step 3: Identify what the question is asking for

- Having a clear goal can prevent you from losing track of what you're doing and can help you stay focused on the task at hand.

Step 4: Solve for the wanted element (often by using substitution)

- The ability to perform every step accurately and efficiently is critical to success on the GMAT—practice makes perfect!

Now that we've gone through the basic steps, it's time to practice translating word problems into equations. But first, here are some common mathematical relationships found on the GMAT, words and phrases you might find used to describe them, and their translations. Use them to help you with the drill sets at the end of this chapter.

*Manhattan*GMAT*Prep
the new standard

Common Word Problem Phrases

Addition
Add, Sum, Total(of parts), More Than: +
The sum of x and y: $x + y$
The sum of the three funds combined: $a + b + c$
When fifty is added to his age: $a + 50$
Six pounds heavier than Dave: $d + 6$
A group of men and women: $m + w$
The cost is marked up: $c + m$

Subtraction
Minus, Difference, Less Than: −
x minus five: $x - 5$
The difference between Quentin's and Rachel's heights (if Quentin is taller): $q - r$
Four pounds less than expected: $e - 4$
The profit is the revenue minus the cost: $P = R - C$

Multiplication
The product of h and k: $h \times k$
The number of reds times the number of blues: $r \times b$
One fifth of y: $(1/5) \times y$
n persons have x beads each: total number of beads $= nx$
Go z miles per hour for t hours: distance $= zt$ miles

Ratios and Division
Quotient, Per, Ratio, Proportion: ÷ or /
Five dollars every two weeks: (5 dollars/2 weeks) → 2.5 dollars a week
The ratio of x to y: x/y
The proportion of girls to boys: g/b

Average or Mean (sum of terms divided by the total number of terms)

The average of a and b: $\dfrac{a+b}{2}$

The average salary of the three doctors: $\dfrac{x+y+z}{3}$

A student's average score on 5 tests was 87: $\dfrac{\text{sum}}{5} = 87$ or $\dfrac{a+b+c+d+e}{5} = 87$

Chapter Review: Drill Sets

DRILL SET 1:

Drill 1: Translate the following statements into equations and/or inequalities.

1. The total amount of money saved equals $2,000.
2. The number of cars is three fewer than the number of trucks.
3. There are twice as many computers as there are printers.
4. John ran twice as far as Mary.
5. There are 35 marbles in the jar, some green and some blue.

Drill 2: Translate the following statements into equations and/or inequalities.

1. Container A is three times as big as Container B.
2. One half of the students are learning French.
3. Max earned one-third of what Jerome earned.
4. The number of people on the team is three times the number of employees, minus four.
5. There are 10 more grapes than apples, and one-fourth as many apples as pears.

DRILL SET 2:

Drill 1: Translate and solve the following problems.

1. There are five more computers in the office than employees. If there are 10 employees in the office, how many computers are there?

2. If −5 is 7 more than z, what is $z/4$?

3. Each player on the team is required to purchase a uniform that costs $25. If there are 20 players on the team, what will be the total cost of the uniforms?

4. There are two trees in the front yard of a school. The trees have a combined height of 60 feet, and the taller tree is 3 times the height of the shorter tree. How high is the shorter tree?

5. A clothing store bought a container of 100 shirts for $20. If the store sold all of the shirts at $0.50 per shirt, what is the store's gross profit on the box?

Drill 2: Translate and solve the following problems.

1. A bag of 60 marbles is separated into two groups. If the first group contains 16 more marbles than the second group, how many marbles are in the larger group?

2. Two parking lots can hold a total of 115 cars. The Green lot can hold 35 fewer cars than the Red lot. How many cars can the Red lot hold?

3. At the county fair, two people are competing to see who can eat the most hot dogs. One competitor eats 7 less than the other competitor. If the competitor who eats fewer hot dogs eats 25 hot dogs, how many hot dogs did the two people eat, combined?

4. Ben and Sarah run a combined 30 kilometers. Ben runs 8 kilometers less than Sarah. How many kilometers did Ben run?

5. A class went to a donut shop, where 13 of the students ate 3 donuts each. Another 7 students were really hungry, and ate 8 donuts each. How many total donuts did the class eat?

Drill 3: Translate and solve the following problems.

1. Three friends sit down to eat 14 slices of pizza. If two of the friends eat the same number of slices, and the third eats two more slices than each of the other two, how many slices are eaten by the third friend?

2. A plane leaves Chicago in the morning, and makes three flights before returning. The first flight traveled twice as far as the second flight, and the second flight traveled three times as far as the third flight. If the third flight was 45 miles, how many miles was the first flight?

3. A rubber ball is thrown and bounces twice before it is caught. The first time the ball bounces it goes 5 times as high as the second time it bounces. If the second bounce goes 5 feet high, what is the combined height of the two bounces?

4. A museum tour guide can take 1 class through the museum in 30 minutes. If each class has 30 students, how many students will go through the museum in 2 hours?

5. A band on a concert tour played 10 concerts. The first concert had 100 people, and the last concert had 6 times as many people. If the sixth concert had 1/2 as many people as the last concert, how many people were at the sixth concert?

Drill 4: Translate and solve the following problems.

1. Movie theater X charges $6 per ticket, and each movie showing costs the theatre $1,750. If 300 people bought tickets for a certain showing, and the theater averaged $2 in concessions (popcorn, etc.) per ticket-holder, what was the theater's profit for that showing?

2. Three health clubs are competing to attract new members. One company runs an ad campaign and recruits 120 new members. The second company runs a similar campaign and recruits 2/3 as many members. The third company recruits 10 more members than the second company. How many new members are recruited by the three companies combined?

3. It costs a certain bicycle factory $10,000 to operate for one month, plus $300 for each bicycle produced during the month. Each of the bicycles sells for a retail price of $700. The gross profit of the factory is measured by total income from sales minus the production costs of the bicycles. If 50 bicycles are produced and sold during the month, what is the factory's gross profit?

*Manhattan*GMAT*Prep
the new standard

4. If a harbor cruise can shuttle 50 people per trip, and each trip takes 3 hours, how long will it take for 350 people to complete the tour?

5. Alfred and Nick cooked a total of 49 pies. If twice the number of pies that Alfred cooked was 14 pies more than the number of pies that Nick cooked, how many pies did Alfred cook?

Drill 5: Translate and solve the following problems.

1. Arnaldo earns $11 for each ticket that he sells, and a bonus of $2 per ticket for each ticket he sells over 100. If Arnaldo was paid $2,400, how many tickets did he sell?

2. Alicia is producing a magazine that costs $3 per magazine to print. In addition, she has to pay $10,500 to her staff to design the issue. If Alicia sells each magazine for $10, how many magazines must she sell to break even?

3. Eleanor's football team has won 3 times as many games as Christina's football team. Christina's football team has won four fewer games than Joanna's team. If Joanna's team won 10 games, how many games did Eleanor's team win?

4. The distance between Town *X* and Town *Y* is twice the distance between Town *X* and Town *Z*. The distance between Town *Z* and Town *W* is 2/3 the distance between Town *Z* and Town *X*. If the distance between Town *Z* and Town *W* is 18 miles, how far is Town *X* from Town *Y*?

5. Every week, Renee is paid 40 dollars per hour for the first 40 hours she works, and 80 dollars per hour for each hour she works after the first 40 hours. If she earned $2,000 last week, how many hours did she work?

DRILL SET 3:

Drill 1: Translate and solve the following word problems involving age.

1. Norman is 12 years older than Michael. In 6 years, he will be twice as old as Michael. How old is Norman now?

2. Louise is three times as old as Mary. In 5 years, Louise will be twice as old as Mary. How old is Mary now?

3. Chris is 14 years younger than Sam. In 3 years, Sam will be 3 times as old as Chris. How old is Sam now?

4. Toshi is 7 years older than his brother Kosuke, who is twice as old as their younger sister Junko. If Junko is 8 years old, how old is Toshi?

5. Amar is 30 years younger than Lauri. In 5 years, Lauri will be three times as old as Amar. How old will Lauri be in 10 years?

Drill 2: Translate and solve the following word problems involving averages. For the purpose of these problems "average" means the arithmetic mean.

Remember that $A = \dfrac{S}{n}$, where A = average, n = the number of terms, and S = the sum of the terms.

1. 3 lawyers earn an average of $300 per hour. How much money have they earned in total after they each worked 4 hours?

2. The average of 2, 13 and x is 10. What is x?

3. Last year, Nancy earned twice the amount of money that Janet earned. Kate earned three times the amount Janet earned. If Kate earned $45,000 last year, what was the average salary of the three women?

4. John buys 5 books with an average price of $12. If John then buys another book with a price of $18, what is the average price of the six books?

5. If the average of the five numbers $x - 3$, x, $x + 3$, $x + 4$, and $x + 11$ is 45, what is the value of x?

Drill 3: Translate and solve the following word problems involving rates. Remember that $d = rt$, where d = distance, r = rate and t = time.

1. Bill drove to the store at a rate of 30 miles per hour. If the store is 90 miles away, how long did it take him to get there?

2. Maria normally walks at a rate of 4 miles per hour. If she walks at one half of her normal rate, how long will it take her to walk 4 miles?

3. A train traveled at a constant rate from New York to Chicago in 9 hours. If the distance between New York and Chicago is 630 miles, how fast was the train going?

4. Randy completed a 12 mile run in 4 hours. If Betty ran 3 miles per hour faster than Randy, how long did it take her to complete the same 12 mile run?

5. A truck uses 1 gallon of gasoline every 15 miles. If the truck travels 3 hours at 60 miles per hour, how many gallons of gasoline will it use?

*Manhattan*GMAT*Prep
the new standard

Drill Set Answers

DRILL SET 1:

Set 1, Drill 1:

1. The total amount of money saved equals $2,000. $m = \$2{,}000$

2. The number of cars is three fewer than the number of trucks. $c = t - 3$

3. There are twice as many computers as there are printers. $c = 2p$

4. John ran twice as far as Mary. $j = 2m$

5. There are 35 marbles in the jar, some green and some blue. $35 = g + b$

Set 1, Drill 2:

1. Container A is three times as big as Container B. $A = 3B$

2. One half of the students are learning French. $1/2\, S = F$

3. Max earned one-third of what Jerome earned. $M = 1/3 J$

4. The number of people on the team is three times the number of employees, minus four. $t = 3e - 4$

5. There are 10 more grapes than apples, and one-fourth as many apples as pears. $g = a + 10$
$a = 1/4\, p$

DRILL SET 2:

Set 2, Drill 1:

1. There are five more computers in the office than employees. If there are 10 employees in the office, how many computers are there?

Let c = number of computers
Let e = number of employees

$c = e + 5$

If $e = 10$, then $c = (10) + 5$
$c = 15$

2. If -5 is 7 more than z, what is $z/4$? $-5 = z + 7$
$z = -12$
$z/4 = -3$

3. Each player on the team is required to purchase a uniform that costs $25. If there are 20 players on the team, what will be the total cost of the uniforms?

Let u = cost of each uniform
Let p = number of players
Let C = the total cost of the uniforms

$C = u \times p$

If p = 20, and u = $25, then

$C = (\$25) \times (20) = \$500$

4. There are two trees in the front yard of a school. The trees have a combined height of 60 feet, and the taller tree is 3 times the height of the shorter tree. How high is the shorter tree?

Let s = the height of the shorter tree
Let t = the height of the taller tree

$s + t = 60$
$3s = t$

$s + (3s) = 60$
$4s = 60$

$s = 15$

5. A clothing store bought a container of 100 shirts for $20. If the store sold all of the shirts at $0.50 per shirt, what is the store's gross profit on the box?

Let p = profit
Let r = revenue
Let c = cost

$Profit = Revenue - Cost$
$p = r - c$
$r = 100 \times \$0.50$
$c = \$20$

$p = (100 \times \$0.50) - (\$20)$
$p = \$50 - \$20 = \$30$

Set 2, Drill 2:

1. A bag of 60 marbles is separated into two groups. If the first group contains 16 more marbles than the second group, how many marbles are in the larger group?

Let f = the number of marbles in the first group
Let s = the number of marbles in the second group

$f + s = 60$
$f = s + 16$
$(s + 16) + s = 60$
$2s + 16 = 60$
$2s = 44$

*Manhattan*GMAT*Prep
the new standard

$s = 22$

$f = (22) + 16 = 38$

Answer: The larger group has 38 marbles.

2. Two parking lots can hold a total of 115 cars. The Green lot can hold 35 fewer cars than the Red lot. How many cars can the Red lot hold?

Let g = the number of cars that the Green lot can hold
Let r = the number of cars that the Red lot can hold

$g + r = 115$
$g = r - 35$

$(r - 35) + r = 115$
$2r - 35 = 115$
$2r = 150$
$r = 75$

$g = r - 35 = 75 - 35 = 40$

Red lot: 75 cars
Green lot: 40 cars

Answer: The Red lot can hold 75 cars.

3. At the county fair, two people are competing to see who can eat the most hot dogs. One competitor eats 7 less than the other competitor. If the competitor who eats fewer hot dogs eats 25 hot dogs, how many hot dogs did the two people eat, combined?

Let f = the number of hot dogs eaten by the first competitor (assume he or she ate fewer)
Let s = the number of hot dogs eaten by the second competitor

$f = s - 7$
$f = 25$

Therefore,

$(25) = s - 7$
$s = 32$

$25 + 32 = 57$

Answer: 57 hot dogs were eaten.

4. Ben and Sarah run a combined 30 kilometers. Ben runs 8 kilometers less than Sarah. How many kilometers did Ben run?

Let B = the number of kilometers run by Ben
Let S = the number of kilometers run by Sarah

$B + S = 30$
$B = S - 8$

$B + 8 = S$

$(B + 8) + B = 30$
$2B + 8 = 30$
$2B = 22$
$B = 11$

Answer: Ben ran 11 kilometers.

5. A class went to a donut shop, where 13 of the students ate 3 donuts each. Another 7 students were really hungry, and ate 8 donuts each. How many total donuts did the class eat?

13 students ate 3 donuts each: $13 \times 3 = 39$
7 students ate 8 donuts each: $7 \times (8) = 56$

Total = $39 + 56 = 95$

Answer: The class ate 95 donuts.

Set 2, Drill 3:

1. Three friends sit down to eat 14 slices of pizza. If two of the friends eat the same number of slices, and the third eats two more slices than each of the other two, how many slices are eaten by the third friend?

Let P = the number of slices of pizza eaten by each of the two friends who eat the same amount.
Let T = the number of slices of pizza eaten by the third friend.

$T = P + 2$

$P + P + T = 14$
$P + P + (P + 2) = 14$
$3P + 2 = 14$
$3P = 12$
$P = 4$

$T = P + 2 = 4 + 2 = 6$

Answer: 6 slices of pizza

2. A plane leaves Chicago in the morning, and makes three flights before returning. The first flight traveled twice as far as the second flight, and the second flight traveled three times as far as the third flight. If the third flight was 45 miles, how many miles was the first flight?

Let F = the distance of the first flight
Let S = the distance of the second flight
Let T = the distance of the third flight

$F = 2S$
$S = 3T$
$T = 45$

$S = 3 \times (45) = 135$
$F = 2 \times (135) = 270$

Answer: 270 miles

3. A rubber ball is thrown and bounces twice before it is caught. The first time the ball bounces it goes 5 times as high as the second time it bounces. If the second bounce goes 5 feet high, what is the combined height of the two bounces?

Let a = the height of the first bounce
Let b = the height of the second bounce

$a = 5 \times b$
$b = 5$

$a = 5 \times (5) = 25$

Total height = $a + b = 25 + 5 = 30$

Answer: 30 feet

4. A museum tour guide can take 1 class through the museum in 30 minutes. If each class has 30 students, how many students will go through the museum in 2 hours?

If each tour takes 30 minutes, a guide can complete 4 tours in 2 hours.

4 tours × 30 students = 120 students

Answer: 120 students

5. A band on a concert tour played 10 concerts. The first concert had 100 people, and the last concert had 6 times as many people. If the sixth concert had 1/2 as many people as the last concert, how many people were at the sixth concert?

Let f = the number of people at the first concert
Let l = the number of people at the last concert
Let s = the number of people at the sixth concert

$f = 100$
$l = 6\,f = 6 \times (100) = 600$
$s = 1/2\,(l) = 1/2 \times (600) = 300$

Answer: 300 people

Set 2, Drill 4:

1. Movie theater X charges $6 per ticket, and each movie showing costs the theater $1,750. If 300 people bought tickets for a certain showing, and the theater averaged $2 in concessions (popcorn, etc.) per ticket-holder, what was the theater's profit for that showing?

Profit = Revenue − Cost

Revenue = 300 × 6 + 300 × 2 = 1,800 + 600 = 2,400
Cost = 1,750

Profit = 2,400 − 1,750 = 650

Answer: $650

2. Three health clubs are competing to attract new members. One company runs an ad campaign and recruits 120 new members. The second company runs a similar campaign and recruits 2/3 as many members. The third company recruits 10 more members than the second company. How many new members are recruited by the three companies combined?

Let a = the number of new members recruited by the first company
Let b = the number of new members recruited by the second company
Let c = the number of new members recruited by the third company

$a = 120$
$b = 2/3\ (a) = 2/3 \times (120) = 80$
$c = b + 10 = (80) + 10 = 90$

$a + b + c = 120 + 80 + 90 = 290$

Answer: 290 new members

3. It costs a certain bicycle factory \$10,000 to operate for one month, plus \$300 for each bicycle produced during the month. Each of the bicycles sells for a retail price of \$700. The gross profit of the factory is measured by total income from sales minus the production costs of the bicycles. If 50 bicycles are produced and sold during the month, what is the factory's gross profit?

Profit = Revenue − Cost
Revenue = 50 × 700 = 35,000

Cost = 10,000 + (50 × 300) = 10,000 + 15,000 = 25,000
Profit = 35,000 − 25,000 = 10,000

Answer: \$10,000

4. If a harbor cruise can shuttle 50 people per trip, and each trip takes 3 hours, how long will it take for 350 people to complete the tour?

First, let's figure out how many trips we need. If each trip can accommodate 50 people, then we will need:

350 people / 50 = 7 trips

7 trips × 3 hours = 21 hours

Answer: 21 hours

5. Alfred and Nick cooked a total of 49 pies. If twice the number of pies that Alfred cooked was 14 pies more than the number of pies that Nick cooked, how many pies did Alfred cook?

Let A = the number of pies that Alfred cooked.
Let N = the number of pies that Nick cooked.

$A + N = 49$
$2A = N + 14 \quad 2A - 14 = N$

$A + (2A - 14) = 49$
$3A - 14 = 49$
$3A = 63$
$A = 21$

Answer: 21 pies

Set 2, Drill 5:

1. Arnaldo earns $11 for each ticket that he sells, and a bonus of $2 per ticket for each ticket he sells over 100. If Arnaldo was paid $2,400, how many tickets did he sell?

Let x = the total number of tickets sold.

Therefore, $(x - 100)$ = the number of tickets sold over 100

$11x + 2(x - 100) = 2,400$
$11x + 2x - 200 = 2,400$
$13x = 2,600$
$x = 200$

Answer: 200 tickets

2. Alicia is producing a magazine that costs $3 per magazine to print. In addition, she has to pay $10,500 to her staff to design the issue. If Alicia sells each magazine for $10, how many magazines must she sell to break even?

Let m = the number of magazines sold
Total cost = $3m + 10,500$
Total revenue = $10m$

Breaking even occurs when total revenue equals total cost, so:

$3m + 10,500 = 10m$
$10,500 = 7m$
$1,500 = m$

Answer: 1,500 magazines

3. Eleanor's football team has won 3 times as many games as Christina's football team. Christina's football team has won four fewer games than Joanna's team. If Joanna's team won 10 games last year, how many games did Eleanor's team win?

Let E = the number of games Eleanor's team won
Let C = the number of games Christine's team won
Let J = the number of games Joanna's team won

$E = 3C$
$C = J - 4$
$J = 10$

$C = (10) - 4 = 6$
$E = 3(6) = 18$

Answer: 18 games

4. The distance between Town X and Town Y is twice the distance between Town X and Town Z. The distance between Town Z and Town W is 2/3 the distance between Town Z and Town X. If the distance between Town Z and Town W is 18 miles, how far is Town X from Town Y?

Let $[XY]$ = the distance between Town X and Town Y
Let $[XZ]$ = the distance between Town X and Town Z
Let $[ZW]$ = the distance between Town Z and Town W

Translating the information in the question, we get:
$[XY] = 2[XZ]$ from the first sentence
$[ZW] = 2/3\ [XZ]$ from the second sentence
$[ZW] = 18$ from the third sentence

$18 = 2/3\ [XZ]$
$54/2 = [XZ]$
$27 = [XZ]$
$[XY] = 2(27) = 54$

Answer: 54 miles

5. Every week, Renee is paid 40 dollars per hour for the first 40 hours she works, and 80 dollars per hour for each hour she works after the first 40 hours. If she earned $2,000 last week, how many hours did she work?

Let h = number of hours Renee worked

$40(40) + (h - 40)(80) = 2,000$
$1,600 + 80h - 3,200 = 2,000$
$80h - 1,600 = 2,000$
$80h = 3,600$
$h = 45$

Answer: 45 hours

DRILL SET 3:

Set 3, Drill 1:

1. Norman is 12 years older than Michael. In 6 years, he will be twice as old as Michael. How old is Norman now?

Let N = Norman's age now	$(N + 6)$ = Norman's age in 6 years.
Let M = Michael's age now	$(M + 6)$ = Michael's age in 6 years.

$N = M + 12$	Translate the first sentence into an equation.
$N + 6 = 2(M + 6)$	Translate the second sentence into an equation.

$N - 12 = M$	Rewrite the first equation to put it in terms of M.

$N + 6 = 2(N - 12 + 6)$	Insert $N - 12$ for M in the second equation.
$N + 6 = 2(N - 6)$	
$N + 6 = 2N - 12$	

$18 = N$	Solve for N.

Answer: Norman is 18 years old.

2. Louise is three times as old as Mary. In 5 years, Louise will be twice as old as Mary. How old is Mary now?

Let L = Louise's age now	$(L + 5)$ = Louise's age 5 years from now
Let M = Mary's age now	$(M + 5)$ = Mary's age 5 years from now

$L = 3M$	Translate the first sentence into an equation.
$(L + 5) = 2(M + 5)$	Translate the second sentence into an equation.

$(3M + 5) = 2(M + 5)$	Insert $3M$ for L in the second equation.
$3M + 5 = 2M + 10$	Make sure you distribute the 2.
$M = 5$	Solve for M

Answer: Mary is 5 years old.

3. Chris is 14 years younger than Sam. In 3 years, Sam will be 3 times as old as Chris. How old is Sam now?

Let C = Chris' age now	$(C + 3)$ = Chris' age 3 years from now
Let S = Sam's age now	$(S + 3)$ = Sam's age 3 years from now

$C = S - 14$	Translate the first sentence into an equation.
$3(C + 3) = (S + 3)$	Translate the second sentence into an equation.

$3C + 9 = S + 3$
$3(S - 14) + 9 = S + 3$ Insert $S - 14$ for C in the second equation.
$3S - 42 + 9 = S + 3$
$3S - 33 = S + 3$
$2S - 33 = 3$
$2S = 36$
$S = 18$ Solve for S.

Answer: 18 years old

4. Toshi is 7 years older than his brother Kosuke, who is twice as old as their younger sister Junko. If Junko is 8 years old, how old is Toshi?

Let T = Toshi's age
Let K = Kosuke's age
Let J = Junko's age

$J = 8$
$B = 2 \times J = 2 \times (8) = 16$
$T = B + 7 = (16) + 7 = 23$

Answer: 23 years old

5. Amar is 30 years younger than Lauri. In 5 years, Lauri will be three times as old as Amar. How old will Lauri be in 10 years?

Let A = Amar's age now $(A + 5)$ = Amar's age 5 years from now
Let L = Lauri's age now $(L + 5)$ = Lauri's age 5 years from now

We're looking for Lauri's age in 10 years: $L + 10$

$A = L - 30$ Translate the first sentence into an equation.
$L + 5 = 3 (A + 5)$ Translate the second sentence into an equation.

$L + 5 = 3(L - 30 + 5)$ Insert $L - 30$ for A in the second equation.
$L + 5 = 3(L - 25)$
$L + 5 = 3L - 75$
$80 = 2L$
$40 = L$

Remember, we're looking for Lauri's age in 10 years:

$L + 10 = 40 + 10 = 50$

Answer: 50 years old

Set 3, Drill 2:

1. 3 lawyers earn an average of $300 per hour. How much money have they earned in total after they each worked 4 hours?

Each lawyer worked 4 hours, earning $300 per hour. $4 \times \$300 = \$1,200$

There are 3 lawyers. $\$1,200 \times 3 = \$3,600$

Answer: They earned $3,600 in total.

2. The average of 2, 13, and x is 10. What is x?

$$A = \frac{S}{n}$$

Here, $10 = A$, S is the sum of the 3 terms (2, 13, x), and 3 is the number of terms.

$$\frac{2 + 13 + x}{3} = 10$$
$$2 + 13 + x = 30$$
$$15 + x = 30$$
$$x = 15$$

3. Last year, Nancy earned twice the amount of money that Janet earned. Kate earned three times the amount Janet earned. If Kate earned $45,000 last year, what was the average salary of the three women?

Let N = the amount of money Nancy earned
Let J = the amount of money Janet earned
Let K = the amount of money Kate earned
Let A = the average salary

$N = 2J$
$K = 3J$
$K = \$45,000$
$(\$45,000) = 3J$
$\$15,000 = J$
$N = 2(\$15,000)$
$N = \$30,000$

$$\frac{N + K + J}{3} = A$$

$$\frac{\$30,000 + \$15,000 + \$45,000}{3} = A$$

$$\frac{\$90,000}{3} = A$$
$$\$30,000 = A$$

*Manhattan*GMAT*Prep

4. John buys 5 books with an average price of $12. If John then buys another book with a price of $18, what is the average price of the six books?

$$\frac{\text{Sum}}{\text{Number}} = \text{Average}$$

First, we need to know the cost of the 5 books.

Sum = (Average)(Number) = ($12)(5) = $60

Sum of the cost of all 6 books = $60 + $18 = $78
Number of total books = 6

$$\frac{\$78}{6} = \text{Average}$$

$13 = Average

5. If the average of the five numbers $x - 3$, x, $x + 3$, $x + 4$, and $x + 11$ is 45, what is the value of x?

$$\frac{(x-3)+(x)+(x+3)+(x+4)+(x+11)}{5} = 45$$

$$\frac{5x+15}{5} = 45$$

$x + 3 = 45$
$x = 42$

Set 3, Drill 3:

1. Bill drove to the store at a rate of 30 miles per hour. If the store is 90 miles away, how long did it take him to get there?

Let r = rate
Let t = time
Let d = distance

$r \times t = d$
(30 m/hr) $\times t$ = 90 miles
t = 90/30 = 3 hours

2. Maria normally walks at a rate of 4 miles per hour. If she walks at one half of her normal rate, how long will it take her to walk 4 miles?

Let r = rate
Let t = time
Let d = distance

$r = 4$ miles/hr
$1/2 \times r = 2$ miles/hr
$d = 4$ miles

$r \times t = d$
2 miles/hr $\times t = 4$ miles
$2t = 4$
$t = 2$ hours

3. A train traveled at a constant rate from New York to Chicago in 9 hours. If the distance between New York and Chicago is 630 miles, how fast was the train going?

$d = rt$
630 miles $= r$(9 hours)
70 miles per hour $= r$

Answer: 70 miles per hour

4. Randy completed a 12 mile run in 4 hours. If Betty ran 3 miles per hour faster than Randy, how long did it take her to complete the same 12 mile run?

r = rate at which Randy ran
$r + 3$ = the rate at which Betty ran

12 miles $= r$(4 hours)
$r = 3$ miles per hour

$12 = (r + 3)(t)$
$12 = (3 + 3)(t)$
$12 = 6t$
$2 = t$

Answer: 2 hours

5. A truck uses 1 gallon of gasoline every 15 miles. If the truck travels 3 hours at 60 miles per hour, how many gallons of gasoline will it use?

Let d = distance traveled

$d = (60$ mph$)(3$ hours$) = 180$ miles

180 miles/15 miles per gallon = 12 gallons

Answer: 12 gallons of gasoline

Chapter 4
of
FOUNDATIONS OF GMAT MATH

DIVISIBILITY

In This Chapter . . .

- Divisibility Rules
- Factors
- Prime Numbers
- Prime Factors
- The Factor Foundation Rule
- The Factor/Prime Factorization Connection
- Unknown Numbers and Divisibility
- Unknown Numbers and Divisibility (cont.)

DIVISIBILITY

In This Chapter:

- Divisibility rules
- How to find the factors of a number
- The connection between factors and divisibility
- How to answer questions on the GMAT related to divisibility

There is a group of problems on the GMAT that tests what could broadly be referred to as "Number Properties." They are focused on a very important subset of numbers known as integers. Before we go any further, let's do a brief overview of what integers are.

Integers are whole numbers. That means that they are numbers that do not have any decimals or fractions attached. Some people think of them as counting numbers, i.e. 1, 2, 3... etc. Integers can be positive, and they can also be negative. −1, −2, −3... etc. are all integers as well. And there's one more important number that qualifies as an integer: 0.

So numbers such as 7, 15,003, −346, and 0 are all integers. Numbers such as 1.3, 3/4, and π are not integers.

Now that we know what integers are, let's see what we know about them when dealing with the four basic operations: addition, subtraction, multiplication and division.

integer + integer = always an integer   ex. $4 + 11 = 15$

integer − integer = always an integer   ex. $-5 - 32 = -37$

integer × integer = always an integer   ex. $14 \times 3 = 42$

None of these properties of integers turn out to be very interesting. But what happens when we *divide* an integer by another integer? Well, $18 \div 3 = 6$, which is an integer, but $12 \div 8 = 1.5$, which is not an integer.

If an integer divides another integer and the result, or quotient, is an integer, we say the first number is divisible by the second. So 18 is divisible by 3 because $18 \div 3 =$ an integer. On the other hand, we would say that 12 is NOT divisible by 8, because $12 \div 8$ is not an integer.

Divisibility Rules

On this test, being able to quickly identify which numbers are divisible by some integer will be an important skill. There are some easy-to-remember rules to help you make this identification for numbers that often show up on this test.

An integer is divisible by:

2 if the integer is even.

> Any even number is, by definition, divisible by 2. The even numbers are easy to identify. Any number that ends in 0, 2, 4, 6 or 8 is even.

3 if the sum of the integer's digits is a multiple of 3.

Take the number 147. Its digits are 1, 4 and 7. 1 + 4 + 7 = 12, which is a multiple of 3, which means that 147 is divisible by 3.

5 if the integer ends in 0 or 5

75 and 80 are divisible by 5, but 77 and 84 are not.

9 if the sum of the integer's digits is a multiple of 9.

This rule is very similar to the divisibility rule for 3. Take the number 144. 1 + 4 + 4 = 9, so 144 is divisible by 9.

10 if the integer ends in 0.

8,730 is divisible by 10, but 8,753 is not.

Check Your Skills

1. Is 123,456,789 divisible by 2?
2. Is 732 divisible by 3?
3. Is 989 divisible by 9?

Answers can be found on page 121.

Factors

Let's continue to explore the question of divisibility by asking the question, what numbers is 6 divisible by? Questions related to divisibility are only interested in positive integers, so we really only have 6 possible numbers: 1, 2, 3, 4, 5, and 6. So let's see which numbers 6 is divisible by.

$6 \div 1 = 6$ Any number divided by 1 equals itself, so an integer divided by 1 will be an integer.

$6 \div 2 = 3$
$6 \div 3 = 2$ Note that these form a pair

$6 \div 4 = 1.5$
$6 \div 5 = 1.2$ Not integers, so 6 is NOT divisible by 4 or by 5.

$6 \div 6 = 1$ Any number divided by itself equals 1, so an integer is always divisible by itself.

So 6 is divisible by 1, 2, 3 and 6. That means that 1, 2, 3 and 6 are **factors** of 6. There are a variety of ways you might see this relationship expressed on the GMAT.

2 is a factor of 6	6 is a multiple of 2
2 is a divisor of 6	6 is divisible by 2
2 divides 6	2 goes into 6

Sometimes it will be necessary to find the factors of a number in order to answer a question. An easy way to find all the factors of a small number is to use factor pairs. Factor pairs for any integer are the pairs of factors that, when multiplied together, yield that integer.

Here's a step-by-step way to find all the factors of the number 60 using a **factor pairs table:**

(1) Make a table with 2 columns labeled "Small" and "Large."

(2) Start with 1 in the small column and 60 in the large column. (The first set of factor pairs will always be 1 and the number itself)

(3) The next number after 1 is 2. If 2 is a factor of 60, then write "2" underneath the "1" in your table. It is, so divide 60 by 2 to find the factor pair: $60 \div 2 = 30$. Write "30" in the large column.

Small	Large
1	60
2	30
3	20
4	15
5	12
6	10

(4) The next number after 2 is 3. Repeat this process until the numbers in the small and the large columns run into each other. In this case, we find that 6 and 10 are a factor pair. But 7, 8 and 9 are not factors of 60, and the next number after 9 is 10, which appears in the large column, so we can stop.

The advantage of using this method, as opposed to thinking of factors and listing them out, is that this is an organized, methodical approach that makes it easier to find *every* factor of a number quickly. Let's practice. (This is also a good opportunity to practice your long division.)

Check Your Skills

4. Find all the factors of 90.
5. Find all the factors of 72.
6. Find all the factors of 105.
7. Find all the factors of 120.

Answers can be found on pages 121–122.

Prime Numbers

Let's backtrack a little bit and ask the question, what numbers is 7 divisible by? Our only possibilities are the positive integers less than or equal to 7, so let's check every possibility.

$7 \div 1 = 7$ Every number is divisible by 1—no surprise there!

$7 \div 2 = 3.5$

$7 \div 3 = 2.33...$

$7 \div 4 = 1.75$ 7 is not divisible by *any* integer besides 1 and itself

$7 \div 5 = 1.4$

$7 \div 6 = 1.16...$

$7 \div 7 = 1$ Every number is divisible by itself—boring!

So 7 only has two factors—1 and itself. Numbers that only have 2 factors are known as **prime numbers.** As we will see, prime numbers play a very important role in answering questions about divisibility. Because they're so important, it's important to be able to identify what numbers are prime and what numbers aren't.

The prime numbers that appear most frequently on the test are prime numbers less than 20. They are 2, 3, 5, 7, 11, 13, 17 and 19. Two things to note about this list: 1 is not prime, and out of *all* the prime numbers, 2 is the *only* even prime number.

> **Nerd Note:** Why isn't 1 prime? Actually, 1 used to be prime—but then mathematicians decided to define prime numbers as having exactly two different positive factors. 1 has only one factor (1), so it's no longer considered prime.

2 is prime because it has only two factors—1 and itself. The reason that it's the only even prime number is that *every* even number is divisible by 2, and thus has another factor besides 1 and itself. For instance, we can immediately tell that 12,408 can't be prime, because we know that it has at least one factor besides 1 and itself: 2.

So every positive integer can be placed into one of two categories—prime or not prime.

Primes   Non-Primes

2, 3, 5, 7, 11, etc.   4, 6, 8, 9, 10, etc.

exactly two factors: 1 and itself   *more than* 2 factors

ex. $7 = 1 \times 7$ ex. $6 = 1 \times 6$

only factor pair   *and* $6 = 2 \times 3$

more than 2 factors *and*

more than 1 factor pair

> **Nerd Note:** 1 is a non-prime, but is a special case and has many properties distinct from other non-primes. (e.g. it only has 1 factor).

Check Your Skills

8. List all the prime numbers between 20 and 50.

The answer can be found on page 122.

Prime Factorization

Let's take another look at 60. When we found the factor pairs of 60, we discovered that it had 12 factors and 6 factor pairs.

$60 = 1 \times 60$ Always the first factor pair—boring!

and 2×30

and 3×20

and 4×15 } 5 other factor pairs—interesting!
Let's look at these in a little more detail.

and 5×12

and 6×10

> **Safety Tip:** From here on, we will be referring to boring and interesting factor pairs. These are not technical terms, but the boring factor pair is the factor pair that involves 1 and the number itself. All other pairs are interesting pairs. Keep reading to see why!

Manhattan **GMAT** Prep
the new standard

Let's look at one of these factor pairs—4 × 15. One way to think about this pair is that 60 *breaks down* into 4 and 15. One way to express this relationship visually is to use a **factor tree.**

Now, the question arises—can we go further? Sure! Neither 4 nor 15 is prime, which means they both have factor pairs that we might find *interesting*. 4 breaks down into 2 × 2, and 15 breaks down into 3 × 5:

Can we break it down any further? Not with *interesting* factor pairs. We could say that 2 = 2 × 1, for instance, but that doesn't provide us any new information. The reason we can't go any further is that 2, 2, 3 and 5 are all *prime numbers*. Prime numbers only have one boring factor pair. So when we find a prime factor, we know that that branch of our factor tree has reached its end. We can go one step further and circle every prime number as we go, reminding us that we can't break down that branch any further. The factor tree for 60 would look like this:

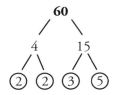

So after we broke down 60 into 4 and 15, and broke 4 and 15 down, we ended up with 60 = 2 × 2 × 3 × 5.

What if we start with a different factor pair of 60? Let's create a factor tree for 60 in which the first breakdown we make is 6 × 10.

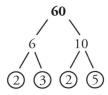

According to this factor tree 60 = 2 × 3 × 2 × 5. Notice that, even though they're in a different order, this is the same group of prime numbers we had before. In fact, *any* way we break down 60, we will end up with the same prime factors: two 2's, one 3 and one 5. Another way to say this is that 2 × 2 × 3 × 5 is the **prime factorization** of 60.

One way to think about prime factors is that they are the DNA of a number. Every number has a unique prime factorization. 60 is the only number that can be written as $2 \times 2 \times 3 \times 5$. Breaking down numbers into their prime factors is the key to answering many divisibility problems.

As we proceed through the chapter, we'll discuss what prime factors can tell us about a number and some different types of questions the GMAT may ask. But because the prime factorization of a number is so important, first we need a fast, reliable way to find the prime factorization of *any* number.

A factor tree is the best way to find the prime factorization of a number. A number like 60 should be relatively straightforward to break down into primes, but what if you need the prime factorization of 630?

For large numbers, it's often best to start with the smallest prime factors and work your way toward larger primes. This is why it's good to know your divisibility rules!

Take a second to try on your own, and then we'll go through it together on the next page.

Start by finding the smallest prime number that 630 is divisible by. The smallest prime number is 2. 630 is even, so we know it must be divisible by 2. 630 divided by 2 is 315, so our first breakdown of 630 is into 2 and 315.

Now we still need to factor 315. It's not even, so we know it's not divisible by 2. Is it divisible by 3? If the digits of 315 add up to a multiple of 3, it is. $3 + 1 + 5 = 9$, which is a multiple of 3, so 315 is divisible by 3. 315 divided by 3 is 105, so our factor tree now looks like this:

> **Safety Tip:** Don't forget to circle primes as you go! Those branches are broken down as far as they'll go.

If 315 was not divisible by 2, then 105 won't be either (we will discuss why later), but 105 might still be divisible by 3. $1 + 0 + 5 = 6$, so 105 is divisible by 3. $105 \div 3 = 35$, so our tree now looks like this:

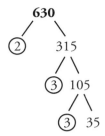

35 is not divisible by 3 (3 + 5 = 8, which is not a multiple of 3), so the next number to try is 5. 35 ends in a 5, so we know it is divisible by 5. 35 ÷ 5 = 7, so our tree now looks like this:

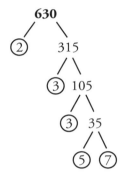

Every number on the tree has now been broken down as far as it can go. So the prime factorization of 630 is $2 \times 3 \times 3 \times 5 \times 7$.

Alternatively, you could have split 630 into 63 and 10, since it's easy to see that 630 is divisible by 10. Then you would proceed from there. Either way will get you to the same set of prime factors.

Now it's time to get a little practice doing prime factorizations. (These are the same numbers from the first Check Your Skills section in this chapter. We'll discuss the connection later in the chapter.)

Check Your Skills

9. Find the prime factorization of 90.
10. Find the prime factorization of 72.
11. Find the prime factorization of 105.
12. Find the prime factorization of 120.

Answers can be found on pages 122–123

The Factor Foundation Rule

This discussion begins with the **factor foundation rule.** The factor foundation rule states that if a is divisible by b, and b is divisible by c, then a is divisible by c as well. In other words, if we know that 12 is divisible by 6, and 6 is divisible by 3, then 12 is divisible by 3 as well.

This rule also works in reverse to a certain extent. If d is divisible by two different primes, *e* and *f*, *d* is also divisible by *e* × *f*. In other words, if 20 is divisible by 2 and by 5, then 20 is also divisible by 2 × 5 (10).

Another way to think of this rule is that divisibility travels up and down the factor tree. Let's walk through the factor tree of 150. We'll break it down, and then we'll build it back up.

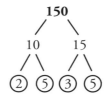

150 is divisible by 10 and by 15, so 150 is also divisible by *everything* that 10 and 15 are divisible by. 10 is divisible by 2 and 5, so 150 is also divisible by 2 and 5. 15 is divisible by 3 and 5, so 150 is also divisible by 3 and 5. Taken all together, we know that the prime factorization of 150 is 2 × 3 × 5 × 5. We could represent that information like this:

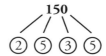

Think of prime factors as building blocks. In the case of 150, we have one 2, one 3 and two 5's at our disposal to build other factors of 150. In our first example, we went down the tree —from 150 down to 10 and 15, and then down again to 2, 5, 3 and 5. But we can also build upwards, starting with our four building blocks. For instance, 2 × 3 = 6, and 5 × 5 = 25, so our tree could also look like this:

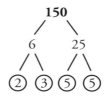

(Even though 5 and 5 are not different primes, 5 appears twice on 150's tree. So we are allowed to multiply those two 5's together to produce another factor of 150, namely 25.)

The tree above isn't even the only other possibility. These are all trees that we could build using different combinations of our prime factors.

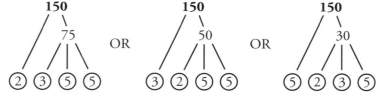

We began with four prime factors of 150: 2, 3, 5 and 5. But we were able to build different factors by multiplying 2, 3 or even all 4 of those primes together in different combinations. As it turns out, *all* of the factors of a number (except for 1) can be built with different combinations of its prime factors.

The Factor/Prime Factorization Connection

Let's take one more look at the number 60 and its factors. Specifically, let's look at the prime factorizations of all the factors of 60.

	Small	Large	
1	1	60	$2 \times 2 \times 3 \times 5$
2	2	30	$2 \times 3 \times 5$
3	3	20	$2 \times 2 \times 5$
2×2	4	15	3×5
5	5	12	$2 \times 2 \times 3$
2×3	6	10	2×5

All the factors of 60 are just different combinations of the prime numbers that make up the prime factorization of 60. To say this another way, every factor of a number can be expressed as the product of a combination of its prime factors. Take a look back at your work for Check Your Skills questions 4–7 and 9–12. Break down all the factor pairs from the first section into their prime factors. This relationship between factors and prime factors is true of every number.

Now that you know why prime factors are so important, it's time for the next step. An important skill on the GMAT is to take the given information in a question and go further with it. For example, if a question tells you that a number n is even, what else do you know about it? Every even number is a multiple of 2, so n is a multiple of 2. These kinds of inferences often provide crucial information necessary to correctly solving problems.

So now that we know the connection between factors and prime factors, we need to make sure that if a question tells us about factors of a number, we know *everything* that goes along with that information.

So far, we've been finding factors and prime factors of numbers—but the GMAT will often ask divisibility questions about *variables*. In the next section, we'll take our discussion of divisibility to the next level and bring variables into the picture. But first, we'll recap what we've learned so far and what tools we'll need going forward.

1. If a is divisible by b, and b is divisible by c, then a is divisible by c as well. (ex. 100 is divisible by 20, and 20 is divisible by 4, so 100 is divisible by 4 as well.)

2. If d has e and f as prime factors, d is also divisible by $e \times f$. (ex. 90 is divisible by 5 and by 3, so 90 is also divisible by $5 \times 3 = 15$.) You can let e and f be the same prime, as long as there are at least 2 copies of that prime in d's factor tree.

3. Every factor of a number (except 1) is the product of a different combination of that number's prime factors. For example, $30 = 2 \times 3 \times 5$. Its factors are 1, 2, 3, 5, 6 (2×3), 10 (2×5), 15 (3×5) and 30 ($2 \times 3 \times 5$).

4. To find *all* the factors of a number in an easy, methodical way, set up a factor pairs table.

5. To find *all* the prime factors of a number, use a factor tree. With larger numbers, start with the smallest primes and work your way up to larger primes.

> **Safety Tip:** Whenever you make a factor tree of an unknown number (or variable), include a branch with a question mark to remind you there may be other factors that you don't know.

Check Your Skills

13. The prime factorization of a number is 3 × 5. What is the number and what are all its factors?
14. The prime factorization of a number is 2 × 5 × 7. What is the number and what are all its factors?
15. The prime factorization of a number is 2 × 3 × 13. What is the number and what are all its factors?

Answers can be found on pages 123

Unknown Numbers and Divisibility

Let's say that you are told some unknown positive number x is divisible by 6. How can you represent this on paper? There are many ways, depending on the problem. You could say that you know that x is a multiple of 6, or you could say that $x = 6 \times$ an integer. You could also represent the information with a factor tree. Careful though—although we've had a lot of practice drawing factor trees, there is one important difference now that we're dealing with an unknown number. We know that x is divisible by 6, but x may be divisible by other numbers as well. We have to treat what they have told us as incomplete information, and remind ourselves there are other things about x we don't know. To represent that on the page, our factor tree could look like this:

Now the question becomes—what else do we know about x? If a question on the GMAT told you that x is divisible by 6, what could you definitely say about x? Take a look at these three statements, and for each statement, decide whether it *must* be true, whether it *could* be true, or whether it *cannot* be true.

     I. x is divisible by 3

     II. x is even

     III x is divisible by 12

We'll deal with each statement one at a time. Let's begin with statement I—x is divisible by 3. One approach to take here is to think about the multiples of 6. If x is divisible by 6, then we know that x is a multiple of 6. Let's list out the first several multiples of 6, and see if they're divisible by 3.

Manhattan **GMAT** Prep
the new standard

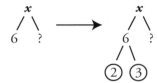

x is a number on this list	6	$6 \div 3 = 2$
	12	$12 \div 3 = 4$
	18	$18 \div 3 = 6$
	24	$24 \div 3 = 8$
	...	...

All of these numbers are also divisible by 3.

At this point, we can be fairly certain that *x* is divisible by 3. In fact, listing out possible values of a variable is often a great way to begin answering a question in which you don't know the value of the number you are asked about.

But can we do better than say we're fairly certain *x* is divisible by 3? Is there a way to definitively say *x* *must* be divisible by 3? As it turns out, there is. Let's return to our factor tree, but let's make one modification to it.

> **Safety Tip:** Note that there could still be other unknown factors, which is why there is still a question mark included in our tree.

Remember, the ultimate purpose of the factor tree is to break numbers down into their fundamental building blocks: prime numbers. Now that the factor tree is broken down as far as it will go, we can apply the factor foundation rule. *x* is divisible by 6, and 6 is divisible by 3, so we can say definitively that *x* *must* be divisible by 3.

In fact, questions like this one are the reason we spent so much time discussing the factor foundation rule and the connection between prime factors and divisibility. Prime factors provide the foundation for a way to make definite statements about divisibility. With that in mind, let's look at statement II.

Statement II says *x* is even. This question is about divisibility, so the question becomes, what is the connection between divisibility and a number being even? Remember, an important part of this test is the ability to make inferences based on the given information.

What's the connection? Well, being even means being divisible by 2. So if we know that *x* is divisible by 2, then we can guarantee that *x* is even. Let's return to our factor tree.

We can once again make use of the factor foundation rule—6 is divisible by 2, so we know that *x* *must* be divisible by 2 as well. And if *x* is divisible by 2, then we know that *x* *must* be even as well.

That just leaves the final statement. Statement III says *x* is divisible by 12. Let's look at this

*Manhattan*GMAT*Prep

question from the perspective of factor trees. Let's compare the factor tree of x with the factor tree of 12.

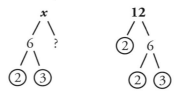

What would we have to know about x to guarantee that it is divisible by 12? Well, when 12 is broken down all the way, we see that 12 is $2 \times 2 \times 3$. 12's building blocks are two 2's and a 3. For x to be divisible by 12, it would have to also have two 2's and one 3 among its prime factors. In other words, for x to be divisible by 12, it has to be divisible by *everything* that 12 is divisible by.

We need x to be divisible by two 2's and one 3 in order to say it *must* be divisible by 12. But looking at our factor tree, we only see one 2 and one 3. Because there is only one 2, we can't say that x *must* be divisible by 12. But then the question becomes, *could* x be divisible by 12? Think about the question for a second, and then keep reading.

The key to this question is the question mark that we put on x's factor tree. That question mark reminds us that we don't know everything about x. x could have other prime factors. What if one of those unknown factors was another 2? Then our tree would look like this:

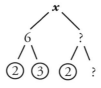

So *if* one of those unknown factors were a 2, then x would be divisible by 12. The key here is that we have no way of knowing for sure whether there is a 2. x may be divisible by 12, it may not. In other words, x *could* be divisible by 12.

To confirm this, we can go back to the multiples of 6. We still know that x must be a multiple of 6, so let's start by listing out the first several multiples and see if they are divisible by 12.

$$
x \text{ is a number on this list}
\left\{
\begin{array}{ll}
6 & 6 \div 12 = 0.5 \\
12 & 12 \div 12 = 1 \\
18 & 18 \div 12 = 1.5 \\
24 & 24 \div 12 = 2 \\
\dots & \dots
\end{array}
\right\}
\text{Some, but not all, of these numbers are also divisible by 12.}
$$

Once again, we see that some of the possible values of x are divisible by 12, and some aren't. The best we can say is that x *could* be divisible by 12.

Check Your Skills

For these statements, the following is true: *x* is divisible by 24. For each statement, say whether it *must* be true, *could* be true, or *cannot* be true.

16. *x* is divisible by 6
17. *x* is divisible by 9
18. *x* is divisible by 8

Answers can be found on pages 124.

Unknown Numbers and Divisibility (cont.)

Let's answer another question, this time with an additional twist. Once again, there will be three statements. Decide whether each statement *must* be true, *could* be true, or *cannot* be true. Answer this question on your own, then we'll discuss each statement one at a time on the next page.

x is divisible by 3 and by 10.

     I. *x* is divisible by 2

     II. *x* is divisible by 15

     III. *x* is divisible by 45

Before we dive into the statements, let's spend a moment to organize the information the question has given us. We know that *x* is divisible by 3 and by 10, so we can create two factor trees to represent this information.

Now that we have our trees, let's get started with statement I. Statement I says that *x* is divisible by 2. The way to determine whether this statement is true should be fairly familiar by now—we need to use the factor foundation rule. First of all, our factor trees aren't quite finished. Factor trees should always be broken down all the way until every branch ends in a prime number. Really, our factor trees should look like this:

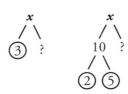

Now we are ready to decide whether statement I is true. *x* is divisible by 10, and 10 is divisible by 2, so we know that *x* is divisible by 2. Statement I *must* be true.

That brings us to statement II. This statement is a little more difficult. It also requires us to take another look at our factor trees. We have two separate trees, but they're giving us information about the same variable—x. Neither tree gives us complete information about x, but we do know a couple of things with absolute certainty. From the first tree, we know that x is divisible by 3, and from the second tree we know that x is divisible by 10—which really means we know that x is divisible by 2 and by 5. We can actually combine those two pieces of information and represent them on one factor tree.

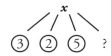

Now we know three prime factors of x: 2, 3 and 5. Let's return to the statement. Statement II says that x is divisible by 15. What do we need to know to say that x *must* be divisible by 15? If we can guarantee that x has all the prime factors that 15 has, then we can guarantee that x is divisible by 15.

15 breaks down into the prime factors 3 and 5. So to guarantee that x is divisible by 15, we need to know it's divisible by 3 and 5. Looking back up at our factor tree, we see that x has both a 3 and a 5, which means that we know x is divisible by 15. Therefore, statement II *must* be true.

We can also look at this question more visually. Remember, prime factors are like building blocks—we also know that x is divisible by any combination of these prime factors. We can combine the prime factors in a number of different ways.

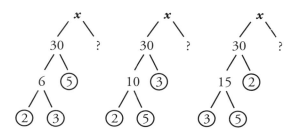

Each of these factor trees can tell us different factors of x. But what's really important is what they have in common. No matter what way you combine the prime factors, each tree ultimately leads to 2 × 3 × 5, which equals 30. So we know that x is divisible by 30. And if x is divisible by 30, it is also divisible by everything 30 is divisible by. We know how to identify every number 30 is divisible by—we can use a factor pair table. The factor pair table of 30 looks like this.

Small	Large
1	30
2	15
3	10
5	6

Again, statement II says that x is divisible by 15. We know x is divisible by 30, and 30 is divisible by 15, so x *must* be divisible by 15.

That brings us to statement III. Statement III says that x is divisible by 45. What do we need to know to say that x *must* be divisible by 45? Build a factor tree of 45, which looks like this.

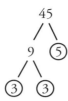

45 is divisible by 3, 3 and 5. For x to be divisible by 45, we need to know that it has all the same prime factors. Does it?

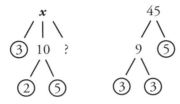

45 has one 5 and two 3's. We know that x has a 5, but we only know that x has one 3. That means that we can't say for sure that x is divisible by 45. x *could* be divisible by 45, because we don't know what the question mark contains. If it contains a 3, then x is divisible by 45. If it doesn't contain a 3, then x is not divisible by 45. Without more information, we can't say for sure either way. So statement III *could* be true.

Now it's time to recap what we've covered in this chapter. When we deal with questions about divisibility, we need a quick, accurate way to identify *all* the factors of a number. A factor pair table provides a reliable to make sure you find every factor of a number.

Prime factors provide essential information about a number or variable. They are the fundamental building blocks of every number. In order for a number or variable to be divisible by another number, it must contain all the same prime factors that the other number contains. In our last example, we could definitely say that x was divisible by 15, because x contained a 3 and a 5. But we could not say that it was divisible by 45, because 45 has a 5 and two 3's, but x only had a 5 and one 3.

Check Your Skills

For these statements, the following is true: x is divisible by 28 and by 15. For each statement, say whether it *must* be true, *could* be true, or *cannot* be true.

19. x is divisible by 14.
20. x is divisible by 20.
21. x is divisible by 24.

Answers can be found on page 125.

Check Your Skills Answer Key:

1.   Is 123,456,789 divisible by 2?

123,456,789 is an odd number, because it ends in 9. So 123,456,789 is not divisible by 2.

2.   Is 732 divisible by 3?

The digits of 732 add up to a multiple of 3 (7 + 3 + 2 = 12). 732 is divisible by 3.

3.   Is 989 divisible by 9?

The digits of 989 do not add up to a multiple of 9 (9 + 8 + 9 = 26). 989 is not divisible by 9.

4.   Find all the factors of 90.

Small	Large
1	90
2	45
3	30
5	18
6	15
9	10

5.   Find all the factors of 72.

Small	Large
1	72
2	36
3	24
4	18
6	12
8	9

6.   Find all the factors of 105.

Small	Large
1	105
3	35
5	21
7	15

7.   Find all the factors of 120.

Small	Large
1	120
2	60
3	40
4	30
5	24
6	20
8	15
10	12

8.   List all the prime numbers between 20 and 50.

        23, 29, 31, 37, 41, 43, and 47.

9.   Find the prime factorization of 90.

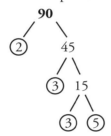

10.   Find the prime factorization of 72.

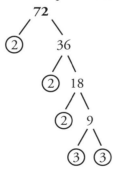

11.   Find the prime factorization of 105.

12.   Find the prime factorization of 120.

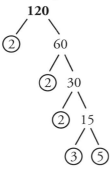

13.   The prime factorization of a number is 3×5. What is the number and what are all its factors?

$3 \times 5 = 15$

Small	Large
1	15
3	5

14.   The prime factorization of a number is $2 \times 5 \times 7$. What is the number and what are all its factors?

$2 \times 5 \times 7 = 70$

	Small	Large	
1	1	70	$2 \times 5 \times 7$
2	2	35	5×7
5	5	14	2×7
7	7	10	2×5

15.   The prime factorization of a number is $2 \times 3 \times 13$. What is the number and what are all its factors?

$2 \times 3 \times 13 = 78$

	Small	Large	
1	1	78	$2 \times 3 \times 13$
2	2	39	3×13
3	3	26	2×13
2×3	6	13	13

For questions 16–18, x is divisible by 24.

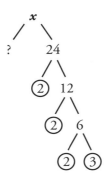

16. x is divisible by 6

For x to be divisible by 6, we need to know that it contains the same prime factors as 6. 6 contains a 2 and a 3. x also contains a 2 and a 3, therefore x *must* be divisible by 6.

17. x is divisible by 9

For x to be divisible by 9, we need to know that it contains the same prime factors as 9. 9 contains two 3's. x only contains one 3 that we know of. But the question mark means x may have other prime factors, and may contain another 3. For this reason, x *could* be divisible by 9.

18. x is divisible by 8

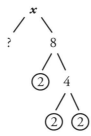

For x to be divisible by 8, we need to know that it contains the same prime factors as 8. 8 contains three 2's. x also contains three 2's, therefore x *must* be divisible by 8.

For questions 19–21, x is divisible by 28 and by 15.

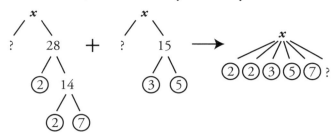

19. x is divisible by 14.

For x to be divisible by 14, we need to know that it contains the same prime factors as 14. 14 contains a 2 and a 7. x also contains a 2 and a 7, therefore x *must* be divisible by 14.

20. x is divisible by 20.

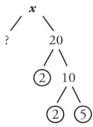

For x to be divisible by 20, we need to know that it contains the same prime factors as 20. 20 contains two 2's and a 5. x also contains two 2's and a 5, therefore x *must* be divisible by 20.

21. x is divisible by 24.

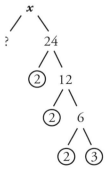

For x to be divisible by 24, we need to know that it contains the same prime factors as 24. 24 contains three 2's and a 3. x contains a 3, but only two 2's that we know of. But the question mark means x may have other prime factors, and may contain another 2. For this reason, x *could* be divisible by 24.

Chapter Review: Drill Sets

DRILL SET 1:

Drill 1

1. Is 4,005 divisible by 5?
2. Does 51 have any factors besides 1 and itself?
3. $x = 20$
   The prime factors of x are:
   The factors of x are:

Drill 2

1. Is 123 divisible by 3?
2. Does 23 have any factors besides 1 and itself?
3. $x = 100$
   The prime factors of x are:
   The factors of x are:

Drill 3

1. Is 285,284,901 divisible by 10?
2. Is 539,105 prime?
3. $x = 42$
   The prime factors of x are:
   The factors of x are:

Drill 4

1. Is 9,108 divisible by 9 and/or by 2?
2. Is 937,184 prime?
3. $x = 39$
   The prime factors of x are:
   The factors of x are:

Drill 5

1. Is 43,360 divisible by 5 and/or by 3?
2. Is 81,063 prime?
3. $x = 37$
   The prime factors of x are:
   The factors of x are:

Drill 6: Which of the following are prime numbers?

Determine which of the following numbers are prime numbers. Remember, you only need to find one factor other than the number itself to prove that the number is not prime.

2	3	5	6
7	9	10	15
17	21	27	29
31	33	258	303
655	786	1,023	1,325

DRILL SET 2:

Drill 1

1. If x is divisible by 33, what other numbers is x divisible by?
2. The prime factorization of a number is $3 \times 3 \times 7$. What is the number and what are all its factors?
3. If x is divisible by 8 and by 3, is x also divisible by 12?

Drill 2

1. If 40 is a factor of x, what other numbers are factors of x?
2. The only prime factors of a number are 5 and 17. What is the number and what are all its factors?
3. 5 and 6 are factors of n. Is n divisible by 15?

Drill 3

1. If 64 divides n, what other divisors does n have?
2. The prime factorization of a number is $2 \times 2 \times 3 \times 11$. What is the number and what are all its factors?
3. 14 and 3 divide n. Is 12 a factor of n?

Drill 4

1. If x is divisible by 4 and by 15, is x a multiple of 18?
2. 91 and 2 go into n. Does 26 divide n?
3. n is divisible by 5 and 12. Is n divisible by 24?

Drill 5

1. If n is a multiple of both 21 and 10, is 30 a divisor of n?
2. 4, 21 and 55 are factors of n. Does 154 divide n?
3. If n is divisible by 196 and by 15, is 210 a factor of n?

Drill Set Answers

Set 1, Drill 1

1.   Is 4,005 divisible by 5?

      4,005 ends in 5, so it is divisible by 5.

2.   Does 51 have any factors besides 1 and itself?

      The digits of 51 add up to a multiple of 3 (5 + 1 = 6), so 3 is a factor of 51. Yes, 51 has factors besides 1 and itself.

3. $x = 20$

      The prime factors of x are:

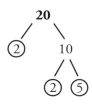

      The factors of x are:

Small	Large
1	20
2	10
4	5

Set 1, Drill 2

1.   Is 123 divisible by 3?

      The digits of 123 add up to a multiple of 3 (1 + 2 + 3 = 6), so 123 is divisible by 3.

2.   Does 23 have any factors besides 1 and itself?

      23 is a prime number. It has no factors besides 1 and itself.

3. $x = 100$

      The prime factors of x are:

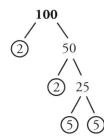

The factors of x are:

Small	Large
1	100
2	50
4	25
5	20
10	10

Set 1, Drill 3

1.   Is 285,284,901 divisible by 10?

285,284,901 ends in a 1, not a 0. It is not divisible by 10.

2.   Is 539,105 prime?

539,105 ends in a 5, so 5 is a factor of 539,105. So are 1 and 539,105. Prime numbers have only two factors, so 539,105 is not prime.

3. $x = 42$

The prime factors of x are:

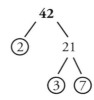

The factors of x are:

Small	Large
1	42
2	21
3	14
6	7

Set 1, Drill 4

1.   Is 9,108 divisible by 9 and/or by 2?

The digits of 9,108 add up to a multiple of 9 ($9 + 1 + 0 + 8 = 18$), so it is a multiple of 9. 9,108 ends in 8, so it is even, which means it is divisible by 2.

2.   Is 937,184 prime?

937,184 ends in 4, which means it's even. Therefore, it's divisible by 2. Prime numbers have only two factors (1 and themselves), so 937,184 is not prime.

3. $x = 39$

The prime factors of x are:

The factors of x are:

Small	Large
1	39
3	13

Set 1, Drill 5

1.   Is 43,360 divisible by 5 and/or by 3?

      43,360 ends in 0, so it is divisible by 5. The digits of 43,360 do not add up to a multiple of 3 (4 + 3 + 3 + 6 + 0 = 16) so it is not divisible by 3.

2.   Is 81,063 prime?

      The digits of 81,063 add up to a multiple of 3 (8 + 1 + 0 + 6 + 3 = 18), so 3 is a factor of 81,063. 1 and 81,063 are also factors of 81,063. Prime numbers have only two factors, so 81,063 is not prime.

3. $x = 37$
      The prime factors of x are: 37
      The factors of x are:

Small	Large
1	37

Set 1, Drill 6: Which of the following are prime numbers?

The numbers in bold below are prime numbers.

2	**3**	**5**	6
7	9	10	15
17	21	27	**29**
31	33	258	303
655	786	1,023	1,325

Prime numbers: 2, 3, 5, 7, 17, 29, 31

Not prime:

All of the even numbers other than 2 (6, 10, 258, 655, 786), since they are divisible by 2.

All of the multiples of 5 (15, 655, 1325)

All of the remaining numbers whose digits add up to a multiple of 3, since they are divisible by 3, by definition: 303 (digits add to 6), 1,023 (digits add to 6). Again, both numbers are divisible by 3.

Set 2, Drill 1

1.   If x is divisible by 33, what other numbers is x divisible by?

      If x is divisible by 33, then x is also divisible by everything 33 is divisible by. The factors of 33 are:

Small	Large
1	33
3	11

So x is also divisible by 1, 3 and 11.

2.   The prime factorization of a number is $3 \times 3 \times 7$. What is the number and what are all its factors?

$3 \times 3 \times 7 = 63$

Small	Large
1	63
3	21
7	9

3.   If x is divisible by 8 and by 3, is x also divisible by 12?

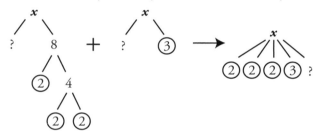

For x to be divisible by 12, we need to know that it contains the same prime factors as 12. $12 = 2 \times 2 \times 3$. Therefore 12 contains two 2's and a 3. x also contains two 2's and a 3, therefore x is divisible by 12.

Set 2, Drill 2

1.   If 40 is a factor of x, what other numbers are factors of x?

If 40 is a factor of x, then any factor of 40 is also a factor of x.

Small	Large
1	40
2	20
4	10
5	8

2.   The only prime factors of a number are 5 and 17. What is the number and what are all its factors?

If 5 and 17 are the only prime factors of the number, then the number = 5×17, which means the number is 85.

Small	Large
1	85
5	17

3.   5 and 6 are factors of n. Is n divisible by 15?

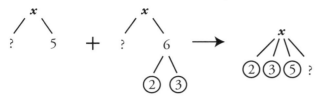

For n to be divisible by 15, we need to know that it contains the same prime factors as 15. $15 = 3 \times 5$. Therefore 15 contains a 3 and a 5. n also contains a 3 and a 5, therefore n is divisible by 15.

Set 2, Drill 3

1.   If 64 divides n, what other divisors does n have?

      If 64 divides n, then any divisors of 64 will also be divisors of n.

Small	Large
1	64
2	32
4	16
8	8

2.   The prime factorization of a number is $2 \times 2 \times 3 \times 11$. What is the number and what are all its factors?

      $2 \times 2 \times 3 \times 11 = 132$

Small	Large
1	132
2	66
3	44
4	33
6	22
11	12

3.   14 and 3 divide *n*. Is 12 a factor of *n*?

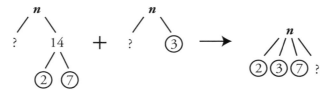

For 12 to be a factor of *n*, *n* must contain all the same prime factors as 12. 12 = 2 × 2 × 3, so 12 contains two 2s and a 3. *n* also contains a 3 but only contains one 2 that we know of, so we don't know whether 12 is a factor of *n*.

Set 2, Drill 4

1.   If *x* is divisible by 4 and by 15, is *x* a multiple of 18?

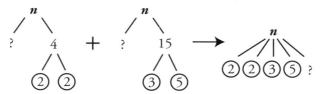

For *x* to be a multiple of 18, *x* would have to be divisible by 18. For *x* to be divisible by 18, it has to contain all the same prime factors as 18. 18 = 2 × 2 × 3 × 3, so 18 contains two 2's and two 3's. *x* contains two 2's, but it only contains one 3 that we know of, so we don't know whether *x* is a multiple of 18.

2.   91 and 2 go into *n*. Does 26 divide *n*?

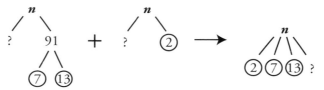

For 26 to divide *n*, *n* has to contain all the same prime factors as 26. 26 = 2 × 13, so 26 contains a 2 and a 13. *n* also contains a 2 and a 13, so 26 divides *n*.

3.   *n* is divisible by 5 and 12. Is *n* divisible by 24?

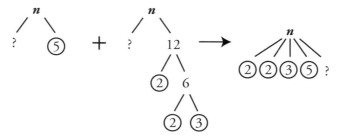

For *n* to be divisible by 24, it has to contain all the same prime factors as 24. 24 = 2 × 2 × 2 × 3, so 24 contains three 2's and a 3. *n* contains a 3, but only contains two 2's, so we don't know whether *n* is divisible by 24.

Set 2, Drill 5

1.   If *n* is a multiple of both 21 and 10, is 30 a divisor of *n*?

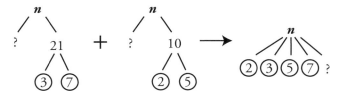

For 30 to be a divisior of *n*, *n* has to contain all the same prime factors that 30 contains. $30 = 2 \times 3 \times 5$, so 30 contains a 2, a 3 and a 5. *n* also contains a 2, a 3 and a 5, so 30 is a divisor of *n*.

2.   4, 21 and 55 are factors of *n*. Does 154 divide *n*?

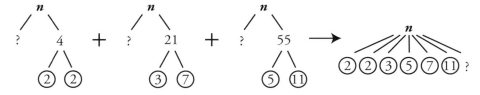

For 154 to divide *n*, *n* has to contain all the same prime factors as 154. $154 = 2 \times 7 \times 11$, so 154 contains a 2, a 7 and an 11. *n* also contains a 2, a 7 and an 11, so 154 divides *n*.

3.   If *n* is divisible by 196 and by 15, is 210 a factor of *n*?

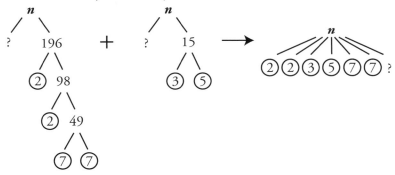

For 210 to be a factor of *n*, *n* must contain all the same prime factors as 210. $210 = 2 \times 3 \times 5 \times 7$, so 210 contains a 2, a 3, a 5 and a 7. *n* contains a 2, a 3, a 5 and a 7, so 210 is a factor of *n*.

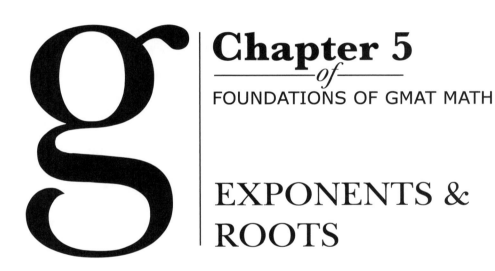

Chapter 5
of
FOUNDATIONS OF GMAT MATH

EXPONENTS & ROOTS

In This Chapter . . .

- Exponents
    - Combining Exponential Terms
    - Additional Exponent Rules
- Roots
    - Basic Properties of Roots
    - Multiplication and Division of Roots
    - Simplifying Roots
- Rewriting Bases
- Solving Algebraic Equations Involving Exponential Terms
    - Unknown Base
    - Unknown Exponent

EXPONENTS

In This Chapter:

- Introduction to exponents and roots
- Simplifying expressions and equations that contain exponents and roots
- Solving for variables in equations that contain exponents and roots

In this chapter we will discuss exponents and roots. More specifically, we'll be talking about how to simplify exponential expressions and how to solve equations that contain exponential terms.

We'll begin with exponents. Exponents are shorthand for one number multiplied by itself repeatedly. Once again, we're working with factors and multiplication. For example:

$$5^3 = 5 \times 5 \times 5 \qquad a^4 = a \times a \times a \times a$$

Every exponential term has two pieces: the **base** and the **exponent,** also known as the power.

$$\text{base} \rightarrow 7^5 \leftarrow \text{exponent}$$

"seven to the fifth power" or just "seven to the fifth"

Two exponential terms can sometimes be combined if they have a common **base.**

Combining Exponential Terms

Imagine that we have a string of five a's (all multiplied together, not added), and we want to multiply this by a string of three a's (again, all multiplied together). How many a's would we end up with?

Let's write it out:

$$(a \times a \times a \times a \times a) \times (a \times a \times a) = a \times a \times a \times a \times a \times a \times a \times a$$

If we wrote each element of this equation exponentially, it would read:

$$a^5 \quad \times \quad a^3 \quad = \quad a^8$$

"a to the fifth, times a cubed, equals a to the eighth"

This leads us to our first rule:

1. When multiplying exponential terms that share a common base, add the exponents.

Other examples:

Exponentially	Written Out
$7^3 \times 7^2 = 7^5$	$(7 \times 7 \times 7) \times (7 \times 7) = 7 \times 7 \times 7 \times 7 \times 7$
$5 \times 5^2 \times 5^3 = 5^6$	$5 \times (5 \times 5) \times (5 \times 5 \times 5) = 5 \times 5 \times 5 \times 5 \times 5 \times 5$
$f^3 \times f^1 = f^4$	$(f \times f \times f) \times f = f \times f \times f \times f$

Manhattan **GMAT** Prep
the new standard

Now let's imagine that we are dividing a string of five a's by a string of three a's. (Again, these are strings of multiplied a's.) What would be the result?

$$\frac{a \times a \times a \times a \times a}{a \times a \times a} \quad \begin{array}{c}\textit{We can cancel}\\ \textit{out from top}\\ \textit{and bottom}\end{array} \quad \rightarrow \quad \frac{a \times \cancel{a} \times \cancel{a} \times \cancel{a} \times a}{\cancel{a} \times \cancel{a} \times \cancel{a}} \quad \rightarrow \quad a \times a$$

If we wrote this out exponentially, it would read

$$\boxed{a^5 \;\div\; a^3 \;=\; a^2}$$ "a to the fifth, divided by a cubed, equals a squared"

Which leads us to our second rule:

2. When dividing exponential terms with a common base, subtract the exponents.

Other examples:

Exponentially	Written Out
$7^5 \div 7^2 = 7^3$	$(7 \times 7 \times 7 \times 7 \times 7) / (7 \times 7) = 7 \times 7 \times 7$
$5^5 \div 5^4 = 5$	$(5 \times 5 \times 5 \times 5 \times 5) / (5 \times 5 \times 5 \times 5) = 5$
$f^4 \div f^1 = f^3$	$(f \times f \times f \times f) / (f) = f \times f \times f$

These are our first 2 exponent rules:

Rule Book: Multiplying and Dividing Like Terms with Different Exponents	
When multiplying exponential terms that share a common base, add the exponents.	**When dividing exponential terms with a common base, subtract the exponents.**
$$a^3 \times a^2 = a^5$$	$$a^5 \div a^2 = a^3$$

Check Your Skills

Simplify the following expressions by combining like terms.

1. $b^5 \times b^7 =$
2. $(x^3)(x^4) =$
3. $\dfrac{y^5}{y^2} =$
4. $\dfrac{d^8}{d^7} =$

Answers can be found on page 149.

These are the most commonly used rules, but there are some other important things to know about exponents.

Additional Exponent Rules

1. When something with an exponent is raised to another power, multiply the two exponents together.

$$(a^2)^4 = a^8$$

> **Safety Tip:** There is **no** rule for adding or subtracting exponential terms with the same base. So, if you're told that $x^5 + x^3 = k$, you cannot simplify this by adding x^5 and x^3.

If you have four pairs of *a*'s, you will have a total of eight *a*'s.

$$(a \times a) \times (a \times a) \times (a \times a) \times (a \times a) = a \times a \times a \times a \times a \times a \times a \times a = a^8$$

2. Anything with an exponent of 0 equals 1.

$$a^0 = 1$$

Here's why…

Let's imagine we divide a string of five *a*'s by a string of five *a*'s. What would we get?

Using longhand, we can see that we get 1.

$$\frac{a \times a \times a \times a \times a}{a \times a \times a \times a \times a} = 1$$

Using exponential division rules, we get $\frac{a^5}{a^5} = a^{5-5} = a^0$.

Therefore, $a^0 = 1$.

3. Anything with a negative exponent is the reciprocal of that same thing with a positive exponent.

$$a^{-2} = \frac{1}{a^2}$$

> **Safety Tip:** The reciprocal of x is $1/x$. There's more on reciprocals in the next chapter.

Here's why…

Let's imagine we divide a string of three *a*'s by a sting of five *a*'s. What would we get?

Using longhand, we would get…

$$\frac{a \times a \times a}{a \times a \times a \times a \times a} = \frac{1}{a \times a} = \frac{1}{a^2}$$

Using exponential division rules, we would get $\frac{a^3}{a^5} = a^{3-5} = a^{-2}$.

Therefore, $a^{-2} = \frac{1}{a^2}$.

4. Negative terms remain negative when taken to an odd exponent, but become positive when taken to an even exponent.

$(-3)^1 =$	$-3 =$	-3
$(-3)^2 =$	$-3 \times -3 =$	9
$(-3)^3 =$	$-3 \times -3 \times -3 =$	-27
$(-3)^4 =$	$-3 \times -3 \times -3 \times -3 =$	81

Safety Tip: Remember this rule from earlier in the book? An odd number of negative signs will give you a negative number, while an even number of negative signs will give you a positive number.

It is important to remember that the exponent rules we just discussed apply to negative exponents as well as to positive exponents. For instance, there are two ways to combine the expression $2^5 \times 2^{-3}$.

1. The first way is to rewrite the negative exponent as a positive exponent, and then combine.

$$2^5 \times 2^{-3} = 2^5 \times \frac{1}{2^3} = \frac{2^5}{2^3} = 2^{5-3} = 2^2 = 4$$

2. Add the exponents directly.

$$2^5 \times 2^{-3} = 2^{5+(-3)} = 2^2 = 4$$

Check Your Skills

Simplify the following expressions.

5. $(x^3)^4$
6. $(5^2)^3$
7. $123,456^0$
8. 2^{-3}

Answers can be found on page 149.

Roots

Basic Properties of Roots

In Chapter 1, we discussed what it means to take the square root or cube root of a number. Now we're going to discuss some of the ways roots are incorporated into expressions and equations and the ways we are allowed to manipulate them.

Before getting into some of the more complicated rules, it is important to remember that any square root times itself will equal whatever is inside the square root. For instance, $\sqrt{2} \times \sqrt{2} = 2$. $\sqrt{18} \times \sqrt{18} = 18$. We can even apply this rule to variables. $\sqrt{y} \times \sqrt{y} = y$. So our first rule for the roots rule book is

$$\sqrt{x} \times \sqrt{x} = x$$

Multiplication and Division of Roots

Suppose you were to see the equation $3 + \sqrt{4} = x$, and you were asked to solve for x. What would you do? Well, $\sqrt{4} = 2$, so you could rewrite the equation as $3 + 2 = x$, so you would know that $x = 5$. 4 is a perfect square, so we were able to simply evaluate the root, and continue to solve the problem. But what if the equation were $\sqrt{8} \times \sqrt{2} = x$, and you were asked to find x. What would you do then? Neither 8 nor 2 is a perfect square, so we can't easily find a value for either root.

It is important to realize that, on the GMAT, sometimes you will be able to evaluate roots, (when asked to take the square root of a perfect square or the cube root of a perfect cube) but other times it will be necessary to manipulate the roots. We'll discuss the different ways that we are allowed to manipulate roots, and then see some examples of how these manipulations may help us arrive at a correct answer on GMAT questions involving roots.

Let's go back to the previous question. If $\sqrt{8} \times \sqrt{2} = x$, what is x?

When two roots are multiplied by each other, we can take what's inside each root, and multiply everything together all inside of one root. What that means is that we can rewrite $\sqrt{8} \times \sqrt{2}$ as $\sqrt{8 \times 2}$, which equals $\sqrt{16}$. And $\sqrt{16}$ equals 4, which means that $x = 4$.

This property also works for division. If $x = \dfrac{\sqrt{27}}{\sqrt{3}}$, what is x? We can divide the numbers inside the square roots and put them inside one square root. So $\dfrac{\sqrt{27}}{\sqrt{3}}$ becomes $\sqrt{\dfrac{27}{3}}$ which becomes $\sqrt{9}$. And $\sqrt{9}$ equals 3, so $x = 3$.

Note that these rules apply if there are any number of roots being multiplied or divided. These rules can also be combined with each other. For instance, $\dfrac{\sqrt{15} \times \sqrt{12}}{\sqrt{5}}$ becomes $\sqrt{\dfrac{15 \times 12}{5}}$. The numbers inside can be combined, and ultimately you end up with $\sqrt{36}$, which equals 6.

Check Your Skills
Solve for x.

9. $x = \sqrt{20} \times \sqrt{5}$

10. $x = \sqrt{98} / \sqrt{2}$

11. $x = \sqrt{2} \times \sqrt{6} \times \sqrt{12}$

12. $x = \dfrac{\sqrt{384}}{\sqrt{2} \times \sqrt{3}}$

Answers can be found on page 149.

Simplifying Roots

Just as multiple roots can be combined to create one root, we can also take one root and break it apart into multiple roots. You may be asking, why would we ever want to do that? Well, suppose a question said, if $x = \sqrt{2} \times \sqrt{6}$, what is x? You would combine them, and say that x equals $\sqrt{12}$. Unfortunately, $\sqrt{12}$ will never be a correct answer on the GMAT. The reason is that $\sqrt{12}$ can be simplified, and correct answers on the GMAT are presented in their simplest forms. So now the question becomes, how can we simplify $\sqrt{12}$?

What if we were to rewrite $\sqrt{12}$ as $\sqrt{4 \times 3}$? As mentioned, we could also break this apart into two separate roots that are multiplied together, namely $\sqrt{4} \times \sqrt{3}$. And we already know that $\sqrt{4}$ equals 2, so we could simplify to $2\sqrt{3}$. And in fact, that is the simplified form of $\sqrt{12}$ and could potentially appear as the correct answer to a question on the GMAT. Just to recap, the progression of simplifying $\sqrt{12}$ was as follows:

$$\sqrt{12} \;\rightarrow\; \sqrt{4 \times 3} \;\rightarrow\; \sqrt{4} \times \sqrt{3} \;\rightarrow\; 2\sqrt{3}$$

Now the question becomes, how can we simplify *any* square root? What if we can't just see that 12 equals 4 times 3, and 4 is a perfect square? Amazingly enough, the method for simplifying square roots will involve something you're probably quite comfortable with at this point—prime factorizations. Take a look at the prime factorization of 12. The prime factorization of 12 is $2 \times 2 \times 3$. So $\sqrt{12}$ can be rewritten as $\sqrt{2 \times 2 \times 3}$. Recall our first roots rule—any root times itself will equal the number inside. If $\sqrt{12}$ can be rewritten as $\sqrt{2 \times 2 \times 3}$, we can take that one step further and say it is $\sqrt{2} \times \sqrt{2} \times \sqrt{3}$. And we know that $\sqrt{2} \times \sqrt{2} = 2$.

We can generalize from this example and say that when we take the prime factorization of a number inside a square root, any prime factor that we can pair off can effectively be brought out of the square root. Let's try another example to practice applying this concept.

What is the simplified form of $\sqrt{360}$? Let's start by taking the prime factorization of 360.

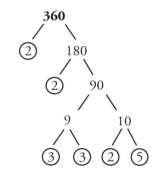

$$360 = 2 \times 2 \times 2 \times 3 \times 3 \times 5$$

Again, we are looking for primes that we can pair off and ultimately remove from the square root. In this case, we have a pair of 2's and a pair of 3's, so let's separate them.

$$\sqrt{360} \;\rightarrow\; \sqrt{2 \times 2 \times 2 \times 3 \times 3 \times 5} \;\rightarrow\; \sqrt{2 \times 2} \times \sqrt{3 \times 3} \times \sqrt{2 \times 5}$$

Notice that the prime factorization of 360 included three 2's. Two 2's could be paired off, but that still left one 2 without a partner. $\sqrt{2 \times 5}$ represents the prime factors that cannot be paired off. This expression can now be simplified to $2 \times 3 \times \sqrt{2 \times 5}$ which is $6\sqrt{10}$.

You might have seen right away that $360 = 36 \times 10$, so $\sqrt{360} = \sqrt{36 \times 10} = \sqrt{36} \times \sqrt{10} = 6\sqrt{10}$. The advantage of the prime factor method is that it will always work, even when you don't spot a shortcut.

Check Your Skills
Simplify the following roots.

13. $\sqrt{75}$

14. $\sqrt{96}$

15. $\sqrt{441}$

Answers can be found on page 149.

Rewriting Bases

So now you know how to combine exponential expressions when they share a common base. But what can you do when presented an expression such as $5^3 \times 25^2$? At first, it may seem that no further simplification is possible.

The trick here is to realize that 25 is actually 5^2. Because they are equivalent values, we can replace 25 with 5^2 and see what we get.

$5^3 \times (5^2)^2$ can be rewritten as $5^3 \times 5^4$. This expression can now be combined and we end up with 5^7.

When dealing with exponential expressions, you need to be on the lookout for perfect squares and perfect cubes that can be rewritten. In our last example, 25 is a perfect square and can be rewritten as 5^2. In general, it is good to know all the perfect squares up to 15^2, and the more common perfect cubes, as well as the powers of 2 and 3. Here's a brief list of some of the numbers likely to appear on the GMAT.

The powers of 2: 2, 4, 8, 16, 32, 64, 128
The powers of 3: 3, 9, 27, 81

$4^2 = 16$	$10^2 = 100$	$4^3 = 64$
$5^2 = 25$	$11^2 = 121$	$5^3 = 125$
$6^2 = 36$	$12^2 = 144$	
$7^2 = 49$	$13^2 = 169$	
$8^2 = 64$	$14^2 = 196$	
$9^2 = 81$	$15^2 = 225$	

*Manhattan*GMAT*Prep

Let's try another example. How would you combine the expression $2^3 \times 8^4$? Try it out for yourself.

Again, the key is to recognize that 8 is 2^3. The expression can be rewritten as $2^3 \times (2^3)^4$, which becomes $2^3 \times 2^{12}$ which equals 2^{15}.

Check Your Skills
Combine the following expressions.

16. $2^4 \times 16^3$
17. $7^5 \times 49^8$
18. $9^3 \times 81^3$

Answers can be found on pages 149.

Solving Algebraic Equations Involving Exponential Terms
GMAT exponent problems often give you an equation, and ask you to solve for either an unknown base, or an unknown exponent.

Unknown Base	Unknown Exponent
$x^3 = 8$	$2^x = 8$

Unknown Base

As we discussed in the first chapter of this book, the key to solving algebraic expressions with an unknown base is to make use of the fact that exponents and roots can effectively cancel each other out. In the equation $x^3 = 8$, x is raised to the third power, so to eliminate the exponent we can take the cube root of both sides of the equation.

$$\sqrt[3]{x^3} = \sqrt[3]{8} \quad \rightarrow \quad x = 2$$

This process also works in reverse. If we are presented with the equation $\sqrt{x} = 6$, we can eliminate the square root by squaring both sides. Square root and raising something to the second power cancel each other out in the same way that cube root and raising something to the third power cancel each other out. So to solve this equation, we can square both sides and get $(\sqrt{x})^2 = 6^2$, which can be simplified to $x = 36$.

There is one additional danger. Remember that when solving an equation where a variable has been squared, you should be on the lookout for two solutions. To solve for y in the equation $y^2 = 100$, we need to remember that y can equal either 10 OR −10.

Check Your Skills
Solve the following equations.

19. $x^3 = 64$
20. $\sqrt[3]{x} = 6$
21. $x^2 = 121$

Answers can be found on page 149.

Unknown Exponent

Unlike examples in the previous section, we can't make use of the relationship between exponents and roots to help us solve for a variable in the equation $2^x = 8$. Instead, the key is to once again recognize that 8 is equivalent to 2^3, and rewrite the equation so that we have the same base on both sides of the equal sign. If we replace 8 with its equivalent value, the equation becomes $2^x = 2^3$.

Now that we have the same base on both sides of the equation, there is only one way for the value of the expression on the left side of the equation to equal the value of the expression on the right side of the equation—the exponents must be equal. We can effectively ignore the bases and set the exponents equal to each other. We now know that $x = 3$.

By the way, when you see the expression 2^x, always call it "two TO THE xth power" or "two TO THE x." Never call it "two x." "Two x" is $2x$, or 2 times x, which is simply a different expression. Don't get lazy with names; that's how you can confuse yourself.

The process of finding the same base on each side of the equation can be applied to more complicated exponents as well. Take a look at the equation $3^{x+2} = 27$. Once again, we must first rewrite one of the bases so that the bases are the same on both sides of the equation. 27 is equivalent to 3^3, so the equation can be rewritten as $3^{x+2} = 3^3$. We can now ignore the bases (because they are the same) and set the exponents equal to each other.

$x + 2 = 3$, which means that $x = 1$.

Check Your Skills

Solve for x the following equations.

22. $2^x = 64$
23. $7^{x-2} = 49$
24. $5^{3x} = 125$

Answers can be found on page 150.

Check Your Skills Answer Key:

1. $b^5 \times b^7 = b^{(5+7)} = b^{12}$

2. $(x^3)(x^4) = x^{(3+4)} = x^7$

3. $\dfrac{y^5}{y^2} = y^{(5-2)} = y^3$

4. $\dfrac{d^8}{d^7} = d^{(8-7)} = d$

5. $(x^3)^4 = x^{3 \times 4} = x^{12}$

6. $(5^2)^3 = 5^{2 \times 3} = 5^6$

7. $123,456^0 = 1$

8. $2^{-3} = \dfrac{1}{8}$

9. $x = \sqrt{20} \times \sqrt{5} = \sqrt{20 \times 5} = \sqrt{100} = 10$

10. $x = \sqrt{98} / \sqrt{2} = \sqrt{98/2} = \sqrt{49} = 7$

11. $x = \sqrt{2} \times \sqrt{6} \times \sqrt{12} = \sqrt{2 \times 6 \times 12} = \sqrt{144} = 12$

12. $x = \dfrac{\sqrt{384}}{\sqrt{2} \times \sqrt{3}} = \sqrt{\dfrac{384}{2 \times 3}} = \sqrt{\dfrac{384}{6}} = \sqrt{64} = 8$

13. $\sqrt{75} \rightarrow \sqrt{3 \times 5 \times 5} \rightarrow \sqrt{5 \times 5} \times \sqrt{3} = 5\sqrt{3}$

14. $\sqrt{96} = \sqrt{2 \times 2 \times 2 \times 2 \times 2 \times 3} = \sqrt{2 \times 2} \times \sqrt{2 \times 2} \times \sqrt{2 \times 3} = 2 \times 2 \times \sqrt{6} = 4\sqrt{6}$

15. $\sqrt{441} \rightarrow \sqrt{3 \times 3 \times 7 \times 7} \rightarrow \sqrt{3 \times 3} \times \sqrt{7 \times 7} = 3 \times 7 = 21$

16. $2^4 \times 16^3 = 2^4 \times (2^4)^3 = 2^4 \times 2^{4 \times 3} = 2^4 \times 2^{12} = 2^{4+12} = 2^{16}$

17. $7^5 \times 49^8 = 7^5 \times (7^2)^8 = 7^5 \times 7^{2 \times 8} = 7^5 \times 7^{16} = 7^{5+16} = 7^{21}$

18. $9^3 \times 81^3 = (3^2)^3 \times (3^4)^3 = 3^{2 \times 3} \times 3^{4 \times 3} = 3^6 \times 3^{12} = 3^{6+12} = 3^{18}$

19. $x^3 = 64$

   $\sqrt[3]{x^3} = \sqrt[3]{64}$

   $x = 4$

20. $\sqrt[3]{x} = 6$

   $(\sqrt[3]{x})^3 = (6)^3$

   $x = 216$

21. $x^2 = 121$

   $\sqrt{x^2} = \sqrt{121}$

   $x = 11 \ \text{OR} \ -11$

22. $2^x = 64$

$2^x = 2^6$

$x = 6$

23. $7^{x-2} = 49$

$7^{x-2} = 7^2$

$x - 2 = 2$

$x = 4$

24. $5^{3x} = 125$

$5^{3x} = 5^3$

$3x = 3$

$x = 1$

Chapter Review: Drill Sets

DRILL SET 1:

Drill 1: Simplify the following expressions by combining the terms.

1. $x^5 \times x^3 =$
2. $7^6 \times 7^9 =$
3. $3^2 \times 3^5 =$
4. $9^2 \times 9^4 =$
5. $5^5/5^3 =$
6. $5^3/5^5 =$
7. $4^{-2} \times 4^5 =$
8. $(-3)^a/(-3)^2 =$
9. $11^4/11^x =$
10. $7^5 \times 5^3 =$

Drill 2: Combine the following expressions.

1. $x^2 \times x^3 \times x^5 =$
2. $3^4 \times 3^2 \times 3 =$
3. $y^3 \times y^{-5} =$
4. $\dfrac{x^5 \times x^6}{x^2} =$
5. $\dfrac{5^6 \times 5^{4x}}{5^4} =$
6. $y^7 \times y^8 \times y^{-6} =$
7. $\dfrac{x^4}{x^{-3}} =$
8. $6^2 \times 6^{-7} \times 6^4 =$
9. $\dfrac{z^5 \times z^{-3}}{z^{-8}} =$
10. $\dfrac{3^{2x} \times 3^{6x}}{3^{-3y}} =$

Drill 3: Simplify the following expressions by combining the terms.

1. $(a^3)^2 =$
2. $(2^2)^4 =$
3. $(3^2)^{-3} =$
4. $(5^2)^x =$
5. $(y^3)^{-4} =$

Drill 4: Combine the following expressions.

1. $(x^2)^6 \times x^3 =$
2. $y^3 \times (y^3)^{-4} =$

3. $\dfrac{(3^5)^2}{3^4} =$

4. $(z^6)^x \times z^{3x} =$

5. $\dfrac{5^3 \times (5^4)^y}{(5^y)^3} =$

Drill 5: Rewrite each negative exponent as a positive exponent.

1. x^{-2}
2. 4^{-4}
3. $y^{-4}z^{-4}$
4. 6^{-3}
5. $x^5 \times x^{-9}$

DRILL SET 2:

Drill 1: Combine the following expressions and solve for x.

1. $x = \sqrt{3} \times \sqrt{27}$

2. $x = \sqrt{2} \times \sqrt{18}$

3. $x = \dfrac{\sqrt{48}}{\sqrt{3}}$

4. $x = \sqrt{5} \times \sqrt{45}$

5. $x = \dfrac{\sqrt{5{,}000}}{\sqrt{50}}$

Drill 2: Combine the following expressions and solve for x.

1. $x = \sqrt{36} \times \sqrt{4}$

2. $x = \dfrac{\sqrt{128}}{\sqrt{2}}$

3. $\dfrac{\sqrt{54} \times \sqrt{3}}{\sqrt{2}}$

4. $x = \dfrac{\sqrt{640}}{\sqrt{2} \times \sqrt{5}}$

5. $x = \dfrac{\sqrt{30}\sqrt{12}}{\sqrt{10}}$

Drill 3: Simplify the following roots.

1. $\sqrt{32}$
2. $\sqrt{24}$

3. $\sqrt{180}$

4. $\sqrt{490}$

5. $\sqrt{450}$

Drill 4: Simplify the following roots.

1. $\sqrt{135}$

2. $\sqrt{224}$

3. $\sqrt{343}$

4. $\sqrt{208}$

5. $\sqrt{432}$

DRILL SET 3:

Drill 1: Simplify the following expressions.

1. $8^3 \times 2^6$
2. $3^4 \times 9^5$
3. $49^2 \times 7^7$
4. $4^3 \times 8^5$
5. $11^8 \times 121^{2x}$

Drill 2: Simplify the following expressions.

1. $25^4 \times 125^3$
2. $9^{-2} \times 27^2$
3. $2^{-7} \times 8^2$
4. $7^{3x} \times 49^{-3}$
5. $4^{5x} \times 32^{-2x}$

Drill 3: Solve the following equations.

1. $x^3 = 27$
2. $y^2 = 81$
3. $2x^3 = 128$
4. $z^2 + 18 = 54$
5. $3x^5 = 96$

Drill 4: Solve the following equations.

1. $3^x = 81$
2. $6^{y-3} = 36$
3. $7^{4x-11} = 7$
4. $5^{-4} = 25^{2x}$
5. $4^2 = 16^{3y-8}$

Drill Set Answers

Set 1, Drill 1:

1. $x^5 \times x^3 = x^{(5+3)} = x^8$
2. $7^6 \times 7^9 = 7^{(6+9)} = 7^{15}$
3. $3^2 \times 3^5 = 3^{(2+5)} = 3^7$
4. $9^2 \times 9^4 = 9^{(2+4)} = 9^6$
5. $5^5/5^3 = 5^{(5-3)} = 5^2$
6. $5^3/5^5 = 5^{(3-5)} = 5^{-2}$
7. $4^{-2} \times 4^5 = 4^{(-2+5)} = 4^3$
8. $(-3)^a/(-3)^2 = (-3)^{(a-2)}$
9. $11^4/11^x = 11^{(4-x)}$
10. $7^5 \times 5^3 =$ Can't simplify—no common bases or exponents!

Set 1, Drill 2:

1. $x^2 \times x^3 \times x^5 = x^{(2+3+5)} = x^{10}$
2. $3^4 \times 3^2 \times 3 = 3^{(4+2+1)} = 3^7$
3. $y^3 \times y^{-5} = y^{(3-5)} = y^{-2}$
4. $\dfrac{x^5 \times x^6}{x^2} = x^{(5+6-2)} = x^9$
5. $\dfrac{5^6 \times 5^{4x}}{5^4} = 5^{(6+4x-4)} = 5^{4x+2}$
6. $y^7 \times y^8 \times y^{-6} = y^{(7+8+(-6))} = y^9$
7. $\dfrac{x^4}{x^{-3}} = x^{(4-(-3))} = x^7$
8. $6^2 \times 6^{-7} \times 6^4 = 6^{(2+(-7)+4)} = 6^{-1}$
9. $\dfrac{z^5 \times z^{-3}}{z^{-8}} = x^{(5+(-3)-(-8))} = x^{10}$
10. $\dfrac{3^{2x} \times 3^{6x}}{3^{-3y}} = 3^{(2x+6x-(-3y))} = 3^{8x+3y}$

Set 1, Drill 3:

1. $(a^3)^2 = a^{(3 \times 2)} = a^6$
2. $(2^2)^4 = 2^{(2 \times 4)} = 2^8$
3. $(3^2)^{-3} = 3^{(2 \times -3)} = 3^{-6}$
4. $(5^2)^x = 5^{(2 \times x)} = 5^{2x}$
5. $(y^3)^{-4} = y^{(3 \times -4)} = y^{-12}$

Set 1, Drill 4:

1. $(x^2)^6 \times x^3 = x^{(2 \times 6 + 3)} = x^{(12+3)} = x^{15}$

2. $y^3 \times (y^3)^{-4} = y^{(3 + 3 \times -4)} = y^{(3 + (-12))} = y^{-9}$

3. $\dfrac{(3^5)^2}{3^4} = 3^{(5\times2-4)} = 3^{(10-4)} = 3^6$

4. $(z^6)^x \times z^{3x} = z^{(6\,\times\,x\,+\,3x)} = z^{(6x\,+\,3x)} = z^{9x}$

5. $\dfrac{5^3 \times (5^4)^y}{(5^y)^3} = 5^{(3+(4\times y)-(y\times3))} = 5^{(3+4\,y-3\,y)} = 5^{y+3}$

Set 1, Drill 5:

1. $x^{-2} = \dfrac{1}{x^2}$

2. $4^{-4} = \dfrac{1}{4^4} = \dfrac{1}{256}$

3. $y^{-4}z^{-4} = \dfrac{1}{y^4 z^4}$

4. $6^{-3} = \dfrac{1}{6^3} = \dfrac{1}{216}$

5. $x^5 \times x^{-9} = x^{5+(-9)} = x^{-4} = \dfrac{1}{x^4}$

Set 2, Drill 1:

1. $x = \sqrt{3} \times \sqrt{27} = \sqrt{3\times27} = \sqrt{81} = 9$

2. $x = \sqrt{2} \times \sqrt{18} = \sqrt{2\times18} = \sqrt{36} = 6$

3. $x = \dfrac{\sqrt{48}}{\sqrt{3}} = \sqrt{\dfrac{48}{3}} = \sqrt{16} = 4$

4. $x = \sqrt{5} \times \sqrt{45} = \sqrt{5\times45} = \sqrt{225} = 15$

5. $x = \dfrac{\sqrt{5,000}}{\sqrt{50}} = \sqrt{\dfrac{5,000}{50}} = \sqrt{100} = 10$

Set 2, Drill 2:

1. $x = \sqrt{36} \times \sqrt{4} = \sqrt{36\times4} = \sqrt{144} = 12$ OR

   $x = \sqrt{36} \times \sqrt{4} = 6 \times 2 = 12$

2. $x = \dfrac{\sqrt{128}}{\sqrt{2}} = \sqrt{\dfrac{128}{2}} = \sqrt{64} = 8$

3. $x = \dfrac{\sqrt{54} \times \sqrt{3}}{\sqrt{2}} = \sqrt{\dfrac{54 \times 3}{2}} = \sqrt{81} = 9$

4. $x = \dfrac{\sqrt{640}}{\sqrt{2} \times \sqrt{5}} = \sqrt{\dfrac{640}{2 \times 5}} = \sqrt{64} = 8$

5. $x = \dfrac{\sqrt{30}\sqrt{12}}{\sqrt{10}} = \sqrt{\dfrac{30 \times 12}{10}} = \sqrt{36} = 6$

Set 2, Drill 3:

1. $\sqrt{32} = \sqrt{2 \times 2 \times 2 \times 2 \times 2} = \sqrt{2 \times 2} \times \sqrt{2 \times 2} \times \sqrt{2} = 2 \times 2 \times \sqrt{2} = 4\sqrt{2}$

2. $\sqrt{24} = \sqrt{2 \times 2 \times 2 \times 3} = \sqrt{2 \times 2} \times \sqrt{2 \times 3} = 2\sqrt{6}$

3. $\sqrt{180} = \sqrt{2 \times 2 \times 3 \times 3 \times 5} = \sqrt{2 \times 2} \times \sqrt{3 \times 3} \times \sqrt{5} = 2 \times 3 \times \sqrt{5} = 6\sqrt{5}$

4. $\sqrt{490} = \sqrt{2 \times 5 \times 7 \times 7} = \sqrt{7 \times 7} \times \sqrt{2 \times 5} = 7\sqrt{10}$

5. $\sqrt{450} = \sqrt{2 \times 3 \times 3 \times 5 \times 5} = \sqrt{3 \times 3} \times \sqrt{5 \times 5} \times \sqrt{2} = 3 \times 5 \times \sqrt{2} = 15\sqrt{2}$

Set 2, Drill 4:

1. $\sqrt{135} = \sqrt{3 \times 3 \times 3 \times 5} = \sqrt{3 \times 3} \times \sqrt{3 \times 5} = 3\sqrt{15}$

2. $\sqrt{224} = \sqrt{2 \times 2 \times 2 \times 2 \times 2 \times 7} = \sqrt{2 \times 2} \times \sqrt{2 \times 2} \times \sqrt{2 \times 7} = 2 \times 2 \times \sqrt{14} = 4\sqrt{14}$

3. $\sqrt{343} = \sqrt{7 \times 7 \times 7} = \sqrt{7 \times 7} \times \sqrt{7} = 7\sqrt{7}$

4. $\sqrt{208} = \sqrt{2 \times 2 \times 2 \times 2 \times 13} = \sqrt{2 \times 2} \times \sqrt{2 \times 2} \times 13 = 2 \times 2 \times \sqrt{13} = 4\sqrt{13}$

5. $\sqrt{432} = \sqrt{2 \times 2 \times 2 \times 2 \times 3 \times 3 \times 3} = \sqrt{2 \times 2} \times \sqrt{2 \times 2} \times \sqrt{3 \times 3} \times \sqrt{3} = 2 \times 2 \times 3 \times \sqrt{3} = 12\sqrt{3}$

Set 3, Drill 1:

1. $8^3 \times 2^6 = (2^3)^3 \times 2^6 = 2^9 \times 2^6 = 2^{15}$

2. $3^4 \times 9^5 = 3^4 \times (3^2)^5 = 3^4 \times 3^{10} = 3^{14}$

3. $49^2 \times 7^7 = (7^2)^2 \times 7^7 = 7^4 \times 7^7 = 7^{11}$

4. $4^3 \times 8^5 = (2^2)^3 \times (2^3)^5 = 2^6 \times 2^{15} = 2^{21}$

5. $11^8 \times 121^{2x} = 11^8 \times (11^2)^{2x} = 11^8 \times 11^{4x} = 11^{4x + 8}$

Set 3, Drill 2:

1. $25^4 \times 125^3 = (5^2)^4 \times (5^3)^3 = 5^8 \times 5^9 = 5^{17}$

2. $9^{-2} \times 27^2 = (3^2)^{-2} \times (3^3)^2 = 3^{-4} \times 3^6 = 3^2$

3. $2^{-7} \times 8^2 = 2^{-7} \times (2^3)^2 = 2^{-7} \times 2^6 = 2^{-1}$

4. $7^{3x} \times 49^{-3} = 7^{3x} \times (7^2)^{-3} = 7^{3x} \times 7^{-6} = 7^{3x-6}$

5. $4^{5x} \times 32^{-2x} = (2^2)^{5x} \times (2^5)^{-2x} = 2^{10x} \times 2^{-10x} = 2^0 = 1$

Set 3, Drill 3:

1. $x^3 = 27$

      $x = 3$

2. $y^2 = 81$

      $y = 9$ OR -9

3. $2x^3 = 128$

      $x^3 = 64$

      $x = 4$

4. $z^2 + 18 = 54$

      $z^2 = 36$

      $z = 6$ OR -6

5. $3x^5 = 96$

      $x^5 = 32$

      $x = 2$

Set 3, Drill 4:

1. $3^x = 81$

      $3^x = 3^4$

      $x = 4$

2. $6^{y-3} = 36$

      $6^{y-3} = 6^2$

      $y - 3 = 2$

      $y = 5$

3. $7^{4x-11} = 7^1$

$4x - 11 = 1$

$4x = 12$

$x = 3$

4. $5^{-4} = 25^{2x}$

$5^{-4} = (5^2)^{2x}$

$5^{-4} = 5^{4x}$

$-4 = 4x$

$-1 = x$

5. $4^2 = 16^{3y-8}$

$4^2 = (4^2)^{3y-8}$

$4^2 = 4^{6y-16}$

$2 = 6y - 16$

$18 = 6y$

$3 = y$

OR

$(2^2) = ((2^2)^2)^{3y-8}$

$(2^2)^2 = (2^4)^{3y-8}$

$2^4 = 2^{12y-32}$

$4 = 12y - 32$

$2 = 6y - 16$

$18 = 6y$

$3 = y$

OR

$4^2 = 16^{3y-8}$

$16 = 16^{3y-8}$

$16^1 = 16^{3y-8}$

$1 = 3y - 8$

$9 = 3y$

$3 = y$

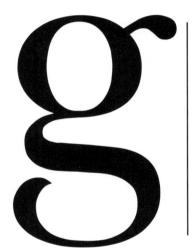

Chapter 6
of
FOUNDATIONS OF GMAT MATH

FRACTIONS

In This Chapter . . .

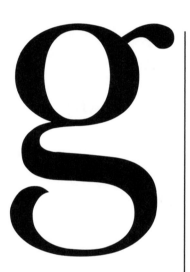

FRACTIONS

This chapter is devoted entirely to understanding what fractions are and how they work. Let's begin by reviewing the two parts of a fraction: the **numerator** and the **denominator.**

$$\frac{3}{4}$$ ← numerator
← denominator

$$\frac{part}{whole}$$

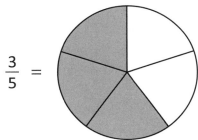

3 pieces = part

4 pieces = whole

In the picture above, each circle represents a whole unit. One full circle means the number 1, 2 full circles is 2, etc. Fractions essentially divide units into parts. The units above have been divided into 4 equal parts, because the denominator of our fraction is 4. In any fraction, the denominator tells you how many equal pieces a unit has been broken into.

The circle at the top has 3 of the pieces shaded in, and one piece unshaded. That's because the top of our fraction is 3. For any fraction, the numerator tells you how many of the equal pieces you have.

Let's see how changes to the numerator and denominator change a fraction. We'll start by seeing how changes affect the denominator. You've already seen what 3/4 looks like; let's see what 3/5 looks like.

$$\frac{3}{5} =$$

The numerator hasn't changed (it's still 3), so we still have 3 shaded pieces. But now the circle has been divided into 5 pieces instead of 4. One effect is that each piece is now smaller. 1/5 is smaller than 1/4. In general, as the denominator of a number gets bigger, the value of the fraction gets smaller. 3/5 is smaller than 3/4, because each fraction has 3 pieces, but when the circle (or number) is divided into 5 equal portions, each portion is smaller, so 3 portions of 1/5 are less than 3 portions of 1/4.

As we split the circle into more and more pieces, each piece gets smaller and smaller. Conversely, as the denominator gets smaller, each piece becomes bigger and bigger.

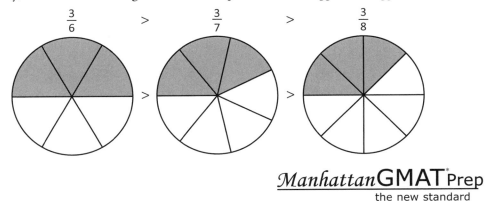

$$\frac{3}{6} \quad > \quad \frac{3}{7} \quad > \quad \frac{3}{8}$$

*Manhattan*GMAT*Prep

Now let's see what happens as we change the numerator. The numerator tells us how many pieces we have, so if we make the numerator smaller, we get fewer pieces.

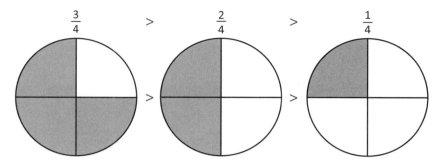

Conversely, if we make the numerator larger, we get more pieces. Let's look more closely what happens as we get more pieces. In particular, we want to know what happens when the numerator becomes equal to or greater than the denominator. First, let's see what happens when we have the same numerator and denominator. If we have 4/4 pieces, this is what our circle looks like.

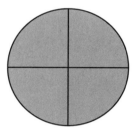

Remember, our circle represents one whole unit. So when all four parts are filled, we have one full unit, or 1. So 4/4 is equal to 1. In general, if the numerator and denominator of a fraction are the same, that fraction equals 1.

Now let's see what happens as the numerator becomes larger than the denominator. What does 5/4 look like?

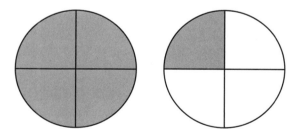

Each circle is only capable of holding 4 pieces, so when we fill up one circle, we have to move on to a second circle and begin filling it up too. So one way of looking at 5/4 is that we have one complete circle, which we know is equivalent to 1, and we have an additional 1/4. So another way to write 5/4 is 1 + 1/4. This can be shortened to $1\frac{1}{4}$ ("one and one fourth").

*Manhattan*GMAT*Prep
the new standard

In the last example, the numerator was only a little larger than the denominator. But that will not always be the case. The same logic applies to any situation. Look at the fraction 15/4. Once again, this means that each number is divided into 4 pieces, and we have 15 pieces.

$\dfrac{15}{4} =$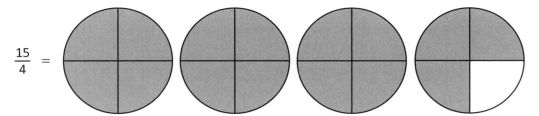

In this case, we have 3 circles completely filled. To fill 3 circles, we needed 12 pieces. (Note: 3 circles × 4 pieces per circle = 12 pieces.) In addition to the 3 full circles, we have 3 additional pieces. So we have $\dfrac{15}{4} = 3 + \dfrac{3}{4} = 3\dfrac{3}{4}$.

Whenever you have both an integer and a fraction in the same number, you have a **mixed number.** Meanwhile, any fraction in which the numerator is larger than the denominator (for example, 5/4) is known as an **improper fraction.** Improper fractions and mixed numbers express the same thing. Later in the chapter we'll discuss how to change from improper fractions to mixed numbers and vice-versa.

Let's review what we've learned about fractions so far. Every fraction has two components: the numerator and the denominator.

The denominator tells you how many equal pieces each unit circle has been broken into. As the denominator gets bigger, each piece gets smaller, so the fraction gets smaller as well.

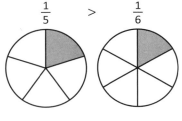

The numerator tells you how many equal pieces you have. As the numerator gets bigger, you have more pieces, so the fraction gets bigger.

When the numerator is smaller than the denominator, the fraction will be less than 1. When the numerator equals the denominator, the fraction equals 1. When the numerator is larger than the denominator, the fraction is greater than 1.

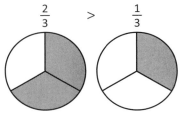

Check Your Skills
For each of the following sets of fractions, decide which fraction is larger.

1. $\dfrac{5}{7}, \dfrac{3}{7}$

2. $\dfrac{3}{10}, \dfrac{3}{13}$

Answers can be found on page 185.

*Manhattan*GMAT*Prep

Manipulating Fractions

In the next two sections, we'll discuss how to add, subtract, multiply and divide fractions. We're already familiar with these four basic manipulations of arithmetic, but when fractions enter the picture, things can become more complicated.

Below, we're going to discuss each manipulation in turn. In each discussion, we'll first talk conceptually about what changes are being made with each manipulation. Then we'll go through the actual mechanics of performing the manipulation.

We'll begin with how to add and subtract fractions.

Fraction Addition and Subtraction

The first thing to recall about addition and subtraction in general is that they affect how many things you have. If you have 3 things, and you add 6 more things, you have $3 + 6 = 9$ things. If you have 7 things and you subtract, or take away, 2 of those things, you now have $7 - 2 = 5$ things. That same basic principle holds true with fractions as well. What this means is that addition and subtraction affect the numerator of a fraction, because the numerator tells us how many things, or pieces, we have.

For example, let's say we want to add the two fractions 1/5 and 3/5. What we are doing is adding 3 fifths to 1 fifth. (A "fifth" is the very specific pie slice we see below.)

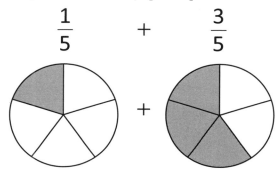

If we were dealing with integers, and we added 3 to 1, we would get 4. The idea is the same with fractions. Now, instead of adding 3 complete units to one complete unit, we're adding 3 fifths to 1 fifth. 1 fifth plus 3 fifths equals 4 fifths.

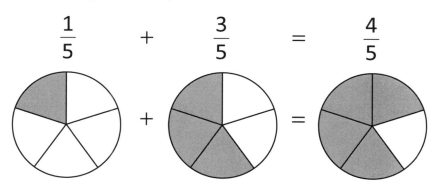

Notice that when we added the two fractions, the denominator stayed the same. Remember, the denominator tells you how many pieces each unit circle has been broken into. In other words, it determines the size of the slice. Adding 3 pieces to 1 piece did nothing to change the size of the pieces. Each unit is still broken into 5 pieces; hence there is no change to the denominator. The only effect of the addition was to end up with more pieces, which means that we ended up with a larger numerator.

Be able to conceptualize what we just did both ways: adding 1/5 and 3/5 to get 4/5, *and* regarding 4/5 as the sum of 1/5 and 3/5.

$$\frac{1}{5} + \frac{3}{5} = \frac{1+3}{5} = \frac{4}{5}$$

$$\frac{4}{5} = \frac{1+3}{5} = \frac{1}{5} + \frac{3}{5}$$

Also, you should be able to handle an x in place of one of the numerators.

$$\frac{1}{5} + \frac{x}{5} = \frac{4}{5} \quad \text{becomes} \quad 1 + x = 4$$
$$x = 3$$

We can apply the same thinking no matter what the denominator is. Say we want to add 3/6 and 5/6. This is how it looks.

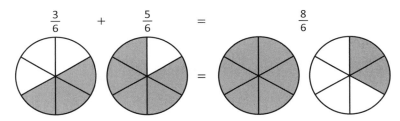

Notice that once again, the only thing that changes during the operation is the numerator. Adding 5 sixths to 3 sixths gives you 8 sixths. The principle is still the same even though we ended up with an improper fraction.

Again, see the operation both ways:

$$\frac{3}{6} + \frac{5}{6} = \frac{3+5}{6} = \frac{8}{6} \qquad \frac{8}{6} = \frac{3+5}{6} = \frac{3}{6} + \frac{5}{6}$$

Be ready for the x as well:

$$\frac{3}{6} + \frac{x}{6} = \frac{8}{6} \quad \text{becomes} \quad 3 + x = 8$$
$$x = 5$$

*Manhattan*GMAT*Prep
the new standard

Now let's look at a slightly different problem. This time we want to add 1/4 and 3/8.

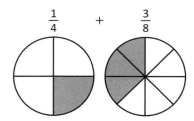

Do you see the problem here? We have one thing on the left and three things on the right, but the denominators are different, so the sizes of the pieces are different. It doesn't make sense in this case simply to add the numerators and get 4 of anything. Fraction addition only works if we can add pieces that are all the same size. So now the question becomes, how can we make all the pieces the same size?

What we need to do is find a new way to express one or both of the fractions so that the slices are the same size. For this particular addition problem, we can take advantage of the fact that one fourth is twice as big as one eighth. Look what happens if we take all the fourths in our first circle and divide them in two.

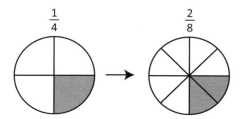

What happened to our fraction? The first thing to note is that we haven't changed the value of our fraction. Originally, we had 1 piece out of 4. Once we divided every part into 2, we ended up with 2 pieces out of 8. So we ended up with twice as many pieces, but each piece was half as big. So we actually ended up with the same amount of stuff overall.

What did we change? We ended up with twice as many pieces, which means we multiplied the numerator by 2, and we broke the circle into twice as many pieces, which means we also multiplied the denominator by 2. So we ended up with $\dfrac{1 \times 2}{4 \times 2} = \dfrac{2}{8}$. We'll come back to this concept later, but for now, simply make sure that you understand that $\dfrac{1}{4} = \dfrac{2}{8}$.

So without changing the value of 1/4, we've now found a way to *rename* 1/4 as 2/8, so we can add it to 3/8. Now our problem looks like this:

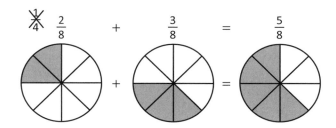

The key to this addition problem was to find what we call a **common denominator.** Finding a common denominator simply means renaming the fractions so they have the same denominator. Then we can add the renamed fractions.

We won't get into all the details of fraction multiplication just yet (don't worry—it's coming), but we need to take a closer look at what we did to the fraction $\dfrac{1}{4}$ in order to rename it. Essentially what we did was multiply this fraction by $\dfrac{2}{2}$. $\dfrac{1}{4} = \dfrac{1}{4} \times \dfrac{2}{2} = \dfrac{1 \times 2}{4 \times 2} = \dfrac{2}{8}$. As we've already discussed, any fraction in which the numerator equals the denominator is 1. So 2/2 = 1. That means that all we did was multiply 1/4 by 1. And anything times 1 equals itself. So we changed the appearance of 1/4 by multiplying the top and bottom by 2, but we did not change its value.

Finding common denominators is a critical skill when dealing with fractions. Let's walk through another example and see how the process works. This time we're going to add 1/4 and 1/3.

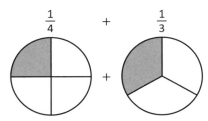

Once again we are adding two fractions with different-sized pieces. There's no way to complete the addition without finding a common denominator. But remember, the only way that we can find common denominators is by multiplying one or both of the fractions by some version of 1 (such as 2/2, 3/3, 4/4, etc.). Because we can only multiply by 1 (the number that won't change the value of the fraction), the only way we can change the denominators is through multiplication. In the last example, the two denominators were 4 and 8. We were able to make them equal because 4 × 2 = 8.

Because all we can do is multiply, what we really need when we look for a common denominator is a common *multiple* of both denominators. In the last example, 8 was a multiple of both 4 and 8.

In this problem, we are adding 1/4 and 1/3. We need to find a number that is a multiple of both 4 and 3. List a few multiples of 4: 4, 8, 12, 16…. Also list a few multiples of 3: 3, 6,

9, 12, stop. 12 is on both lists, so 12 is a multiple of both 3 and 4. Now we need to change both fractions so that they have a denominator of 12.

Let's begin by changing 1/4. We have to ask the question, what times 4 equals 12? The answer is 3. That means that we want to multiply 1/4 by 3/3. $\dfrac{1}{4} \times \dfrac{3}{3} = \dfrac{3}{12}$. So 1/4 is the same as 3/12. Once again, we can look at our circles to verify these fractions are the same.

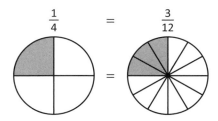

Now we need to change 1/3. Once again, we need to ask, what times 3 equals 12? $4 \times 3 = 12$, so we need to multiply 1/3 by 4/4. $\dfrac{1}{3} = \dfrac{1}{3} \times \dfrac{4}{4} = \dfrac{4}{12}$. Now both of our fractions have a common denominator, so we're ready to add.

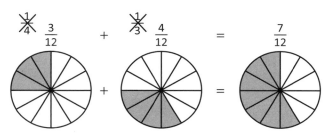

$$\frac{1}{4} + \frac{1}{3} = \frac{1 \times 3}{4 \times 3} + \frac{1 \times 4}{3 \times 4} = \frac{3}{12} + \frac{4}{12} = \frac{7}{12}$$

And now you know everything you need to add any two fractions together.

Let's recap what we've done so far.

When adding fractions, we have to add equal-sized pieces. That means we need the denominators to be the same for any fractions we want to add. **If the denominators are the same, then you add the numerators and keep the denominator the same.**

Ex. $\dfrac{2}{9} + \dfrac{5}{9} = \dfrac{7}{9}$

If the two fractions have different denominators, you need to find a common multiple for the two denominators first.

Ex. $\dfrac{1}{4} + \dfrac{2}{5} = ?$
Common multiple of 4 and 5 = 20

Once you know the common multiple, you need to figure out for each fraction what number times the denominator equals the common multiple.

$\dfrac{1}{4} \times \dfrac{5}{5} = \dfrac{5}{20} \qquad \dfrac{2}{5} \times \dfrac{4}{4} = \dfrac{8}{20}$

Using the number you found in the last step, multiply each fraction that needs to be changed by the appropriate fractional version of 1 (such as 5/5).

Now that the denominators are the same, you can add the fractions.

$\dfrac{5}{20} + \dfrac{8}{20} = \dfrac{13}{20}$

This section would not be complete without a discussion of subtraction. The good news is that subtraction works exactly the same way as addition! The only difference is that when you subtract, you end up with fewer pieces instead of more pieces, so you end up with a smaller numerator.

Let's walk through a subtraction problem together. What is 5/7 − 1/3?

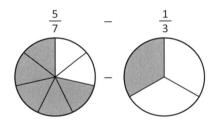

Just like addition, subtraction of fractions requires a common denominator. So we need to figure out a common multiple of the two denominators: 7 and 3. 21 is a common multiple, so let's use that.

Let's change 5/7 so that its denominator is 21. 3 times 7 equals 21, so let's multiply 5/7 by 3/3. $\dfrac{5}{7} = \dfrac{5}{7} \times \dfrac{3}{3} = \dfrac{15}{21}$. Now we do the same for 1/3. 7 times 3 equals 21, so let's multiply 1/3 by 7/7. $\dfrac{1}{3} = \dfrac{1}{3} \times \dfrac{7}{7} = \dfrac{7}{21}$. Our subtraction problem can be rewritten as $\dfrac{15}{21} - \dfrac{7}{21}$, which we can easily solve.

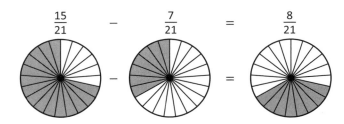

$$\frac{15}{21} - \frac{7}{21} = \frac{8}{21}$$

Finally, if you have an x in the addition, nothing really changes. One way or another, you still have to find a common denominator.

Solve: $\dfrac{1}{4} + \dfrac{x}{5} = \dfrac{13}{20}$

First, subtract 1/4 from each side:

$$\frac{x}{5} = \frac{13}{20} - \frac{1}{4}$$

Perform the subtraction by finding the common denominator, which is 20.

$$\frac{13}{20} - \frac{1 \times 5}{4 \times 5} = \frac{13}{20} - \frac{5}{20} = \frac{8}{20}$$

So we have $\dfrac{x}{5} = \dfrac{8}{20}$

There are several options at this point. The one we'll use right now is to convert to the common denominator again (which is still 20).

$$\frac{x \times 4}{5 \times 4} = \frac{4x}{20} = \frac{8}{20}$$

Now we can set the numerators equal: $4x = 8$

Divide by 4: $x = 2$

If we had spotted the common denominator of all 3 fractions at the start, we could have saved work:

$$\frac{1}{4} + \frac{x}{5} = \frac{13}{20}$$

Convert to a common denominator of 20: $\dfrac{1 \times 5}{4 \times 5} + \dfrac{x \times 4}{5 \times 4} = \dfrac{13}{20}$

Clean up: $\dfrac{5}{20} + \dfrac{4x}{20} = \dfrac{13}{20}$

Set numerators equal: $5 + 4x = 13$

Subtract 5: $4x = 8$

Divide by 4: $x = 2$

Check Your Skills

Evaluate the following expressions.

3. $\dfrac{1}{2} + \dfrac{3}{4} =$

4. $\dfrac{2}{3} - \dfrac{3}{8} =$

5. Find x. $\dfrac{x}{5} + \dfrac{2}{5} = \dfrac{13}{5}$

6. Find x. $\dfrac{x}{3} - \dfrac{4}{9} = \dfrac{8}{9}$

Answers can be found on page 185.

Simplifying Fractions

Suppose you were presented with this question on the GMAT.

$$\frac{5}{9} + \frac{1}{9} = ?$$

   a. 4/9   b. 5/9   c. 2/3

This question involves fraction addition, which we know how to do. So let's begin by adding the two fractions. $\dfrac{5}{9} + \dfrac{1}{9} = \dfrac{5+1}{9} = \dfrac{6}{9}$. But 6/9 isn't one of the answer choices. Did we do something wrong? No, we didn't, but we did forget an important step.

6/9 doesn't appear as an answer choice because it isn't **simplified** (or reduced). To understand what that means, we're going to return to a topic that should be very familiar to you at this point—prime factors. Let's break down the numerator and denominator into prime factors. $\dfrac{6}{9} \rightarrow \dfrac{2 \times 3}{3 \times 3}$.

Notice how both the numerator and the denominator have a 3 as one of their prime factors. Because neither multiplying nor dividing by 1 changes the value of a number, we can effectively cancel the $\dfrac{3}{3}$, leaving behind only $\dfrac{2}{3}$. That is, $\dfrac{6}{9} = \dfrac{2 \times \cancel{3}}{3 \times \cancel{3}} = \dfrac{2}{3}$.

Let's look at another example of a fraction that can be reduced: $\dfrac{18}{60}$. Once again, we can begin by breaking the numerator and denominator into their prime factors. $\dfrac{18}{60} \rightarrow \dfrac{2 \times 3 \times 3}{2 \times 2 \times 3 \times 5}$. This time, the numerator and the denominator have two factors in common: a 2 and a 3. Once again, we can split this fraction into two pieces.

$\dfrac{2 \times 3 \times 3}{2 \times 2 \times 3 \times 5} \rightarrow \dfrac{3}{2 \times 5} \times \dfrac{2 \times 3}{2 \times 3} \rightarrow \dfrac{3}{10} \times \dfrac{6}{6}$. Once again, $\dfrac{6}{6}$ is the same as 1, so really we have $\dfrac{3}{10} \times 1$, which leaves us with $\dfrac{3}{10}$.

As you practice, you should be able to simplify fractions by recognizing the largest common factor in the numerator and denominator and canceling it out. For example, you should recognize that in the fraction $\dfrac{18}{60}$, both the numerator and the denominator are divisible by

6. That means we could think of it as $\dfrac{3 \times 6}{10 \times 6}$. You can then cancel out the common factors

on top and bottom and simplify the fraction. $\dfrac{18}{60} = \dfrac{3 \times \cancel{6}}{10 \times \cancel{6}} = \dfrac{3}{10}$.

Check Your Skills
Simplify the following fractions.

7. $\dfrac{25}{40}$

8. $\dfrac{16}{24}$

Answers can be found on page 185.

Fraction Multiplication

Now that we know how to add and subtract fractions, we're ready to multiply and divide them. We'll begin with multiplication. First, we'll talk about what happens when we multiply a fraction by an integer.

We'll start by asking the question, what is 1/2 × 6? When we added and subtracted fractions, we were really adding and subtracting pieces of numbers. With multiplication, we are starting with an amount, and leaving a fraction of it behind. For instance, in this example, what we are really asking is, what is 1/2 *of* 6? There are a few ways to visualize what that means.

We want to find one half of six. One way to do that is to split 6 into 2 equal parts and keep one of those parts.

Because the denominator of our fraction is 2, we divide 6 into 2 equal parts of 3. Then, because our denominator is 1, we keep one of those parts. So 1/2 × 6 = 3.

We can also think of this multiplication problem a slightly different way. Consider each unit circle of the 6. What happens if we break each of those circles into 2 parts, and keep 1 part?

We divide every circle into 2 parts, and keep 1 of every 2 parts. We end up with 6 halves, or 6/2, written as a fraction. But 6/2 is the same as 3, so really, 1/2 of 6 is 3.

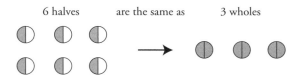

Either way we approach this question, we end up with the same answer. Let's try another example.

What is 2/3 × 12?

Once again, we are really asking, what is 2/3 of 12? In the previous example, when we multiplied a number by 1/2, we divided the number into 2 parts (as indicated by the denominator). Then we kept 1 of those parts (as indicated by the numerator).

By the same logic, if we want to get 2/3 of 12, we need to divide 12 into 3 equal parts, because the denominator is 3. Then we keep 2 of those parts, because the numerator is 2. As with the first example, there are several ways of visualizing this. One way is to divide 12 into 3 equal parts, and keep 2 of those parts.

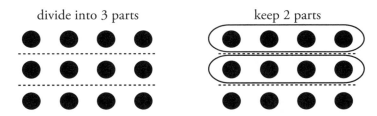

We divided 12 into 3 equal parts of 4, and kept 2 of those parts. 2 groups of 4 is 8, so 2/3 × 12 = 8.

Another way to visualize 2/3 × 12 is to once again look at each unit of 12. If we break each unit into 3 pieces (because the denominator of our fraction is 3) and keep 2 out of every 3 pieces (because our numerator is 2) we end up with this:

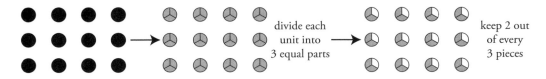

We ended up with 24 thirds, or 24/3. But 24/3 is the same as 8, so 2/3 of 12 is 8.

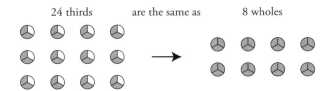

Once again, either way we look at this multiplication problem, we arrive at the same conclusion. $2/3 \times 12 = 8$.

Now that we've seen what happens when we multiply an integer by a fraction, it's time to multiply a fraction by a fraction. It's important to remember that the basic logic is the same. When you multiply any number by a fraction, the denominator of the fraction tells you how many parts to divide your number into, and the numerator tells you how many of those parts to keep. Now let's see how that logic applies to fractions.

What is 1/2 of 3/4?

This question is asking, what is 1/2 of 3/4? So once again, we need to divide 3/4 into 2 equal parts. This time, though, because we're splitting a fraction, we're going to do things a little differently. Because 3/4 is a fraction, it has already broken a number into 4 equal pieces. So what we're going to do is we're going to break each of those pieces into 2 smaller pieces.

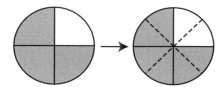

Cut each piece in half

Now that we've divided each piece into 2 smaller pieces, we want to keep 1 of those smaller pieces.

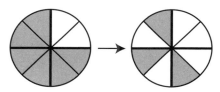

Keep 1 out of 2 resulting pieces.

So what did we end up with? First of all, our product is going to remain a fraction. Our original number was 3/4. In other words, a number was broken into 4 parts, and we had 3 of those parts. Now the number has been broken into 8 pieces, not 4, so our denominator is now 8. However, we still have 3 of those parts, so our numerator is still 3. So 1/2 of 3/4 is 3/8.

Let's try one more. What is 5/6 of 1/2? Once again, we have to start by dividing our fraction into 6 equal pieces.

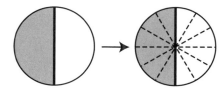

Cut each piece into 6 smaller pieces

Now we want to keep 5 out of every 6 parts.

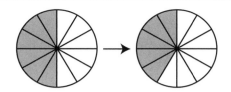

Keep 5 of the 6

So what did we end up with? Now we have a number divided into 12 parts, so our denominator is 12, and we have 5 parts, so the numerator is 5. 5/6 of 1/2 is 5/12.

Now, multiplying fractions would get very cumbersome if we always resorted to slicing circles up into increasingly tiny pieces. So let's talk about the mechanics of multiplying a number by a fraction.

First, note the following crucial difference between two types of arithmetic operations:

Addition & Subtraction:
Only the numerator changes (once you've found a common denominator).

Multiplication & Division:
Both numerator and denominator typically change.

Now, to multiply fractions, you just multiply together the numerators to get the new numerator. You multiply the denominators together to get the new denominator. Then you simplify.

$$\frac{1}{2} \times \frac{6}{1} = \frac{1 \times 6}{2 \times 1} = \frac{6}{2} = 3$$

$$\frac{2}{3} \times \frac{12}{1} = \frac{2 \times 12}{3 \times 1} = \frac{24}{3} = 8$$

> **Safety Tip:** Any integer can be rewritten as a fraction with a denominator of 1. For instance $6 = 6/1$, $13 = 13/1$ etc.

$$\frac{1}{2} \times \frac{3}{4} = \frac{1 \times 3}{2 \times 4} = \frac{3}{8}$$

$$\frac{5}{6} \times \frac{1}{2} = \frac{5 \times 1}{6 \times 2} = \frac{5}{12}$$

In practice, when you are multiplying fractions, don't worry about the conceptual foundation, which is much harder to grasp than the mechanics.

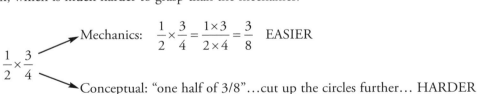

Mechanics: $\frac{1}{2} \times \frac{3}{4} = \frac{1 \times 3}{2 \times 4} = \frac{3}{8}$ EASIER

$\frac{1}{2} \times \frac{3}{4}$

Conceptual: "one half of 3/8"…cut up the circles further… HARDER

Lastly, whenever we multiply fractions, we should always look to cancel common factors, in order to reduce our answer without doing unnecessary work.

$$\frac{33}{7} \times \frac{14}{3} = ?$$

Long way: $33 \times 14 =$

$$\begin{array}{r} {}^{1}33 \\ \times\ 14 \\ \hline 132 \\ 330 \\ \hline 462 \end{array}$$

$7 \times 3 = 21$

You wind up with $\dfrac{462}{21}$.

$$\begin{array}{r} 22 \\ 21\overline{)462} \\ -42 \\ \hline 42 \\ -42 \\ \hline \end{array}$$

This work can be simplified greatly by canceling parts of each fraction before multiplying. Shortcut: Look for common factors in the numerator and denominator.

$$\frac{33}{7} \times \frac{14}{3} = \frac{3 \times 11}{7} \times \frac{2 \times 7}{3}$$

We can now see that the numerator of the first fraction has a 3 as a factor, which can be canceled out by the 3 in the denominator of the second fraction. Similarly, the 7 in the denominator of the first fraction can be canceled out by the 7 in the numerator of the second fraction. By cross-canceling these factors, we can save ourselves a lot of work.

$$\frac{\cancel{3} \times 11}{\cancel{7}} \times \frac{2 \times \cancel{7}}{\cancel{3}} = \frac{11}{1} \times \frac{2}{1} = \frac{22}{1} = 22$$

Check Your Skills

Evaluate the following expressions. Simplify all fractions.

9. $\dfrac{3}{7} \times \dfrac{6}{10} =$

10. $\dfrac{5}{14} \times \dfrac{7}{20} =$

Answers can be found on page 185.

Fraction Division

Now we're up to the last of our four basic operations (addition, subtraction, multiplication and division). This section will be a little different than the other three. The reason it will be different is that we're actually going to do fraction division by avoiding division altogether!

We can avoid division entirely because of the relationship between multiplication and division. Multiplication and division are two sides of the same coin. Any multiplication problem can be expressed as a division problem, and vice-versa. This is useful because, although the mechanics for multiplication are straightforward, the mechanics for division are complicated. Because division is more difficult to perform than multiplication, we are going to express every fraction division problem as a fraction multiplication problem.

Now the question becomes, how do we rephrase a division problem so that it becomes a multiplication problem? The key is **reciprocals.**

Reciprocals are numbers that, when multiplied together, equal 1. For instance, 3/5 and 5/3 are reciprocals, because $\dfrac{3}{5} \times \dfrac{5}{3} = \dfrac{3 \times 5}{5 \times 3} = \dfrac{15}{15} = 1$.

Another pair of reciprocals is 2 and 1/2, because $2 \times \dfrac{1}{2} = \dfrac{2}{1} \times \dfrac{1}{2} = \dfrac{2 \times 1}{1 \times 2} = \dfrac{2}{2} = 1$. Once again, it is important to remember that every integer can be thought of as a fraction.

The way to find the reciprocal of a number turns out to be very easy—take the numerator and denominator of a number and switch them.

Fraction   Reciprocal   Fraction   Reciprocal

$$\dfrac{3}{5} \diagdown \diagup \dfrac{5}{3} \qquad \text{Integer } 2 = \dfrac{2}{1} \diagdown \diagup \dfrac{1}{2}$$

Reciprocals are important because dividing by a number is the exact same thing as multiplying by its reciprocal. Let's look at an example to clarify.

What is 6 ÷ 2?

This problem shouldn't give you any trouble—6 divided by 2 is 3. But it should also seem familiar. In reality, it's the exact same problem we dealt with in the discussion on fraction multiplication. 6 ÷ 2 is the exact same thing as 6 × 1/2.

6 ÷ 2 = 3   Dividing by 2 is the same as multiplying by 1/2.
6 × 1/2 = 3

To change from division to multiplication, you need to do two things. First, take the divisor (the number to the right of the division sign—in other words, what you are dividing *by*) and replace it with its reciprocal. In this problem, 2 is the divisor, and 1/2 is the reciprocal of 2. Then, switch the division sign to a multiplication sign. So 6 ÷ 2 becomes 6 × 1/2.

Then, proceed to do the multiplication. $6 \div 2 = 6 \times \dfrac{1}{2} = \dfrac{6}{1} \times \dfrac{1}{2} = \dfrac{6 \times 1}{1 \times 2} = \dfrac{6}{2} = 3$.

This is obviously overkill for 6 ÷ 2, but let's try another one. What is 5/6 ÷ 4/7?

Once again, we start by taking the divisor (4/7) and replacing it with its reciprocal (7/4). We then switch the division sign to a multiplication sign. So 5/6 ÷ 4/7 is the same as 5/6 × 7/4.

Now we do fraction multiplication. $\dfrac{5}{6} \div \dfrac{4}{7} = \dfrac{5}{6} \times \dfrac{7}{4} = \dfrac{5 \times 7}{6 \times 4} = \dfrac{35}{24}$. And that's all there is to it.

Note that the fraction bar or slash is another way to express division. After all, $6 \div 2 = 6/2$ $= \dfrac{6}{2} = 3$. In fact, the division sign $\div$ looks like a little fraction. So if you see a "double-decker" fraction, don't worry. It's just one fraction divided by another fraction.

$$\frac{\dfrac{5}{6}}{\dfrac{4}{7}} = \frac{5}{6} \div \frac{4}{7} = \frac{5}{6} \times \frac{7}{4} = \frac{35}{24}$$

Let's recap. When you are confronted with a division problem involving fractions, it is *always* easier to perform multiplication than division. For that reason, every division problem should be rewritten as a multiplication problem.

To do so, replace the divisor with its reciprocal. To find the reciprocal of a number, you simply need to switch the numerator and denominator (ex. 2/9 → 9/2).

Remember that a number multiplied by its reciprocal equals 1.

After that, switch the division symbol to a multiplication symbol, and perform fraction multiplication.

Fraction Reciprocal

$$\frac{2}{9} \quad \rightarrow \quad \frac{9}{2}$$

$$\frac{9}{2} \times \frac{2}{9} = 1$$

$$\frac{3}{4} \div \frac{2}{9} \rightarrow \frac{3}{4} \times \frac{9}{2} = \frac{27}{8}$$

Check Your Skills

Evaluate the following expressions. Simplify all fractions.

11. $\dfrac{1}{6} \div \dfrac{1}{11} =$

12. $\dfrac{8}{5} \div \dfrac{4}{15} =$

Answers can be found on page 186.

<u>Fractions in Equations</u>

When an x appears in a fraction multiplication or division problem, we'll use essentially the same concepts and techniques to solve.

$$\frac{4}{3}x = \frac{15}{8}$$

Divide both sides by $\dfrac{4}{3}$:

$$x = \frac{15}{8} \div \frac{4}{3}$$

$$x = \frac{15}{8} \times \frac{3}{4} = \frac{45}{32}$$

An important tool to add to our arsenal at this point is *cross-multiplication*. This tool comes from the principle of making common denominators.

$$\frac{x}{7} = \frac{5}{8}$$

The common denominator of 7 and 8 is $7 \times 8 = 56$. So we have to multiply the left fraction by 8/8 and the right fraction by 7/7:

$$\frac{8 \times x}{8 \times 7} = \frac{5 \times 7}{8 \times 7}$$

Now we can set the numerators equal: $8x = 5 \times 7 = 35$
$$x = 35/8$$

However, in this situation we can avoid having to determine the common denominator by cross–multiplying each numerator times the other denominator and setting the products equal to each other.

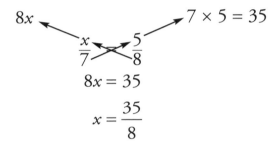

$$8x = 35$$

$$x = \frac{35}{8}$$

Check Your Skills

Solve for x in the following equations.

13. $\dfrac{3}{4}x = \dfrac{3}{2}$

14. $\dfrac{x}{6} = \dfrac{5}{3}$

Answers can be found on page 186.

Switching Between Improper Fractions and Mixed Numbers

Let's return to our discussion of why 5/4 equals $1^{1}/_{4}$ and how to switch between improper fractions and mixed numbers.

To do this we need to talk about the numerator in more detail. The numerator is a description of how many parts you have. The fraction 5/4 tells us that we have 5 parts. But we have some flexibility in how we arrange those 5 parts. For instance, we already expressed it above as 4/4 + 1/4, or 1 + 1/4. Essentially what we did was we split the numerator into two pieces: 4 and 1. If we wanted to express this as a fraction, we could say that 5/4 becomes $\dfrac{4+1}{4}$. This hasn't changed anything, because 4 + 1 equals 5, so we still have the same number of parts.

Then, as we saw above, we can split our fraction into two separate fractions. For instance $\frac{4+1}{4}$ becomes $\frac{4}{4}+\frac{1}{4}$. This is the same as saying that 5 fourths equals 4 fourths plus 1 fourth. So we have several different ways of representing the same fraction. $\frac{5}{4}=\frac{4+1}{4}=\frac{4}{4}+\frac{1}{4}$. Here is a visual representation:

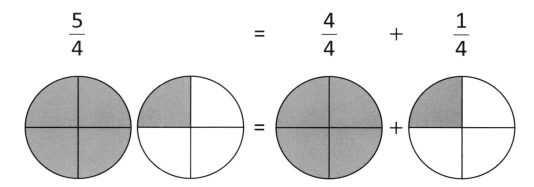

As a general rule, we can always split the numerator into different parts and split a fraction into multiple fractions. This is just reversing the process of adding fractions. When we add fractions, we take two fractions with the same denominator and combine them into one fraction. Here we are doing the exact opposite—turning one fraction into two separate fractions each with the same denominator. And now that our fraction 5/4 is split into two fractions, we can take advantage of the fact that fractions, at their essence, represent division. As we discussed earlier, 4/4 = 1. Our original explanation didn't mention division, but as we mentioned above, another way to think of 4/4 is 4 ÷ 4, which equals 1.

To switch from an improper fraction to a mixed number, we want to figure out how many complete units we have. To do that, we need to figure out the largest multiple of the denominator that is less than or equal to the numerator. For the fraction 5/4, 4 is the largest multiple of 4 that is less than 5. So we split our fraction into 4/4 and 1/4. We then note that 4/4 equals 1, so our mixed number is $1^1/_4$.

Let's try it again with the fraction 15/4. This time, the largest multiple of 4 that is less than 15 is 12. So we can split our fraction 15/4 into 12/4 + 3/4. In other words, $\frac{15}{4}=\frac{12+3}{4}=\frac{12}{4}+\frac{3}{4}$. And 12/4 = 3, so the fraction 15/4 becomes the mixed number $3^3/_4$.

Let's try one with a different denominator. How do we turn the fraction 16/7 into a mixed number? This time we need the largest multiple of 7 that is less than or equal to 16. 14 is the largest multiple of 7 less than 16, so we once again split our fraction 16/7 into 14/7 and 2/7. $\frac{16}{7}=\frac{14+2}{7}=\frac{14}{7}+\frac{2}{7}$. 14 divided by 7 equals 2, so our mixed number is $2^2/_7$.

Check Your Skills

Change the following improper fractions to mixed numbers.

15. $\dfrac{11}{6}$

16. $\dfrac{100}{11}$

Answers can be found on page 186.

Changing Mixed Numbers to Improper Fractions

Now that we know how to change a number from an improper fraction to a mixed number, we also need to be able to do the reverse. Suppose we have the mixed number $5\,{}^{2}/_{3}$. How do we turn this number into a fraction?

To do so, we need to remember that we can think of any number (even an integer) as a fraction. The number 1, for instance, can be thought of any number of different ways. It can be thought of as 1/1. It can also be thought of as 2/2. In other words, a unit circle has been split into 2 equal pieces, and we have 2 of those pieces (forming a single whole again). 1 can also be written as 3/3, 4/4, 5/5, etc.

In fact, we can think of the process of turning mixed numbers into improper fractions as simple fraction addition. $5\,{}^{2}/_{3}$ is the same thing as $5 + 2/3$, so we can think of it as $\dfrac{5}{1}+\dfrac{2}{3}$.

Now we know what to do—we need to change $\dfrac{5}{1}$ so that it has a denominator of 3. The way to do that is to multiply $\dfrac{5}{1}$ by $\dfrac{3}{3}$. $5=\dfrac{5}{1}=\dfrac{5}{1}\times\dfrac{3}{3}=\dfrac{5\times3}{1\times3}=\dfrac{15}{3}$. So our mixed number is really $\dfrac{15}{3}+\dfrac{2}{3}=\dfrac{15+2}{3}=\dfrac{17}{3}$.

Check Your Skills

Change the following mixed numbers to improper fractions.

17. $3\,{}^{3}/_{4}$

18. $5\,{}^{2}/_{3}$

Answers can be found on page 186.

Check Your Skills Answers

1. $\dfrac{5}{7}, \dfrac{3}{7}$ – The denominators of the two fractions are the same, but the numerator of $\dfrac{5}{7}$ is

   bigger, so $\dfrac{5}{7} > \dfrac{3}{7}$.

2. $\dfrac{3}{10}, \dfrac{3}{13}$ – The numerators of the two fractions are the same, but the denominator of $\dfrac{3}{10}$

   is smaller, so $\dfrac{3}{10} > \dfrac{3}{13}$.

3. $\dfrac{1}{2} + \dfrac{3}{4} = \dfrac{1}{2} \times \dfrac{2}{2} + \dfrac{3}{4} = \dfrac{2}{4} + \dfrac{3}{4} = \dfrac{2+3}{4} = \dfrac{5}{4}$ (you have five quarters of a pie)

4. $\dfrac{2}{3} - \dfrac{3}{8} = \dfrac{2}{3} \times \dfrac{8}{8} - \dfrac{3}{8} \times \dfrac{3}{3} = \dfrac{16}{24} - \dfrac{9}{24} = \dfrac{16-9}{24} = \dfrac{7}{24}$

5. Find x. $\dfrac{x}{5} + \dfrac{2}{5} = \dfrac{13}{5}$

   $\dfrac{x}{5} = \dfrac{13}{5} - \dfrac{2}{5}$

   $\dfrac{x}{5} = \dfrac{11}{5}$

   $x = 11$

6. Find x. $\dfrac{x}{3} - \dfrac{4}{9} = \dfrac{8}{9}$

   $\dfrac{x}{3} = \dfrac{8}{9} + \dfrac{4}{9}$

   $\dfrac{x}{3} = \dfrac{12}{9}$

   $\dfrac{x}{3} \times \dfrac{3}{3} = \dfrac{12}{9}$

   $\dfrac{3x}{9} = \dfrac{12}{9}$

   $3x = 12$

   $x = 4$

7. $\dfrac{25}{40} = \dfrac{5 \times 5}{8 \times 5} = \dfrac{5 \times \cancel{5}}{8 \times \cancel{5}} = \dfrac{5}{8}$

8. $\dfrac{16}{24} = \dfrac{2 \times 8}{3 \times 8} = \dfrac{2 \times \cancel{8}}{3 \times \cancel{8}} = \dfrac{2}{3}$

9. $\dfrac{3}{7} \times \dfrac{6}{10} = \dfrac{3}{7} \times \dfrac{3}{5} = \dfrac{9}{35}$

10. $\dfrac{5}{14} \times \dfrac{7}{20} = \dfrac{5}{2 \times 7} \times \dfrac{7}{4 \times 5} = \dfrac{\cancel{5}}{2 \times \cancel{7}} \times \dfrac{\cancel{7}}{4 \times \cancel{5}} = \dfrac{1}{8}$

11. $\dfrac{1}{6} \div \dfrac{1}{11} = \dfrac{1}{6} \times \dfrac{11}{1} = \dfrac{11}{6}$

12. $\dfrac{8}{5} \div \dfrac{4}{15} = \dfrac{8}{5} \times \dfrac{15}{4} = \dfrac{2 \times 4}{5} \times \dfrac{3 \times 5}{4} = \dfrac{2 \times \cancel{4}}{\cancel{5}} \times \dfrac{3 \times \cancel{5}}{\cancel{4}} = \dfrac{6}{1} = 6$

13. $\dfrac{3}{4}x = \dfrac{3}{2}$

$x = \dfrac{3}{2} \div \dfrac{3}{4} = \dfrac{3}{2} \times \dfrac{4}{3}$

$x = \dfrac{3 \times 2 \times 2}{2 \times 3} = \dfrac{\cancel{3} \times \cancel{2} \times 2}{\cancel{2} \times \cancel{3}} = \dfrac{2}{1}$

$x = 2$

14. $\dfrac{x}{6} = \dfrac{5}{3}$

$3 \times x = 5 \times 6$

$3x = 30$

$x = 10$

15. $\dfrac{11}{6} = \dfrac{6+5}{6} = \dfrac{6}{6} + \dfrac{5}{6} = 1 + \dfrac{5}{6} = 1\tfrac{5}{6}$

16. $\dfrac{100}{11} = \dfrac{99+1}{11} = \dfrac{99}{11} + \dfrac{1}{11} = 9 + \dfrac{1}{11} = 9\tfrac{1}{11}$

17. $3\tfrac{3}{4} = 3 + \dfrac{3}{4} = \dfrac{3}{1} \times \dfrac{4}{4} + \dfrac{3}{4} = \dfrac{12}{4} + \dfrac{3}{4} = \dfrac{15}{4}$

18. $5\tfrac{2}{3} = 5 + \dfrac{2}{3} = \dfrac{5}{1} \times \dfrac{3}{3} + \dfrac{2}{3} = \dfrac{15}{3} + \dfrac{2}{3} = \dfrac{17}{3}$

DRILL SET 1:

Drill 1: For each of the following pairs of fractions, decide which fraction is larger

1. $\dfrac{1}{4}, \dfrac{3}{4}$

2. $\dfrac{1}{5}, \dfrac{1}{6}$

3. $\dfrac{53}{52}, \dfrac{85}{86}$

4. $\dfrac{7}{9}, \dfrac{6}{10}$

5. $\dfrac{700}{360}, \dfrac{590}{290}$

Drill 2: Add or subtract the following fractions.

1. $\dfrac{2}{7} + \dfrac{3}{7} =$

2. $\dfrac{5}{8} - \dfrac{4}{8} =$

3. $\dfrac{7}{9} - \dfrac{2}{9} =$

4. $\dfrac{9}{11} + \dfrac{20}{11} =$

5. $\dfrac{3}{4} - \dfrac{10}{4} =$

Drill 3: Add or subtract the following fractions.

1. $\dfrac{2}{3} + \dfrac{5}{9}$

2. $\dfrac{7}{8} - \dfrac{5}{4}$

3. $\dfrac{4}{9} + \dfrac{8}{11}$

4. $\dfrac{20}{12} - \dfrac{5}{3}$

5. $\dfrac{1}{4} + \dfrac{4}{5} + \dfrac{5}{8}$

DRILL 4: Solve for x in the following equations.

1. $\dfrac{1}{5} + \dfrac{x}{5} = \dfrac{4}{5}$

2. $\dfrac{x}{8} - \dfrac{3}{8} = \dfrac{10}{8}$

3. $\dfrac{x}{6} + \dfrac{5}{12} = \dfrac{11}{12}$

4. $\dfrac{2}{7} - \dfrac{x}{21} = -\dfrac{2}{21}$

5. $\dfrac{2}{5} + \dfrac{x}{8} = \dfrac{31}{40}$

DRILL SET 2:

Drill 1: Simplify the following fractions.

1. $\dfrac{6}{9}$

2. $\dfrac{12}{28}$

3. $\dfrac{24}{36}$

4. $\dfrac{35}{100}$

5. $\dfrac{6x}{70}$

Drill 2: Multiply or Divide the following fractions. Final answer must be simplified.

1. $\dfrac{4}{7} \times \dfrac{8}{9}$

2. $\dfrac{9}{4} \div \dfrac{2}{3}$

3. $\dfrac{7}{15} \div \dfrac{8}{5}$

4. $\dfrac{5}{12} \times \dfrac{8}{10}$

5. $\dfrac{3x}{13} \times \dfrac{5}{6}$

Drill 3: Multiply or Divide the following fractions. Final answer must be simplified.

1. $\dfrac{14}{20} \times \dfrac{15}{21}$

2. $\dfrac{6}{25} \div \dfrac{9}{10}$

3. $\dfrac{4}{21} \times \dfrac{14}{13} \times \dfrac{5}{8}$

4. $\dfrac{3}{11} \div \dfrac{3}{11}$

5. $\dfrac{57}{63} \times \dfrac{0}{18}$

Drill 2: Convert the following mixed numbers to improper fractions.

1. $3\frac{2}{3}$

2. $2\frac{1}{6}$

3. $6\frac{3}{7}$

4. $4\frac{5}{9}$

5. $12\frac{5}{12}$

Drill 4: Solve for x in the following equations.

1. $\dfrac{5}{3}x = \dfrac{3}{7}$

2. $\dfrac{2}{x} = \dfrac{7}{3}$

3. $\dfrac{6}{11}x = \dfrac{10}{33}$

4. $\dfrac{2x}{13} = \dfrac{3}{7}$

5. $\dfrac{3x}{4} - \dfrac{5}{6} = \dfrac{17}{12}$

DRILL SET 3:

DRILL 1: Convert the following improper fractions to mixed numbers.

1. $\dfrac{9}{4}$

2. $\dfrac{31}{7}$

3. $\dfrac{47}{15}$

4. $\dfrac{70}{20}$

5. $\dfrac{91}{13}$

Drill Set Answers

Set 1, Drill 1

1. $\frac{1}{4}, \frac{3}{4}$ – The denominators are the same, but the numerator of $\frac{3}{4}$ is larger, so $\frac{3}{4} > \frac{1}{4}$.

2. $\frac{1}{5}, \frac{1}{6}$ – The numerators are the same, but the denominator of $\frac{1}{5}$ is smaller, so $\frac{1}{5} > \frac{1}{6}$.

3. $\frac{53}{52}, \frac{85}{86}$ – In the first fraction, $\frac{53}{52}$, the numerator is bigger than the denominator, so the fraction is greater than 1. In the second fraction, $\frac{85}{86}$, the denominator is bigger than the numerator, so the fraction is less than 1. $\frac{53}{52} > \frac{85}{86}$.

4. $\frac{7}{9}, \frac{6}{10}$ – The second fraction, $\frac{6}{10}$, has both a smaller numerator and a larger denominator than the first fraction. Therefore, $\frac{6}{10} < \frac{7}{9}$.

5. $\frac{700}{360}, \frac{590}{290}$ – The first fraction is greater than 1 but less than 2, because 700 is less than twice 360 ($2 \times 360 = 720$). The second fraction is greater than 2, because 590 is more than twice 290 ($2 \times 290 = 580$). $\frac{590}{290} > \frac{700}{360}$

Set 1, Drill 2

1. $\frac{2}{7} + \frac{3}{7} = \frac{2+3}{7} = \frac{5}{7}$

2. $\frac{5}{8} - \frac{4}{8} = \frac{5-4}{8} = \frac{1}{8}$

3. $\frac{7}{9} - \frac{2}{9} = \frac{7-2}{9} = \frac{5}{9}$

4. $\frac{9}{11} + \frac{20}{11} = \frac{9+20}{11} = \frac{29}{11}$

5. $\frac{3}{4} - \frac{10}{4} = \frac{3-10}{4} = \frac{-7}{4}$

Set 1, Drill 3

1. $\dfrac{2}{3}+\dfrac{5}{9}=\dfrac{2}{3}\times\dfrac{3}{3}+\dfrac{5}{9}=\dfrac{2\times3}{3\times3}+\dfrac{5}{9}=\dfrac{6}{9}+\dfrac{5}{9}=\dfrac{6+5}{9}=\dfrac{11}{9}$

2. $\dfrac{7}{8}-\dfrac{5}{4}=\dfrac{7}{8}-\dfrac{5}{4}\times\dfrac{2}{2}=\dfrac{7}{8}-\dfrac{5\times2}{4\times2}=\dfrac{7}{8}-\dfrac{10}{8}=\dfrac{7-10}{8}=\dfrac{-3}{8}$

3. $\dfrac{4}{9}+\dfrac{8}{11}=\dfrac{4}{9}\times\dfrac{11}{11}+\dfrac{8}{11}\times\dfrac{9}{9}=\dfrac{4\times11}{9\times11}+\dfrac{8\times9}{11\times9}=\dfrac{44}{99}+\dfrac{72}{99}=\dfrac{116}{99}$

4. $\dfrac{20}{12}-\dfrac{5}{3}=\dfrac{20}{12}-\dfrac{5}{3}\times\dfrac{4}{4}=\dfrac{20}{12}-\dfrac{5\times4}{3\times4}=\dfrac{20}{12}-\dfrac{20}{12}=0$

5. $\dfrac{1}{4}+\dfrac{4}{5}+\dfrac{5}{8}=\dfrac{1}{4}\times\dfrac{10}{10}+\dfrac{4}{5}\times\dfrac{8}{8}+\dfrac{5}{8}\times\dfrac{5}{5}=\dfrac{1\times10}{4\times10}+\dfrac{4\times8}{5\times8}+\dfrac{5\times5}{8\times5}=$

   $\dfrac{10}{40}+\dfrac{32}{40}+\dfrac{25}{40}=\dfrac{10+32+25}{40}=\dfrac{67}{40}$

Set 1, Drill 4

1. $\dfrac{1}{5}+\dfrac{x}{5}=\dfrac{4}{5}$

   $\dfrac{x}{5}=\dfrac{4}{5}-\dfrac{1}{5}$

   $\dfrac{x}{5}=\dfrac{4-1}{5}=\dfrac{3}{5}$

   $x=3$

2. $\dfrac{x}{8}-\dfrac{3}{8}=\dfrac{10}{8}$

   $\dfrac{x}{8}=\dfrac{10}{8}+\dfrac{3}{8}$

   $\dfrac{x}{8}=\dfrac{10+3}{8}=\dfrac{13}{8}$

   $x=13$

3. $\dfrac{x}{6}+\dfrac{5}{12}=\dfrac{11}{12}$

   $\dfrac{x}{6}=\dfrac{11}{12}-\dfrac{5}{12}$

   $\dfrac{x}{6}=\dfrac{11-5}{12}=\dfrac{6}{12}$

   $\dfrac{x\times2}{6\times2}=\dfrac{2x}{12}=\dfrac{6}{12}$

   $2x=6$

   $x=3$

4. $\dfrac{2}{7}-\dfrac{x}{21}=-\dfrac{2}{21}$

   $-\dfrac{x}{21}=-\dfrac{2}{21}-\dfrac{2}{7}$

   $-\dfrac{x}{21}=-\dfrac{2}{21}-\dfrac{2\times3}{7\times3}$

   $-\dfrac{x}{21}=-\dfrac{2}{21}-\dfrac{6}{21}=\dfrac{-2-6}{21}=\dfrac{-8}{21}$

   $\dfrac{x}{21}=\dfrac{8}{21}$

   $x=8$

*Manhattan*GMAT*Prep
the new standard

5. $\dfrac{2}{5} + \dfrac{x}{8} = \dfrac{31}{40}$

$\dfrac{x}{8} = \dfrac{31}{40} - \dfrac{2}{5}$

$\dfrac{x}{8} = \dfrac{31}{40} - \dfrac{2 \times 8}{5 \times 8}$

$\dfrac{x}{8} = \dfrac{31}{40} - \dfrac{16}{40}$

$\dfrac{x}{8} = \dfrac{15}{40}$

$\dfrac{x \times 5}{8 \times 5} = \dfrac{5x}{40} = \dfrac{15}{40}$

$5x = 15$

$x = 3$

Set 2, Drill 1

1. $\dfrac{6}{9} = \dfrac{2 \times 3}{3 \times 3} = \dfrac{2}{3} \times \dfrac{3}{3} = \dfrac{2}{3}$

2. $\dfrac{12}{28} = \dfrac{2 \times 2 \times 3}{2 \times 2 \times 7} = \dfrac{3}{7} \times \dfrac{2 \times 2}{2 \times 2} = \dfrac{3}{7}$

3. $\dfrac{24}{36} = \dfrac{2 \times 2 \times 2 \times 3}{2 \times 2 \times 3 \times 3} = \dfrac{2}{3} \times \dfrac{2 \times 2 \times 3}{2 \times 2 \times 3} = \dfrac{2}{3}$

4. $\dfrac{35}{100} = \dfrac{5 \times 7}{2 \times 2 \times 5 \times 5} = \dfrac{7}{2 \times 2 \times 5} \times \dfrac{5}{5} = \dfrac{7}{20}$

5. $\dfrac{6x}{70} = \dfrac{2 \times 3 \times x}{2 \times 5 \times 7} = \dfrac{3 \times x}{5 \times 7} \times \dfrac{2}{2} = \dfrac{3x}{35}$

Set 2, Drill 2

1. $\dfrac{4}{7} \times \dfrac{8}{9} = \dfrac{4 \times 8}{7 \times 9} = \dfrac{32}{63}$

2. $\dfrac{9}{4} \div \dfrac{2}{3} = \dfrac{9}{4} \times \dfrac{3}{2} = \dfrac{9 \times 3}{4 \times 2} = \dfrac{27}{8}$

3. $\dfrac{7}{15} \div \dfrac{8}{5} = \dfrac{7}{15} \times \dfrac{5}{8} = \dfrac{7 \times 5}{3 \times 5 \times 8} = \dfrac{7 \times \cancel{5}}{3 \times \cancel{5} \times 8} = \dfrac{7}{24}$

4. $\dfrac{5}{12} \times \dfrac{8}{10} = \dfrac{5 \times 2 \times 2 \times 2}{2 \times 2 \times 3 \times 2 \times 5} = \dfrac{\cancel{5} \times \cancel{2} \times \cancel{2} \times \cancel{2}}{\cancel{2} \times \cancel{2} \times 3 \times \cancel{2} \times \cancel{5}} = \dfrac{1}{3}$

5. $\dfrac{3x}{13} \times \dfrac{5}{6} = \dfrac{3 \times x \times 5}{13 \times 2 \times 3} = \dfrac{\cancel{3} \times x \times 5}{13 \times 2 \times \cancel{3}} = \dfrac{5x}{26}$

Set 2, Drill 3

1. $\dfrac{14}{20} \times \dfrac{15}{21} = \dfrac{2 \times 7 \times 3 \times 5}{2 \times 2 \times 5 \times 7 \times 3} = \dfrac{\cancel{2} \times \cancel{7} \times \cancel{3} \times \cancel{5}}{2 \times \cancel{2} \times \cancel{5} \times \cancel{7} \times \cancel{3}} = \dfrac{1}{2}$

2. $\dfrac{6}{25} \div \dfrac{9}{10} = \dfrac{6}{25} \times \dfrac{10}{9} = \dfrac{2 \times 3 \times 2 \times 5}{5 \times 5 \times 3 \times 3} = \dfrac{2 \times \cancel{3} \times 2 \times \cancel{5}}{5 \times \cancel{5} \times \cancel{3} \times 3} = \dfrac{4}{15}$

3. $\dfrac{4}{21} \times \dfrac{14}{13} \times \dfrac{5}{8} = \dfrac{2 \times 2 \times 2 \times 7 \times 5}{3 \times 7 \times 13 \times 2 \times 2 \times 2} = \dfrac{\cancel{2} \times \cancel{2} \times \cancel{2} \times \cancel{7} \times 5}{3 \times \cancel{7} \times 13 \times \cancel{2} \times \cancel{2} \times \cancel{2}} = \dfrac{5}{39}$

4. $\dfrac{3}{11} \div \dfrac{3}{11} = \dfrac{3}{11} \times \dfrac{11}{3} = \dfrac{3 \times 11}{11 \times 3} = \dfrac{33}{33} = 1$

5. $\dfrac{57}{63} \times \dfrac{0}{18} = \dfrac{57 \times 0}{63 \times 18} = 0$

Set 2, Drill 4

1. $\dfrac{5}{3}x = \dfrac{3}{7}$

   $x = \dfrac{3}{7} \div \dfrac{5}{3} = \dfrac{3}{7} \times \dfrac{3}{5}$

   $x = \dfrac{9}{35}$

2. $\dfrac{2}{x} = \dfrac{7}{3}$

   $2 \times 3 = 7 \times x$

   $6 = 7x$

   $\dfrac{6}{7} = x$

3. $\dfrac{6}{11}x = \dfrac{10}{33}$

   $x = \dfrac{10}{33} \div \dfrac{6}{11} = \dfrac{10}{33} \times \dfrac{11}{6}$

   $x = \dfrac{2 \times 5 \times 11}{3 \times 11 \times 2 \times 3} = \dfrac{\cancel{2} \times 5 \times \cancel{11}}{3 \times \cancel{11} \times \cancel{2} \times 3}$

   $x = \dfrac{5}{9}$

4. $\dfrac{2x}{13} = \dfrac{3}{7}$

   $2x \times 7 = 3 \times 13$

   $14x = 39$

   $x = \dfrac{39}{14}$

5. $\dfrac{3x}{4} - \dfrac{5}{6} = \dfrac{17}{12}$

$\dfrac{3x}{4} \times \dfrac{3}{3} - \dfrac{5}{6} \times \dfrac{2}{2} = \dfrac{17}{12}$

$\dfrac{9x}{12} - \dfrac{10}{12} = \dfrac{17}{12}$

$9x - 10 = 17$

$9x = 27$

$x = 3$

Set 3, Drill 1

1. $\dfrac{9}{4} = \dfrac{8+1}{4} = \dfrac{8}{4} + \dfrac{1}{4} = 2 + \dfrac{1}{4} = 2\,\tfrac{1}{4}$

2. $\dfrac{31}{7} = \dfrac{28+3}{7} = \dfrac{28}{7} + \dfrac{3}{7} = 4 + \dfrac{3}{7} = 4\,\tfrac{3}{7}$

3. $\dfrac{47}{15} = \dfrac{45+2}{15} = \dfrac{45}{15} + \dfrac{2}{15} = 3 + \dfrac{2}{15} = 3\,\tfrac{2}{15}$

4. $\dfrac{70}{20} = \dfrac{60+10}{20} = \dfrac{60}{20} + \dfrac{10}{20} = 3 + \dfrac{10}{20} = 3 + \dfrac{1}{2} = 3\,\tfrac{1}{2}$

5. $\dfrac{91}{13} = 7$

Set 3, Drill 2

1. $3\,\tfrac{2}{3} = 3 + \dfrac{2}{3} = \dfrac{3 \times 3}{1 \times 3} + \dfrac{2}{3} = \dfrac{9}{3} + \dfrac{2}{3} = \dfrac{11}{3}$

2. $2\,\tfrac{1}{6} = 2 + \dfrac{1}{6} = \dfrac{2 \times 6}{1 \times 6} + \dfrac{1}{6} = \dfrac{12}{6} + \dfrac{1}{6} = \dfrac{13}{6}$

3. $6\,\tfrac{3}{7} = 6 + \dfrac{3}{7} = \dfrac{6 \times 7}{1 \times 7} + \dfrac{3}{7} = \dfrac{42}{7} + \dfrac{3}{7} = \dfrac{45}{7}$

4. $4\,\tfrac{5}{9} = 4 + \dfrac{5}{9} = \dfrac{4 \times 9}{1 \times 9} + \dfrac{5}{9} = \dfrac{36}{9} + \dfrac{5}{9} = \dfrac{41}{9}$

5. $12\,\tfrac{5}{12} = 12 + \dfrac{5}{12} = \dfrac{12 \times 12}{1 \times 12} + \dfrac{5}{12} = \dfrac{144}{12} + \dfrac{5}{12} = \dfrac{149}{12}$

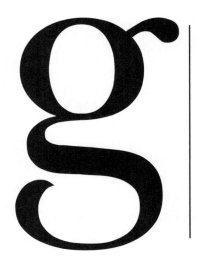

Chapter 7
of
FOUNDATIONS OF GMAT MATH

FRACTIONS, DECIMALS, & PERCENTS

In This Chapter . . .

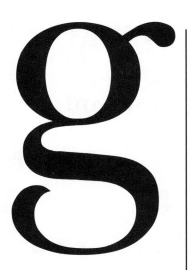

FRACTIONS, DECIMALS, AND PERCENTS

In This Chapter:

- The common thread between fractions, decimals, and percents
- How to convert numbers in one form to another form (e.g., changing percents to decimals)
- How to use fractions, decimals, and percents to solve certain types of GMAT word problems

Fractions, Decimals, and Percents: Three Ways to Say the Same Thing!

Fractions, decimals, and percents are three different ways of representing the same thing: "parts of a whole."

Consider the following:

1/3 of the orange   *2.5 times the distance*   *110% of the sales*

In each of these instances, we're using a fraction, a decimal, or a percent to indicate that we have some portion of a whole. In fact, these different forms are very closely related. For instance, we might say that a container is 1/2 full, which is the same thing as saying that it is 50% full, or filled to 0.5 of its capacity. To illustrate, see the table below. Each row consists of a fraction, a decimal, and a percent representing the same part of a whole.

> **Nerd Note:** The "part" can be greater than the "whole," as it is in 110% or 5/4.

Fraction	**Decimal**	**Percent**
$\frac{1}{4}$ ¼ 1/4	0.25	25%
The container is 1/2 full.	The container is filled to 0.5 of its capacity.	The container is 50% full.
3/2	1.5	150%

Thus, one helpful feature of fractions, decimals, and percents is that we can use whichever form is most convenient to solve a particular problem.

We've already discussed fractions at length in the last chapter, so we'll get started here by investigating percents and decimals in a little more detail. After that, we'll discuss how to change from one form to another (for instance, changing from a fraction to a decimal). Finally, we'll look at some word problems that involve fractions, decimals and percents.

Percents

Percent literally means "per one hundred." Another way to think of it is out of 100. So for instance, if you say "60% of the children like to play tag," what you are saying is that 60 out of every 100 children like to play tag.

Percentages are, for most of us, the most common way we discuss proportions in our everyday lives. We often see signs advertising "20% off," but rarely (if ever) see signs that say "1/5 off," or "0.8 of the original."

However, in terms of performing mathematical computations, percentages are often the *least* useful way to represent a proportion.

In general, you should convert all percentages to decimals before performing computations. You can do this by moving the decimal point two places to the left:

> 85% is the equivalent of 0.85
> 70% is the equivalent of 0.7
> 5% is the equivalent of 0.05

Nerd Note: Moving decimal points in a number is actually multiplying or dividing that number by a power of 10 (depending on how many places you move the point). When 3.5 becomes 35, you've multiplied it by 10, and when 457 becomes 4.57, you've divided it by 100.

Shifting the Decimal Point

An important skill when dealing with decimals is the ability to change numbers by shifting the decimal. You can do this by multiplying or dividing a number by 10 or a power of 10.

When you multiply a number by 10, you move the decimal to the right one place.

> For example: $1.23 \times 10 = 12.3$

When you divide a number by 10, you move the decimal to the left one place.

> For example: $782.95 \div 10 = 78.295$

This also works with powers of 10. Whatever power 10 is raised to is the number of places you move the decimal.

> For example: $43.8723 \times 10^3 = 43,872.3$

10 is raised to the third power, and our number is being multiplied by 10^3, so the decimal is moved to the right 3 places. This rule also works with division.

> For example: $57,234 \div 10^4 = 5.7234$

Check Your Skills

1. $32.753 \times 10^2 =$
2. $43,681 \times 10^{-4} =$

Answers can be found on page 207.

Decimal Addition / Subtraction

When adding or subtracting decimals, make sure to line up decimal points:

Right	**Wrong**

$$
\begin{array}{r}
0.3 \\
+\ 0.65 \\
\hline
0.95
\end{array}
\qquad
\begin{array}{r}
0.3 \\
+\ 0.65 \\
\hline
=\ 0.68
\end{array}
$$

$$
\begin{array}{r}
0.65 \\
-\ 0.50 \\
\hline
0.15
\end{array}
\qquad
\begin{array}{r}
0.65 \\
-\ \ \ 0.5 \\
\hline
0.60
\end{array}
$$

One way to ensure that you line up decimals properly is to add zeroes to make each decimal look the same before adding or subtracting. For example, turn 0.5 into 0.50 before subtracting it from 0.65.

Check Your Skills

3. $3.128 + 0.045 =$
4. $1.8746 - 0.313 =$

Answers can be found on page 207.

Decimal Multiplication

If you have to multiply terms with decimals, one easy way to do it is to account for the decimal at the end of your work.

Imagine that we have to compute the following product.

$0.25 \times 0.5 = ?$

First, just multiply the terms together, ignoring the decimal points.

$25 \times 5 = 125$

Next, count the number of digits that were originally to the right of the decimal point for either term. Then move the decimal point in the answer an equivalent number of places to the left.

In this case, we originally had three digits to the right of the decimal. To account for that, we move our decimal three spots to the left.

$0.\textcircled{2}\textcircled{5} \times 0.\textcircled{5} = ?$

125 becomes 0.125

Therefore, $0.25 \times 0.5 = 0.125$

> **Nerd Note:** A digit is just one of these ten numbers: 0, 1, 2, 3, 4, 5, 6, 7, 8, 9. Most numbers are expressed using more than 1 digit. For instance, "twenty-one" is 21, written using the digits 2 and 1. "Digit" also means "finger," since we usually have ten of those too!

Other examples:

$3.5 \times 20 = ?$

35×20 is 700.   We originally had one digit to the right of a decimal point, so we move the decimal one place to the left:

$3.5 \times 20 = 70.0$

$0.001 \times 0.005 = ?$

$1 \times 5 = 5.$ We originally had six digits to the right of a decimal point so we move the decimal six to the left:

$0.001 \times 0.005 = 0.000005$

Proportional information is often given in the form "the percent of." In these cases, the percentage should be converted to a decimal, and "of" means "times." For example:

50% of the price becomes $0.5p$
70% of $300 becomes $0.7(300) = 210$
25% of x becomes $0.25x$

Check Your Skills

5. $0.6 \times 1.4 =$
6. $0.0004 \times 0.032 =$

Answers can be found on page 207.

Decimal Division

It is difficult to divide with decimal terms. The good news is that there's an easy workaround involving something we are now very comfortable with—fractions. Let's look at an example.

What is $300 \div 0.05$?

The first thing we're going to do is rewrite this division problem as a fraction. Remember, fractions are one way to express division. So our problem now looks like this: $\dfrac{300}{0.05} = ?$

Now, we want to get rid of the decimal in the denominator. We can do this by moving the decimal to the right 2 places, which is really the same thing as multiplying 0.05 by 100. $0.05 \times 100 = 5$. But, we don't want to change the value of the fraction; otherwise we would have an entirely different question! We can get around that by also multiplying the top of the fraction by 100. So we end up with $\dfrac{300}{0.05} = \dfrac{300 \times 100}{0.05 \times 100} = \dfrac{30,000}{5}$. Now we can do normal division and end up with the answer: 6,000.

Notice that this process works the same whether there is only one decimal or both numbers involved are decimals. All we need to do is make sure we multiply both decimals by the same power of 10 and make sure that we eliminate all the decimals. In sum, we can move the decimal points on top and bottom of a fraction—as long as we move them *together* (in

the same direction and for the same number of places). Let's try another one.

What is $12.39 \div 0.003$?

Once again, we start by rewording this division problem as a fraction. $\dfrac{12.39}{0.003}$. Now, we want to make sure that both numbers are turned into integers. 12.39 needs to have the decimal moved to the right 2 places in order to become an integer, while 0.003 needs to have the decimal moved to the right 3 places in order to become an integer. Therefore, if we multiply both the top and bottom by 1,000, we can make sure that both numbers will be integers.

$\dfrac{12.39}{0.003} = \dfrac{12.39 \times 1,000}{0.003 \times 1,000} = \dfrac{12,390}{3}$. Now we can do normal division, and find that $12,390 \div 3 = 4,130$.

Check Your Skills

7. $4 \div 0.05 =$

8. $1.24 \div 0.004 =$

Answers can be found on page 207.

Converting FDPs

From Percent to Decimal or Fraction

Percent to Decimal

As we discussed earlier, to convert from a percent to a decimal, simply move the decimal point two spots to the left.

53% becomes 0.53

40.57% becomes 0.4057

3% becomes 0.03

Percent to Fraction

To convert from a percent to a fraction, remember that *per cent* literally means "per hundred," so put the percent over one hundred and then simplify.

45% becomes 45/100 = 9/20

8% becomes 8/100 = 2/25

Check Your Skills

9. Change 87% to a decimal.
10. Change 30% to a fraction.

Answers can be found on page 207.

From Decimal to Percent or Fraction

Decimal to Percent

To convert from a decimal to a percent, simply move the decimal point two spots to the right.

     0.53 becomes 53%

     0.4057 becomes 40.57%

     0.03 becomes 3%

Decimal to Fraction

To convert from decimal to fraction, it helps to remember the proper names for the digits—the first digit to the right of the decimal point is the tenths digit, next is the hundredth digit, and then the thousandth digit, and so on.

4	5	7	•	1	2	3	5
Hundreds	Tens	Units		Tenths	Hundredths	Thousandths	Ten Thousandths

The number of zeroes in the denominator should match the number of digits in the decimal (besides the 0 in front of the decimal point). For example:

     0.3 is three tenths, or 3/10

     0.23 is twenty-three hundredths, or 23/100

     0.007 is seven thousandths, or 7/1000

Check Your Skills

11. Change 0.37 to a percent.
12. Change 0.25 to a fraction.

Answers can be found on page 207.

From Fraction to Decimal or Percent

Fraction to Decimal

To convert from a fraction to a decimal, long-divide the numerator by the denominator:

3/8 is $3 \div 8 = 0.375$
$$8\overline{)3.000}^{0.375}$$

1/4 is $1 \div 4 = 0.25$
$$4\overline{)1.00}^{0.25}$$

Fraction to Percent

To convert from a fraction to a percent, first convert from fraction to decimal, and then convert that decimal to a percent.

Step 1: $1/2 = 1 \div 2 = 0.50$

Step 2: $0.50 = 50\%$

Dividing the numerator by the denominator can be cumbersome and time consuming. Ideally, you should have the following conversions memorized before test day.

Fraction	Decimal	Percent
1/100	0.01	1%
1/20	0.05	5%
1/10	0.1	10%
1/8	0.125	12.5%
1/5	0.2	20%
1/4	0.25	25%
3/10	0.3	30%
1/3	0.3333…	33.33…%
3/8	0.375	37.5%
2/5	0.4	40%
1/2	0.5	50%
3/5	0.6	60%
5/8	0.625	62.5%
2/3	0.6666…	66.66…%
7/10	0.7	70%
3/4	0.75	75%
4/5	0.8	80%
7/8	0.875	87.5%
9/10	0.9	90%
1	1	100%

Check Your Skills

13. Change 3/5 to a decimal.
14. Change 3/8 to a percent.

Answers can be found on page 207.

FDP Word Problems

As we mentioned earlier, the purpose of fractions, decimals, and percents is to represent the proportions between a part and a whole.

Most FDP Word Problems hinge on these fundamental relationships:

Part = Fraction × Whole

Part = Decimal × Whole

In general, these problems will give you two parts of the equation and ask you to figure out the third. In the examples to come, if you're having trouble setting up equations, refer back to Chapter 3: Word Problems.

Let's look at three examples:

> A quarter of the students attended the pep rally. If there are a total of 200 students, how many of them attended the pep rally?

In this case, we are told the fraction and the total number of students. We are asked to find the number of students who attended the pep rally.

$a = (1/4)(200)$
$a = 50$

Fifty students attended the pep rally.

> At a certain pet shop, there are four kittens, two turtles, eight puppies, and six snakes. If there are no other pets, what percentage of the store's animals are kittens?

Here we are told the part (there are four kittens) and the whole (there are twenty animals total). We are asked to find the percentage.

$4 = x(20)$
$4 \div 20 = x$
$0.2 = x$

To answer the question, we convert the decimal 0.2 to 20%. Twenty percent of the animals are kittens.

> Sally receives a commission equal to thirty percent of her sales. If Sally earned $4,500 in commission last month, what were her total sales?

Here we are given the part, and told what percent that part is, but we don't know the whole. We are asked to solve for the whole.

$4,500 = 0.30s$
$4,500 \div 0.30 = s$
$s = 15,000$

Her total sales for the month were $15,000.

Tip: If in doubt—sound it out! Do you ever get confused on how exactly to set up an equation for a word problem? If so, you're not alone! For instance, consider the following problem:

   x is forty percent of what number?

First, let's assign a variable to the number we're looking for—let's call it *y*.

Do we set this up as $40\% \times x = (y)$, or $x = 40\% (y)$?

If you are unsure of how to set up this equation, try this—say it aloud or to yourself. Often, that will clear up any confusion, and put you on the right track.

Let's illustrate, using our two options.

	Equation	**Read out loud as...**
Option 1:	$40\% \times x = (y)$	40% of $x = y$
Option 2:	$x = 40\% (y)$	x is 40% of y

Now, it's much easier to see that the second option, $x = 40\% (y)$, is the equation that represents our original question.

Check Your Skills
Write the following sentences as equations.

15. *x* is 60% of *y*.
16. 1/3 of *a* is *b*.
17. *y* is 25% of what number?

Answers can be found on pages 207–208.

Typical Complications

Now let's take those three problems and give them a little GMAT twist.

   "A quarter of the students attended the pep rally. If there are a total of 200 students, how many of them did not attend the pep rally?"

Notice here that the fraction we are given, a quarter, represents the students who did attend the pep rally, but we are asked to find the number that did *not* attend the pep rally.

Here are two ways we can solve this:

1. Find the value of one quarter and subtract from the whole.

   $a = (1/4)(200)$
   $a = 50$

Once we figure out 50 students did attend, we can see that $200 - 50 = 150$, so 150 did not attend.

OR

2. Find the value of the remaining portion.

If 1/4 did attend, that must mean 3/4 did not attend:

$$n = (3/4)(200)$$
$$n = 150$$

> "At a certain pet shop, there are four kittens, two turtles, eight puppies, and six snakes. If there are no other pets, what percentage of the store's animals do kittens and puppies represent?"

Here we are asked to combine two different elements. We can take either of two approaches.

1. Figure each percentage out separately and then add.

$$4 = x(20)$$
$$0.2 = x$$

$$8 = y(20)$$
$$0.4 = y$$

$$0.2 + 0.4 = 0.6$$

Kittens and puppies represent 60% of the animals.

OR

2. Add the percentages first and then solve.

There are twelve kittens and puppies:

$$12 = x(20)$$
$$0.6 = x$$

Kittens and puppies represent 60% of the animals.

> "Sally receives a monthly salary of $1,000 plus 30% of her total sales. If Sally earned $5,500 last month, what were her total sales?"

In this case, a constant ($1,000) has been added in to the proportion equation.

Her salary = $1,000 + 0.30(total sales)

$$5,500 = 1000 + 0.3(s)$$
$$4,500 = 0.3(s)$$
$$15,000 = s$$

Check Your Skills

18. A water drum is filled to 1/4 of its capacity. If another 30 gallons of water were added, the drum would be filled. How many gallons of water does the drum currently contain?

The answer can be found on page 208.

Check Your Skills Answer Key

1. $32.753 \times 10^2 = 3,275.3$

2. $43,681 \times 10^{-4} = 4.3681$

3. $\begin{array}{r} 3.128 \\ +\ .045 \\ \hline 3.173 \end{array}$

4. $\begin{array}{r} 1.8746 \\ -\ .313 \\ \hline 1.5616 \end{array}$

5. $0.6 \times 1.4 =$

   $6 \times 14 = 84$ Move the decimal to the left 2 places.

   $0.6 \times 1.4 = 0.84$

6. $0.0004 \times 0.032 =$

   $4 \times 32 = 128$ Move the decimal to the left 7 places.

   $0.0004 \times 0.032 = 0.0000128$

7. $4 \div 0.05 =$

$$\frac{4}{0.05} = \frac{4 \times 100}{0.05 \times 100} = \frac{400}{5} = 80$$

8. $1.24 \div 0.004 =$

$$\frac{1.24}{0.004} = \frac{1.24 \times 1,000}{0.004 \times 1,000} = \frac{1,240}{4} = 310$$

9. Change 87% to a decimal.
   87% becomes 0.87

10. Change 30% to a fraction.
   30% becomes 30/100, which reduces to 3/10

11. Change 0.37 to a percent.
   0.37 becomes 37%

12. Change 0.25 to a fraction.
   0.25 is 25 hundredths, so it becomes 25/100, which reduces to 1/4

13. Change 3/5 to a decimal.
   3/5 is $3 \div 5 = 0.6$

14. Change 3/8 to a percent.
   Step 1: 3/8 is $3 \div 8 = 0.375$
   Step 2: $0.375 = 37.5\%$

15. $x = 60\%\ (y)$
   $x = 0.6(y)$

16. 1/3 of a is b.

    $(1/3)a = b$

17. y is 25% of what number?

    Let x = the number in question.

    $y = 25\% \, (x)$

    $y = 0.25(x)$

18. A water drum is filled to 1/4 of its capacity. If another 30 gallons of water were added, the drum would be filled. How many gallons of water does the drum currently contain?

Let x be the capacity of the water drum. If the drum is 1/4 full, and 30 gallons would make it full, then

$$30 = (1 - 1/4)x, \text{ which means:}$$

$$30 = \frac{3}{4}x$$

Divide both sides by 3/4. This is equivalent to multiplying by 4/3.

$$30 = \frac{3}{4}x$$

$$\frac{4}{3} \times 30 = x$$

$$\frac{120}{3} = x$$

$$40 = x$$

If the total capacity is 40 gallons and the drum is 1/4 full, then the drum currently contains $1/4 \times 40 = 10$ gallons.

FDP DRILL SET 1: WORKING WITH DECIMALS

DRILL 1: Evaluate the following expressions.

1. $6.75 \times 10^3 =$
2. $72.12 \times 10^{-4} =$
3. $2{,}346 \times 10^{-3} =$
4. $27.048 \times 10^2 =$
5. $54.197 / 10^2 =$

DRILL 2: Evaluate the following expressions.

1. $1 + 0.2 + 0.03 + 0.004 =$
2. $0.48 + 0.02 =$
3. $1.21 + 0.38 =$
4. $-0.02 + 0.35 =$
5. $0.370 + 0.042 =$

DRILL 3: Evaluate the following expressions.

1. $0.27 \times 2 =$
2. $0.403 \times 3 =$
3. $0.2 \times 0.2 =$
4. $20 \times 0.85 =$
5. $0.04 \times 0.201 =$

DRILL 4: Evaluate the following expressions.

1. $2.1 \times 0.08 =$
2. $0.063 \times 0.40 =$
3. $0.03 \times 0.005 =$
4. $0.75 (80) + 0.50 (20) =$
5. $100 \times 0.01 \times 0.01 =$

DRILL 5: Evaluate the following expressions.

1. $4/0.2 =$
2. $12.6/0.3 =$
3. $3.20/0.04 =$
4. $0.49/0.07 =$
5. $6/0.5 =$

DRILL SET 2:

DRILL 1: Fill in the missing information in the chart below:

Fraction	Decimal	Percent
1/100	0.01	1%
1/20		
	0.1	
1/8		
	0.2	
		25%
	0.3	
		33.33...%
3/8		
		40%
1/2		
	0.6	
		66.66...%
		70%
	0.75	
4/5	0.8	80%
	0.875	
9/10		
		100%

DRILL 2:

1. Convert 45% to a decimal.
2. Convert 70% to a fraction.
3. Convert 13.25% to a decimal.
4. Convert 36% to a fraction.
5. Convert 0.02% to a decimal.

DRILL 3:

1. Convert 0.20 to a percent.
2. Convert 0.55 to a fraction.
3. Convert 0.304 to a percent.
4. Convert 0.455 to a fraction.
5. Convert 0.375 to a fraction.

DRILL 4:
1. Convert 4/5 to a percent.
2. Convert 3/6 to a percent.
3. Convert 9/12 to a percent.
4. Convert 6/20 to a percent.
5. Convert 3/2 to a percent.

DRILL SET 3:

DRILL 1

1. Forty percent of the balls in a bag are red. If there is a total of 300 balls in the bag, how many of them are red?

2. Sally always puts 15% of her salary in a retirement fund. If she put $6,000 in her retirement fund last year, what was her salary?

3. Sixteen students wear glasses. If there are forty students total, what fraction of the students wear glasses?

4. What is the new price of an eighty-dollar sweater that has been discounted 20%?

5. Billy has twenty dollars and Johnny has thirty dollars. If both Billy and Johnny invest 25% of their money in baseball cards, how much money will they invest?

DRILL 2

1. Last year, a furniture store sold four hundred chairs, two hundred tables, four hundred couches, and nothing else. The chairs made up what percent of the total items sold?

2. At her old job, Sally earned a yearly salary of $80,000. At her new job, Sally earns a salary equal to $40,000 plus a commission of 25% on all her sales. If Sally wants to make a yearly salary at her new job that is the same as that of her old job, how much does she have to produce in terms of yearly sales?

3. Of 250 people surveyed, 36% said they preferred regular soda, 40% said they preferred diet soda, and the rest did not have a preference. How many of the 250 people did not have a preference?

4. A jar contains 1/3 red marbles and 1/2 blue marbles. The remaining 25 marbles are white. How many marbles does the jar contain?

5. Ted has 2/3 as many friends as Billy has, and Chris has 1/2 as many friends as Billy has. The number of friends Chris has is what percent of the number of friends Ted has?

Drill Set Solutions

Set 1, Drill 1

1. $6.75 \times 10^3 = 6,750$ Move the decimal to the right 3 places.

2. $72.12 \times 10^{-4} = 0.007212$ Move the decimal to the left 4 places

3. $2,346 \times 10^{-3} = 2.346$ Move the decimal to the left 3 places.

4. $27.048 \times 10^2 = 2,704.8$ Move the decimal to the right 2 places.

5. $54.197 / 10^2 = 0.54197$ Because we are dividing by 10^2, we move the decimal to the **left** 2 places.

Set 1, Drill 2

1.
$$
\begin{array}{r}
1.000 \\
+\ 0.200 \\
+\ 0.030 \\
+\ 0.004 \\
\hline
1.234
\end{array}
$$

2.
$$
\begin{array}{r}
0.\overset{1}{4}8 \\
+\ 0.02 \\
\hline
0.50
\end{array}
$$

3.
$$
\begin{array}{r}
1.21 \\
+\ 0.38 \\
\hline
1.59
\end{array}
$$

4.
$$
\begin{array}{r}
0.35 \\
-\ 0.02 \\
\hline
0.33
\end{array}
$$

5.
$$
\begin{array}{r}
0.\overset{1}{3}70 \\
+\ 0.042 \\
\hline
0.412
\end{array}
$$

Set 1, Drill 3

1. $0.27 \times 2 =$
   $27 \times 2 = 54$ Move the decimal to the left 2 places.
   $0.27 \times 2 = 0.54$

2. $0.403 \times 3 =$
   $403 \times 3 = 1,209$ Move the decimal to the left 3 places.
   $0.403 \times 3 = 1.209$

3. $0.2 \times 0.2 =$
   $2 \times 2 = 4$ Move the decimal to the left 2 places.
   $0.2 \times 0.2 = 0.04$

4. $20 \times 0.85 =$
   $20 \times 85 = 1,700$ Move the decimal to the left 2 places.
   $20 \times 0.85 = 17$

5. $0.04 \times 0.201 =$
   $4 \times 201 = 1,209$ Move the decimal to the left 5 places.
   $0.04 \times 0.201 = 0.00804$

Set 1, Drill 4

1. $2.1 \times 0.08 =$
   $21 \times 8 = 168$ Move the decimal to the left 3 places.
   $2.1 \times 0.08 = 0.168$

2. $0.063 \times 0.4 =$
   $63 \times 40 = 168$ Move the decimal to the left 5 places.
   $0.063 \times 0.4 = 0.0252$

3. $0.03 \times 0.005 =$
   $3 \times 5 = 15$ Move the decimal to the left 5 places.
   $0.03 \times 0.005 = 0.00015$

4. $0.75(80) + 0.50(20) =$
   $0.75 \times 80 = 60$
   $0.50 \times 20 = 10$
   $60 + 10 = 70$

5. $100 \times 0.01 \times 0.01 =$
   $100 \times 0.01 = 10^2 \times 0.01 = 1$
   $1 \times 0.01 = 0.01$

Set 1, Drill 5

1. $4 / 0.2 =$
   $$\frac{4}{0.2} \times \frac{10}{10} = \frac{40}{2} = 20$$

2. $12.6 / 0.3 =$
   $$\frac{12.6}{0.3} \times \frac{10}{10} = \frac{126}{3} = 42$$

3. $3.20 / 0.04 =$
   $$\frac{3.20}{0.04} \times \frac{100}{100} = \frac{320}{4} = 80$$

4. $0.49 / 0.07 =$

$$\frac{0.49}{0.07} \times \frac{100}{100} = \frac{49}{7} = 7$$

5. $6 / 0.5 =$

$$\frac{6}{0.5} \times \frac{10}{10} = \frac{60}{5} = 12$$

Set 2, Drill 1

Fraction	Decimal	Percent
1/100	0.01	1%
1/20	0.05	5%
1/10	0.1	10%
1/8	0.125	12.5%
1/5	0.2	20%
1/4	0.25	25%
3/10	0.3	30%
1/3	0.3333…	33.33…%
3/8	0.375	37.5%
2/5	0.40	40%
1/2	0.50	50%
3/5	0.6	60%
2/3	0.6666…	66.66…%
7/10	0.7	70%
3/4	0.75	75%
4/5	0.8	80%
7/8	0.875	87.5%
9/10	0.9	90%
1	1.0	100%

Set 2, Drill 2

1. Convert 45% to a decimal.
    45% becomes 0.45
2. Convert 70% to a fraction.
    70% becomes 70/100, which reduces to 7/10
3. Convert 13.25% to a decimal.
    13.25% becomes 0.1325
4. Convert 36% to a fraction.
    36% becomes 36/100, which reduces to 9/25
5. Convert 0.02% to a decimal.
    0.02% becomes 0.0002

Set 2, Drill 3

1. Convert 0.20 to a percent.

   0.20 becomes 20%

2. Convert 0.55 to a fraction.

   0.55 becomes 55/100, which reduces to 11/20

3. Convert 0.304 to a percent.

   0.304 becomes 30.4%

4. Convert 0.455 to a fraction.

   0.455 becomes 455/1000, which reduces to 91/200

5. Convert 0.375 to a fraction.

   0.375 becomes 375/1000, which reduces to 3/8

Set 2, Drill 4

1. Convert 4/5 to a percent.

   Step 1: $4 \div 5 = 0.8$ $5\overline{)4.0}$ = 0.8

   Step 2: 0.8 becomes 80%

2. Convert 3/6 to a percent.

   Step 1: $3 \div 6 = 0.5$ $6\overline{)3.0}$ = 0.5

   Step 2: 0.5 becomes 50%

3. Convert 9/12 to a percent.

   Step 1: $9 \div 12 = 0.75$ $12\overline{)9.00}$ = 0.75

   Step 2: 0.75 becomes 75%

4. Convert 6/20 to a percent.

   Step 1: $6 \div 20 = 0.30$ $20\overline{)6.0}$ = 0.3

   Step 2: 0.30 becomes 30%

5. Convert 3/2 to a percent.

   Step 1: $3 \div 2 = 1.5$ $2\overline{)3.0}$ = 1.5

   Step 2: 1.5 becomes 150%

Set 3, Drill 1

1. Forty percent of the balls in a bag are red. If there is a total of 300 balls in the bag, how many of them are red?

   $300 \times 40\% = 300 \times 4/10 = 120$

2. Sally always puts 15% of her salary in a retirement fund. If she put $6,000 in her retirement fund last year, what was her salary?

Let s = Sally's total salary
$6,000 = 15% of s
$6,000 = 3/20 \times s$
$6,000 \times 20/3 = s$
$40,000 = s$

3. Sixteen students wear glasses. If there are forty students total, what fraction of the students wear glasses?

16/40 = 2/5

4. What is the new price of an eighty–dollar sweater that has been discounted 20%?

If the sweater has been discounted 20%, then the new price is 80% of the original (because 100% − 20% = 80%)
80% × $80 = 4/5 × $80 = $64

5. Billy has twenty dollars and Johnny has thirty dollars. If both Billy and Johnny spend 25% of their money on baseball cards, how much money will they invest?

(0.25 × $20) + (0.25 × $30) = $5 + $7.50 = $12.50

Set 3, Drill 2

1. Last year, a furniture store sold four hundred chairs, two hundred tables, four hundred couches, and nothing else. The chairs made up what percent of the total items sold?

400/(400 + 200 + 400) = 400/1000 = 4/10 = 40%

2. At her old job, Sally earned a yearly salary of $80,000. At her new job, Sally earns a salary equal to $40,000 plus a commission of 25% on all her sales. If Sally wants to make a yearly salary at her new job that is the same as that of her old job, how much does she have to produce in terms of yearly sales?

Let s represent the amount of sales that Sally needs to generate in her new job to equal her previous salary.

$80,000 = $40,000 + $s \times 25%$
$80,000 = $40,000 + 1/4 s
$40,000 = 1/4 s
$160,000 = s$

3. Of 250 people surveyed, 36% said they preferred regular soda, 40% said they preferred diet soda, and the rest did not have a preference. How many of the 250 people did not have a preference?

The percent of people who did not have a preference = 100% − (36% + 40%) = 100% − 76% = 24%

The number of people who did not have a preference = 24% × 250 =

$$\frac{24}{100} \times 250 = \frac{6}{25} \times 250 = \frac{6}{\cancel{25}} \times \frac{\cancel{25} \times 10}{1} = 60$$

4. A jar contains 1/3 red marbles and 1/2 blue marbles. The remaining 25 marbles are white. How many marbles does the jar contain?

First we need to figure out what fraction of the marbles are white. We can do this by figuring out what fraction of the marbles are not white. Add the fractional amounts of red and blue marbles.

1/3 + 1/2 = 2/6 + 3/6 = 5/6.

1 − 5/6 = 1/6   The white marbles are 1/6 of the total number of marbles.

Let x = total number of marbles.
25 = 1/6 x
150 = x

5. Ted has 2/3 as many friends as Billy has, and Chris has 1/2 as many friends as Billy has. The number of friends Chris has is what percent of the number of friends Ted has?

Let T = the number of friends Ted has
Let B = the number of friends Billy has
Let C = the number of friends Chris has

T = 2/3 B
C = 1/2 B

C = x% T ?

B = 3/2 T
C = 1/2 (3/2 T)
C = 3/4 T
C = 75% T

Answer: 75%

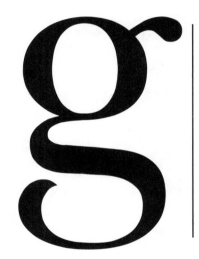

Chapter 8
of

FOUNDATIONS OF GMAT MATH

BEYOND EQUATIONS:
INEQUALITIES AND
ABSOLUTE VALUE

In This Chapter . . .

Beyond Equations: Inequalities and Absolute Value

In This Chapter:

- Introduction to inequalities
- Solving inequalities
- Finding absolute value

Introduction to Inequalities

Earlier we explored how to solve equations. Now let's look at how we can solve *inequalities*.

Inequalities are expressions that use <, >, ≤ or ≥ to describe the relationship between two values.

> *Examples of inequalities:*
>
> $5 > 4$ $\qquad$ $y \le 7$ $\qquad$ $x < 5$ $\qquad$ $2x + 3 \ge 0$

The table below illustrates how the various inequality symbols are translated. Notice that when we translate these inequalities, we read from left to right.

$x < y$	x is less than y	
$x > y$	x is greater than y	
$x \le y$	x is less than or equal to y	x is at most y
$x \ge y$	x is greater than or equal to y	x is at least y

We can also have two inequalities in one statement:

$9 < g < 200$	9 is less than g, and g is less than 200
$-3 < y \le 5$	-3 is less than y, and y is less than or equal to 5
$7 \ge x > 2$	7 is greater than or equal to x, and x is greater than 2

To visualize an inequality, it is helpful to represent it on a number line:

Example 1

$y > 5$

Example 2

$b \le 2$

Note: 5 is *not* included in the line (as shown by the circle around 5), because it is not a part of the solution—y is greater than 5, but not equal to 5.

Here, 2 is included in the solution, because b can equal 2.

Visually, any number covered by the black arrow will make the inequality true and so is a possible solution to the inequality. Conversely, any number not covered by the black arrow will make the inequality untrue and is not a solution.

Check Your Skills

Represent the following equations on the number line provided:

1. $x > 3$

2. $b \geq -2$

3. $y = 4$

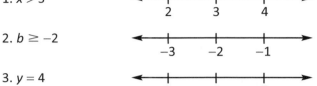

> **Time Saving Tip:** We can flip inequalities around…
>
> $x > 5$ means the same thing as $5 < x$. Similarly, "x is greater than 5" means the same thing as "5 is less than x."

Translate the following into inequality statements:

4. z is greater than v.
5. The total amount is greater than $2,000.

Answers can be found on page 229.

Solving Inequalities

What does it mean to "solve an inequality"?

You may be asking yourself, "I know what it means to solve an equation (such as $x = 2$), but what does it mean to solve an inequality?" Essentially, the principle is the same.

A solution is a number that makes an equation or inequality true. When you plug a solution back into the original equation or inequality, you get a *true statement*. This idea works the same for both equations and inequalities.

However, equations have only one, or just a few, values as solutions, but inequalities give a whole *range* of values as solutions—way too many to list individually.

> **Safety Tip:** Remember: solutions do not need to be integers—they can be fractions, decimals, etc.

Here's an example to help illustrate:

Equation: $x + 3 = 8$

The solution to $x + 3 = 8$ is $x = 5$. 5 is the **only** number that will make the equation true.

Plug back in to check:
$5 + 3 = 8$. True.

Inequality: $x + 3 < 8$

The solution to $x + 3 < 8$ is $x < 5$. Now, 5 itself is not a solution because $5 + 3 < 8$ is not a true statement. But, 4 is a solution because $4 + 3 < 8$ is true. For that matter, 4.99, 3, 2, 2.87, -5, and -100 are all also solutions. And the list goes on. Whichever of the correct answers you plug in, you need to arrive at something that looks like:

(Any number less than 5) $+ 3 < 8$. True.

Check Your Skills

6. Which of the following numbers are solutions to the inequality $x < 10$?

> (A) −3
> (B) 2.5
> (C) −3/2
> (D) 9.999
> (E) All of the above

The answer can be found on page 229.

Cleaning Up Inequalities

As with equations, our objective is to isolate our variable on one side of the inequality. When the variable is by itself, it is easiest to see what the solution (or range of solutions) really is. Although $2x + 6 < 12$ and $x < 3$ provide the same information (the second inequality is a simplified form of the first), we understand the full range of solutions much more easily when we look at the second inequality, which literally tells us that "x is less than 3."

Fortunately, the similarity between equations and inequalities doesn't end there—the techniques we will be using to clean up inequalities are the same that we used in Chapter 1 to clean up equations. (We will discuss one important difference shortly.)

Inequality Addition and Subtraction

If we told you that $x = 5$, what would $x + 3$ equal? $x + 3 = 5 + 3$, or $x = 8$. In other words, if we add the same number to both sides of an equation, the equation is still true.

The same holds true for inequalities. If we add or subtract the same number from both sides of an inequality, the inequality remains true.

Example 1	*Example 2*
$a - 4 > 6$	$y + 7 < 3$
$\underline{+4 \quad +4}$	$\underline{-7 \quad -7}$
$a \quad\quad > 10$	$y \quad\quad < -4$

We can also add or subtract variables from both sides of an inequality. There is no difference between adding/subtracting numbers and adding/subtracting variables.

Check Your Skills

Isolate the variable in the following inequalities.

7. $x - 6 < 13$
8. $y + 11 \geq -13$
9. $x + 7 > 7$

Answers can be found on page 229.

Inequality Multiplication and Division

We can also use multiplication and division to isolate our variables, as long as we recognize one very important distinction. If we multiply or divide by a negative number, we must

Manhattan **GMAT** Prep

switch the direction of the inequality sign. If we are multiplying or dividing by a positive number, the direction of the sign stays the same.

Let's look at a couple of examples to illustrate.

Multiplying or dividing by a POSITIVE number—the sign stays the same.

Example 1	*Example 2*
$2x > 10$	$z/3 \leq 2$
$2x/2 > 10/2$ Divide each side by 2	$z/3 \times (3) \leq 2 \times (3)$ Multiply each side by 3
$x > 5$	$z \leq 6$

In both instances, the sign remains the same because we are multiplying or dividing by a positive number.

Multiplying or Dividing by a NEGATIVE Number—Switch the Sign!

Example 1	*Example 2*
$-2x > 10$	$-4b \geq -8$
$-2x/-2 > 10/-2$ Divide each side by -2	$-4b/-4 \geq -8/-4$ Divide each side by -4
Switch the sign!	Flip the inequality sign!
$x < -5$	$b \leq 2$

Why do we do this? Take a look at the following example that illustrates why we need to switch the signs when multiplying or dividing by a negative number.

Incorrect if you DON'T switch		Switch the sign—Correct!	
$5 < 7$	TRUE	$5 < 7$	TRUE
$(-1) \times 5 < (-1) \times 7$	Multiply both sides by -1	$(-1) \times 5 < (-1) \times 7$	Multiply both sides by -1 AND switch the sign!
$-5 < -7$?!?	NOT TRUE!	$-5 > -7$	STILL TRUE

In each case, we begin with a true inequality statement: $5 < 7$ and then multiply by -1. We see that we have to switch the sign in order for the inequality statement to remain true.

What about multiplying or dividing an inequality by a *variable?* The short answer is… try not to do it! The issue is that you don't know the sign of the "hidden number" that the variable represents. If the variable has to be positive (e.g., it counts people or measures a length), then you can go ahead and multiply or divide, but be careful!

Check Your Skills

Isolate the variable in each equation

10. $x + 3 \geq -2$
11. $2y < 8$
12. $a + 4 \geq 2a$

Answers can be found on page 229.

Absolute Value—The Distance from Zero

The GMAT adds another level of difficulty to equations and inequalities in the form of *absolute value*.

The "absolute value" of a number describes how far that number is away from 0. It is the distance between that number and 0 on a number line. The symbol for absolute value is |number|. For instance, we would write the absolute value of −5 as |−5|.

Example 1: The absolute value of 5 is 5.

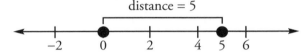

Example 2: The absolute value of −5 is also 5.

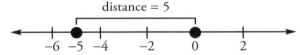

When you face an expression like |4 − 7|, treat the absolute value symbol like parentheses. Solve the arithmetic problem inside first, and then find the absolute value of the answer. In this case, 4 − 7 = −3, and −3 is 3 units from zero, so |4 − 7| = |−3| = 3.

> **Safety Tip: The absolute value of a number will never be negative,** as it always measures the distance from 0. Think of it this way: you could say that you live 4 miles from a certain house, but you would never say that you live −4 miles from the house, even if you live 4 miles south of it.

Check Your Skills

Mark the following expressions as TRUE or FALSE.

13. $|3| = 3$
14. $|-3| = -3$
15. $|3| = -3$
16. $|-3| = 3$
17. $|3 - 6| = 3$
18. $|6 - 3| = -3$

Answers can be found on page 229.

Solving Absolute Value Equations

On the GMAT, many absolute value equations place a variable inside the absolute value signs.

Example: $|y| = 3$

What's the trap here? The trap is that there are two numbers that are 3 units away from 0—3 and −3. That means both of these numbers could be possible values for y. So how do we figure that out? Here, we can't. All we can say is that y could be either the positive value or the negative value; y is *either* 3 or −3.

When there is a variable inside an absolute value, you should look for the variable to have two possible values. Although you will not always be able to determine which of the two is the correct value, it is important to be able to find both values. Next we will go through a step-by-step process for finding all solutions to an equation that contains a variable inside an absolute value.

$|y| = 3$
       Step 1: Isolate the absolute value expression on one side of the equation. In this case, the absolute value expression is already isolated.

$+(y) = 3$ or $-(y) = 3$
       Step 2: Take what's inside the absolute value sign and set up two equations. The first sets the positive value equal to the other side of the equation, and the second sets the negative value equal to the other side.

$y = 3$ or $-y = 3$
$y = 3$ or $y = -3$
       Step 3: Solve both equations.

$y = 3$ or $y = -3$
       Note: We have two possible values.

Sometimes people take a shortcut and go right to "y equals plus or minus 3." This shortcut works as long as the absolute value expression is by itself on one side of the equation.

Here's a slightly more difficult problem, using the same technique:

Example: $6 \times |2x + 4| = 30$

To solve this, you can use the same approach.

$6 \times |2x + 4| = 30$

$\quad |2x + 4| = 5$
       Step 1: Isolate the absolute value expression on one side of the equation or inequality.

$2x + 4 = 5$ or $-(2x + 4) = 5$
$2x + 4 = 5$ or $-2x - 4 = 5$
       Step 2: Set up two equations—the positive and the negative values are set equal to the other side.

$2x = 1$ or $-2x = 9$
       Step 3: Solve both equations/inequalities.

$x = 1/2$ or $x = -9/2$
       Note: We have two possible values.

Check Your Skills

Solve the following equations with absolute values in them:

19. $|a| = 6$
20. $|x + 2| = 5$
21. $|3y - 4| = 17$
22. $4|x + 1/2| = 18$

Answers can be found on page 230.

Putting Them Together: Inequalities and Absolute Values

Some problems on the GMAT include both inequalities and absolute values. We can solve these problems by combining what we have learned about solving inequalities with what we have learned about solving absolute values.

   Example 1: $|x| \geq 4$

Even though we're now dealing with an inequality, and not an equal sign, the basic process is the same. The absolute value is already isolated on one side, so now we need to set up our two equations. The first equation sets the positive value equal to the other side of the equation, and the second sets the negative value equal to the other side.

   $+ (x) \geq 4$ or $- (x) \geq 4$

Now that we have our two equations, we isolate the variable in each equation.

   $+ (x) \geq 4$ $- (x) \geq 4$

   $x \geq 4$ $-x \geq 4$ Divide by -1

                         $x \leq -4$ Remember to flip the sign when dividing by a
                                            negative

So the two solutions to the original equation are $x \geq 4$ and $x \leq -4$. Let's represent that on a number line.

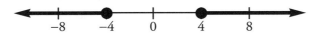

As before, any number that is covered by the black arrow will make the inequality true. Because of the absolute value, there are now two arrows instead of one, but nothing else has changed. Any number to the left of -4 will make the inequality true, as will any number to the right of 4.

Looking back at the inequality $|x| \geq 4$, we can now interpret it in terms of distance. $|x| \geq 4$ means "x is at least 4 units away from zero, in either direction." The black arrows indicate all numbers for which that statement is true.

   Example 2: $|x + 3| < 5$

Once again, the absolute value is already isolated on one side, so now we need to set up our two equations. The first equation sets the positive value equal to the other side of the equation, and the second sets the negative value equal to the other side.

$$+ (x + 3) < 5 \quad \text{and} \quad -(x + 3) < 5$$

Next we isolate the variable in each equation.

$$x + 3 < 5 \qquad -x - 3 < 5$$
$$x < 2 \qquad\qquad -x < 8$$
$$\qquad\qquad\qquad x > -8$$

So our two equations are $x < 2$ and $x > -8$. But now something curious happens if we plot those two equations on our number line.

It seems like every number should be a solution to the equation. But if you start testing numbers, that isn't the case. Test out the number 5 for example. Is $|5 + 3| < 5$? No, it isn't. As it turns out, the only numbers that make the inequality true are those that are true for both inequalities. Really, our number line should look like this:

In our first example, it was the case that x could be greater than or equal to 4 OR less than or equal to -4. For this example, however, it seems to make more sense to say that x is greater than -8 AND less than 2. When solving inequalities, if your two arrows do not overlap, as in the first example, any number that falls in the range of either arrow will be a solution to the inequality. If your two arrows overlap, as in the second example, only the numbers that fall in the range of both arrows will be solutions to the inequality.

It's harder to interpret $|x + 3| < 5$ in terms of distance, but we can do so. The inequality means "$(x + 3)$ is less than 5 units away from from zero, in either direction." The shaded segment indicates all numbers x for which this is true. As the inequalities become more complicated, don't worry about interpreting their meaning—simply solve them algebraically!

Check Your Skills

23. $|x + 1| > 2$
24. $|-x - 4| \geq 8$
25. $|x - 7| < 9$

Answers can be found on page 230.

Check Your Skills Answer Key:

1.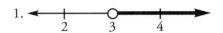

2.

3.

4. $z > v$

5. Let a = amount.
   $$a > \$2{,}000$$

6. The answer is (E) All of the above! All of these numbers are to the left of 10 on the number line.

7. $x - 6 < 13$
   $$x < 19$$

8. $y + 11 \geq -13$
   $$y \geq -24$$

9. $x + 7 > 7$
   $$x > 0$$

10. $x + 3 \geq -2$
    $$x \geq -5$$

11. $2y < 8$
    $$y < 4$$

12. $a + 4 \geq 2a$
    $$4 \geq a$$

13. True

14. False — *(Note that absolute value is always positive!)*

15. False

16. True

17. True ($|3 - 6| = |-3| = 3$)

18. False

19. $|a| = 6$

       $a = 6$ or $a = -6$

20. $|x + 2| = 5$

   + $(x + 2) = 5$ or $-(x + 2) = 5$

       $x + 2 = 5$ or $-x - 2 = 5$

       $x = 3$ or $-x = 7$

                                   $x = -7$

21. $|3y - 4| = 17$

   + $(3y - 4) = 17$ or $-(3y - 4) = 17$

       $3y - 4 = 17$ or $-3y + 4 = 17$

       $3y = 21$ or $-3y = 13$

       $y = 7$ or $y = -13/3$

22. $4|x + 1/2| = 18$

   + $(x + 1/2) = 4.5$ or $-(x + 1/2) = 4.5$

       $x + 1/2 = 4.5$ or $-x - 1/2 = 4.5$

       $x = 4$ or $-x = 5$

                                   $x = -5$

23. $|x + 1| > 2$

   + $(x + 1) > 2$ or $-(x + 1) > 2$

       $x + 1 > 2$ or $-x - 1 > 2$

       $x > 1$ or $-x > 3$

                                $x < -3$

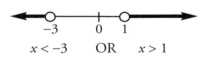

       $x < -3$ OR $x > 1$

24. $|-x - 4| \geq 8$

   + $(-x - 4) \geq 8$ or $-(-x - 4) \geq 8$

       $-x - 4 \geq 8$ or $x + 4 \geq 8$

       $-x \geq 12$ or $x \geq 4$

       $x \leq -12$

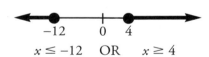

       $x \leq -12$ OR $x \geq 4$

25. $|x - 7| < 9$

   + $(x - 7) < 9$ or $-(x - 7) < 9$

       $x - 7 < 9$ or $-x + 7 < 9$

       $x < 16$ or $-x < 2$

                                $x > -2$

       $x > -2$ AND $x < 16$, $-2 < x < 16$

Chapter Review: Drill Sets

DRILL SET 1:

Drill 1: Draw the following inequalities on the number line provided:

1. $x > 4$

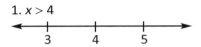

2. $a \geq 3$

3. $y = 2$

4. $x < 5$

5. $5 > x$

DRILL SET 2:

Drill 1: Translate the following into inequality statements:

1. a is less than b.
2. Five times x is greater than 10.
3. Six is less than or equal to $4x$.
4. The price of an apple is greater than the price of an orange.
5. The total number of members is at least 19.

DRILL SET 3:

Drill 1: Solve the following inequalities.

1. $x + 3 \leq -2$
2. $t - 4 \leq 13$
3. $3b \geq 12$
4. $-5x > 25$
5. $-8 < -4y$

Drill 2: Solve the following equations.

1. $2z + 4 \geq -18$

2. $7y - 3 \leq 4y + 9$
3. $b/5 \leq 4$
4. $d + 3/2 < 8$
5. $4x/7 \leq 15 + x$

Drill 3: Solve the following inequalities.

1. $3(x - 7) \geq 9$
2. $\dfrac{x}{3} + 8 < \dfrac{x}{2}$
3. $2x - 1.5 > 7$
4. $\dfrac{8(x + 6)}{9} \geq 0$
5. $\dfrac{2(3 - x)}{5x} \leq 4$

Drill 4: Solve the following inequalities.

1. $3\sqrt{2x + 3} > 12$
2. $\dfrac{2(8 - 3x)}{7} > 4$
3. $0.25x - 3 \leq 1$
4. $2(x - 1)^3 + 3 \leq 19$
5. $\dfrac{4\sqrt[3]{5x - 8}}{3} \geq 4$

DRILL SET 4:

Drill 1: Solve the following absolute value equations.

1. $|x| = 5$
2. $|2y| = 6$
3. $|x + 6| = 3$
4. $|4y + 2| = 18$
5. $|1 - x| = 6$

Drill 2: Solve the following absolute value equations.

1. $3|x - 4| = 16$
2. $2|x + 0.32| = 7$
3. $|3x - 4| = 2x + 6$
4. $|5x - 17| = 3x + 7$
5. $\left|\dfrac{x}{4} + 3\right| = 0.5$

DRILL SET 5:

Drill 1: Solve each of the following inequalities, and then mark the solution on a number line.

1. $|x + 3| < 1$
2. $|3x| \geq 6$
3. $5 \geq |2y + 3|$
4. $7 \geq |-3a + 5|$
5. $|-12a| < 15$

Drill 2: Solve each of the following inequalities, and then mark the solution on a number line.

1. $|-x| \geq 6$
2. $|x + 4|/2 > 5$
3. $|x^3| < 64$
4. $|0.1x - 3| \geq 1$
5. $\left| \dfrac{3x}{2} + 7 \right| \leq 11$

Drill 3: Solve each of the following inequalities, and then mark the solution on a number line.

1. $\left| -\dfrac{4x}{5} + \dfrac{2}{3} \right| \leq \dfrac{7}{15}$
2. $|3x + 7| \geq 2x + 12$
3. $|3 + 3x| < -2x$
4. $|-3 - 5x| \leq -4x$
5. $3\left| \dfrac{5x}{3} - 7 \right| < \dfrac{2x}{3} + 18$

*Manhattan*GMATPrep
the new standard

Drill Set Answers

Set 1, Drill 1: Draw the following inequalities on the number line provided:

1. $x > 4$

2. $a \geq 3$

3. $y = 2$

4. $x < 5$

5. $5 > x$

> Note: We can flip inequalities around... $x < 5$ means the same thing as $5 > x$. "x is less than 5" means the same thing as "5 is greater than x."

Set 2, Drill 1: Translate the following into inequality statements:

1. a is less than b.
   $a < b$

2. Five times x is greater than 10.
   $5x > 10$

3. Six is less than or equal to $4x$.
   $6 \leq 4x$

4. The price of an apple is greater than the price of an orange.
   Let a = the price of an apple
   Let o = the price of an orange

   $a > o$

   Note: In this problem, we set up our variables to refer to prices—not the number of apples and oranges.

5. The total number of members is at least 19.
   Let m = the number of members
   $m \geq 19$

Set 3, Drill 1:

1. $x + 3 \leq -2$
   $x \leq -5$

2. $t - 4 \leq 13$
   $t \leq 17$

3. $3b \geq 12$
   $b \geq 4$

4. $-5x > 25$
   $x < -5$

5. $-8 < -4y$
   $2 > y$

Set 3, Drill 2:

1. $2z + 4 \geq -18$
   $2z \geq -22$
   $z \geq -11$

2. $7y - 3 \leq 4y + 9$
   $3y - 3 \leq 9$
   $3y \leq 12$
   $y \leq 4$

3. $b/5 \leq 4$
   $b \leq 20$

4. $d + 3/2 < 8$
   $d < 8 - 3/2$
   $d < 16/2 - 3/2$
   $d < 13/2$

5. $4x/7 \leq 15 + x$
   $4x \leq 105 + 7x$
   $-3x \leq 105$
   $x \geq -35$

Set 3, Drill 3:

1. $3(x - 7) \geq 9$
   $x - 7 \geq 3$
   $x \geq 10$

2. $\dfrac{x}{3} + 8 < \dfrac{x}{2}$

   $6\left(\dfrac{x}{3} + 8\right) < 6\left(\dfrac{x}{2}\right)$ Multiply by 6 to get rid of fractions

   $2x + 48 < 3x$
   $48 < x$

3. $2x - 1.5 > 7$
   $2x > 8.5$
   $x > 4.25$

4. $\dfrac{8(x+6)}{9} \geq 0$

$8(x+6) \geq 0$

$x+6 \geq 0$

$x \geq -6$

5. $\dfrac{2(3-x)}{5x} \leq 4$

$2(3-x) \leq 20x$

$3-x \leq 10x$

$3 \leq 11x$

$\dfrac{3}{11} \leq x$

Set 3, Drill 4:

1. $3\sqrt{2x+3} > 12$

$\sqrt{2x+3} > 4$

$2x+3 > 16$ We can square both sides of an inequality as long as both sides are positive

$2x > 13$

$x > \dfrac{13}{2}$

2. $\dfrac{2(8-3x)}{7} > 4$

$2(8-3x) > 28$

$8-3x > 14$

$-3x > 6$

$x < -2$

3. $0.25x - 3 \leq 1$

$0.25x \leq 4$

$x \leq 16$

4. $2(x-1)^3 + 3 \leq 19$

$2(x-1)^3 \leq 16$

$(x-1)^3 \leq 8$

$x - 1 \leq 2$ We can take the cube root of both sides of an inequality

$x \leq 3$

5. $\dfrac{4\sqrt[3]{5x-8}}{3} \geq 4$

   $4\sqrt[3]{5x-8} \geq 12$

   $\sqrt[3]{5x-8} \geq 3$ We can cube both sides of an inequality

   $5x - 8 \geq 27$

   $5x \geq 35$

   $x \geq 7$

Set 4, Drill 1:

1. $|x| = 5$

   $+ \quad (x) = 5$ or $-x = 5$

   $\quad\quad x = 5$ $x = -5$

   $\quad\quad x = 5$ or -5

2. $|2y| = 6$

   $+ \quad (2y) = 6$ or $-(2y) = 6$

   $\quad\quad 2y = 6$ $-2y = 6$

   $\quad\quad\ y = 3$ $y = -3$

   $\quad\quad\ y = 3$ or -3

3. $|x + 6| = 3$

   $+ \quad (x + 6) = 3$ or $-(x + 6) = 3$

   $\quad\quad x + 6$ $-x - 6 = 3$

   $\quad\quad x = -3$ $-x = 9$

   $\quad\quad\quad\quad\quad\quad\quad\quad\quad\quad\ x = -9$

   $\quad\quad\ x = -3$ or -9

4. $|4y + 2| = 18$

   $+ \quad (4y + 2) = 18$ or $-(4y + 2) = 18$

   $\quad\quad 4y + 2 = 18$ $-4y - 2 = 18$

   $\quad\quad 4y = 16$ $-4y = 20$

   $\quad\quad\ y = 4$ $y = -5$

   $\quad\quad\ y = 4$ or -5

5. $|1 - x| = 6$

   $+ \quad (1 - x) = 6$ or $-(1 - x) = 6$

   $\quad\quad -x = 5$ $-1 + x = 6$

   $\quad\quad\ x = -5$ $x = 7$

   $\quad\quad\ x = -5$ or 7

Set 4, Drill 2:

1. $3|x - 4| = 16$

$$|x - 4| = \frac{16}{3}$$

+ $(x - 4) = 16/3$ or $-(x - 4) = 16/3$
$x - 4 = 16/3$ $-x + 4 = 16/3$
$x = 16/3 + 4$ $-x = 16/3 - 4$
$x = 16/3 + 12/3$ $-x = 16/3 - 12/3$
$x = 28/3$ $-x = 4/3$
                              $x = -4/3$

$x = 28/3$ or $-4/3$

2. $2|x + 0.32| = 7$
$|x + 0.32| = 3.5$

+ $(x + 0.32) = 3.5$ or $-(x + 0.32) = 3.5$
$x + 0.32 = 3.5$ $-x - 0.32 = 3.5$
$x = 3.18$ $-x = 3.82$
                             $x = -3.82$

$x = 3.18$ or -3.82

3. $|3x - 4| = 2x + 6$

+ $(3x - 4) = 2x + 6$ or $-(3x - 4) = 2x + 6$
$3x - 4 = 2x + 6$ $-3x + 4 = 2x + 6$
$x - 4 = 6$ $4 = 5x + 6$
$x = 10$ $-2 = 5x$

$$-\frac{2}{5} = x$$

$x = 10$ or $-2/5$

4. $|5x - 17| = 3x + 7$

+ $(5x - 17) = 3x + 7$ or $-(5x - 17) = 3x + 7$
$5x - 17 = 3x + 7$ $-5x + 17 = 3x + 7$
$2x - 17 = 7$ $17 = 8x + 7$
$2x = 24$ $10 = 8x$

$x = 12$

$$\frac{10}{8} = x$$

$$\frac{5}{4} = x$$

$x = 12$ or $5/4$

5. $\left|\dfrac{x}{4}+3\right|=0.5$

$+\quad\left(\dfrac{x}{4}+3\right)=0.5$ or $-\left(\dfrac{x}{4}+3\right)=0.5$

$\dfrac{x}{4}+3=0.5$ $\qquad\qquad$ $-\dfrac{x}{4}-3=0.5$

$\dfrac{x}{4}=-2.5$ $\qquad\qquad$ $-\dfrac{x}{4}=3.5$

$x=-10$ $\qquad\qquad\qquad$ $\dfrac{x}{4}=-3.5$

$\qquad\qquad\qquad\qquad\qquad$ $x=-14$

$x=-10$ or -14

Set 5, Drill 1:

1. $|x+3|<1$

$+\quad(x+3)<1$ $\qquad\qquad$ $-(x+3)<1$

$x+3<1$ $\qquad\qquad\qquad$ $-x-3<1$

$x<-2$ $\qquad\qquad\qquad$ $-x<4$

$x+3<1$ $\qquad\qquad\qquad$ $x>-4$

$-4<x<-2$

2. $|3x|\geq 6$

$+\quad(3x)\geq 6$ $\qquad\qquad$ $-(3x)\geq 6$

$3x\geq 6$ $\qquad\qquad\qquad$ $-3x\geq 6$

$x\geq 2$ $\qquad\qquad\qquad$ $x\leq -2$

$x\leq -2$ or $x\geq 2$

3. $5\geq |2y+3|$

$5\geq (2y+3)$ $\qquad\qquad$ $5\geq -(2y+3)$

$5\geq 2y+3$ $\qquad\qquad$ $5\geq -2y-3$

$2\geq 2y$ $\qquad\qquad\qquad$ $8\geq -2y$

$1\geq y$ $\qquad\qquad\qquad$ $-4\leq y$

$-4\leq y\leq 1$

4. $7 \geq |-3a + 5|$

$7 \geq (-3a + 5)$	$7 \geq -(-3a + 5)$
$7 \geq -3a + 5$	$7 \geq 3a - 5$
$2 \geq -3a$	$12 \geq 3a$
$-2/3 \leq a$	$4 \geq a$

$$-2/3 \leq a \leq 4$$

5. $|-12a| < 15$

$+ \quad (-12a) < 15$	$-(-12a) < 15$
$-12a < 15$	$12a < 15$
$a > -15/12$	$a < 15/12$
$a > -5/4$	$a < 5/4$

$$-5/4 < a < 5/4$$

Set 5, Drill 2:

1. $|-x| \geq 6$

$+ \quad (-x) \geq 6$	$-(-x) \geq 6$
$-x \geq 6$	$x \geq 6$
$x \leq -6$	

$$x \leq -6 \quad \text{or} \quad x \geq 6$$

2. $|x + 4|/2 > 5$

$|x + 4| > 10$

$+ \quad (x + 4) > 10$	$-(x + 4) > 10$
$x + 4 > 10$	$-x - 4 > 10$
$x > 6$	$-x > 14$
	$x < -14$

$$x < -14 \text{ or } x > 6$$

3. $|x^3| < 64$

$+ \quad (x^3) < 64$	or	$-(x^3) < 64$
$x^3 < 64$		$-x^3 < 64$
$x < 4$		$x^3 > -64$
		$x > -4$

$$-4 < x < 4$$

4. $|0.1x - 3| \geq 1$

+ $(0.1x - 3) \geq 1$ or $-(0.1x - 3) \geq 1$

     $0.1x - 3 \geq 1$ $-0.1x + 3 \geq 1$

     $0.1x \geq 4$ $-0.1x \geq -2$

     $x \geq 40$ $x \leq 20$

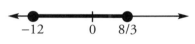

$x \leq 20$ or $x \geq 40$

5. $\left|\dfrac{3x}{2} + 7\right| \leq 11$

+ $\left(\dfrac{3x}{2} + 7\right) \leq 11$ or $-\left(\dfrac{3x}{2} + 7\right) \leq 11$

     $\dfrac{3x}{2} + 7 \leq 11$ $-\dfrac{3x}{2} - 7 \leq 11$

     $\dfrac{3x}{2} \leq 4$ $-\dfrac{3x}{2} \leq 18$

     $3x \leq 8$ $-3x \leq 36$

     $x \leq \dfrac{8}{3}$ $x \geq -12$

$-12 \leq x \leq 8/3$

Set 5, Drill 3:

1. $\left|-\dfrac{4x}{5} + \dfrac{2}{3}\right| \leq \dfrac{7}{15}$

+ $\left(-\dfrac{4x}{5} + \dfrac{2}{3}\right) \leq \dfrac{7}{15}$ or $-\left(-\dfrac{4x}{5} + \dfrac{2}{3}\right) \leq \dfrac{7}{15}$

     $-\dfrac{4x}{5} + \dfrac{2}{3} \leq \dfrac{7}{15}$ $\dfrac{4x}{5} - \dfrac{2}{3} \leq \dfrac{7}{15}$

$15\left(-\dfrac{4x}{5} + \dfrac{2}{3}\right) \leq \left(\dfrac{7}{15}\right)15$ $15\left(\dfrac{4x}{5} - \dfrac{2}{3}\right) \leq \left(\dfrac{7}{15}\right)15$

     $-12x + 10 \leq 7$ $12x - 10 \leq 7$

       $-12x \leq -3$ $12x \leq 17$

          $x \geq \dfrac{1}{4}$ $x \leq \dfrac{17}{12}$

$1/4 \leq x \leq 17/12$

2. $|3x + 7| \geq 2x + 12$

$+ \quad (3x + 7) \geq 2x + 12 \qquad$ or $\qquad -(3x + 7) \geq 2x + 12$

$\qquad 3x + 7 \geq 2x + 12 \qquad\qquad\qquad -3x - 7 \geq 2x + 12$

$\qquad x + 7 \geq 12 \qquad\qquad\qquad\qquad -7 \geq 5x + 12$

$\qquad x \geq 5 \qquad\qquad\qquad\qquad\qquad -19 \geq 5x$

$\qquad\qquad\qquad\qquad\qquad\qquad\qquad -\dfrac{19}{5} \geq x$

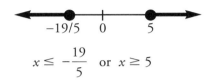

$\qquad x \leq -\dfrac{19}{5} \quad$ or $\quad x \geq 5$

3. $|3 + 3x| < -2x$

$+ \quad (3 + 3x) < -2x \qquad\qquad$ or $\qquad -(3 + 3x) < -2x$

$\qquad 3 + 3x < -2x \qquad\qquad\qquad\qquad -3 - 3x < -2x$

$\qquad 3 + 5x < 0 \qquad\qquad\qquad\qquad\quad -3 < x$

$\qquad 5x < -3$

$\qquad x < -3/5$

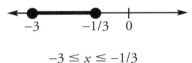

$\qquad\qquad -3 < x < -3/5$

4. $|-3 - 5x| \leq -4x$

$+ \quad (-3 - 5x) \leq -4x \qquad\quad$ or $\qquad -(-3 - 5x) \leq -4x$

$\qquad -3 - 5x \leq -4x \qquad\qquad\qquad\qquad 3 + 5x \leq -4x$

$\qquad -3 \leq x \qquad\qquad\qquad\qquad\qquad 3 \leq -9x$

$\qquad\qquad\qquad\qquad\qquad\qquad\qquad -1/3 \geq x$

$\qquad\qquad -3 \leq x \leq -1/3$

5. $3\left|\dfrac{5x}{3} - 7\right| < \dfrac{2x}{3} + 18$

$\quad \left|\dfrac{5x}{3} - 7\right| < \dfrac{2x}{9} + 6$

$+ \quad \left(\dfrac{5x}{3} - 7\right) < \dfrac{2x}{9} + 6 \qquad$ or $\qquad -\left(\dfrac{5x}{3} - 7\right) < \dfrac{2x}{9} + 6$

$\qquad \dfrac{5x}{3} - 7 < \dfrac{2x}{9} + 6 \qquad\qquad\qquad -\dfrac{5x}{3} + 7 < \dfrac{2x}{9} + 6$

$$\frac{5x}{3} < \frac{2x}{9} + 13$$

$$\frac{5x}{3} - \frac{2x}{9} < 13$$

$$\frac{15x}{9} - \frac{2x}{9} < 13$$

$$\frac{13x}{9} < 13$$

$$13x < 117$$

$$x < 9$$

$$7 < \frac{2x}{9} + \frac{5x}{3} + 6$$

$$1 < \frac{2x}{9} + \frac{5x}{3}$$

$$1 < \frac{2x}{9} + \frac{15x}{9}$$

$$1 < \frac{17x}{9}$$

$$9 < 17x$$

$$\frac{9}{17} < x$$

$$9/17 < x < 9$$

Chapter 9
of
FOUNDATIONS OF GMAT MATH

GEOMETRY

In This Chapter . . .

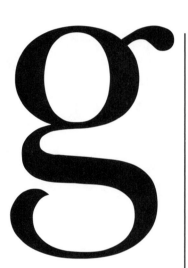

GEOMETRY

In This Chapter:

- Basic shapes that the GMAT tests
- The key elements of each shape
- The equations that define the relationships between these elements
- How to apply these equations to solve GMAT geometry problems
- The coordinate plane

Introduction to Geometry: Shapes and Relationships

For many students, geometry brings to mind complicated shapes and the need to memorize lots of formulas. However, on the GMAT, geometry is fundamentally about *relationships.* Specifically, it is about the relationships between the various elements, or features, of a shape.

Each geometric shape has a set of basic elements—for a circle it might be its radius, its diameter, its circumference and its area. The key relationships among these elements are described by equations (usually not more than 4 or 5 per shape). As an example, the relationship between a circle's radius and its area is described by the equation Area = πr^2 (where r = radius).

In this chapter we'll go over the basic properties of the basic shapes most commonly tested on the GMAT. Then we'll discuss how the GMAT tests your knowledge of these shapes and how to work your way through Geometry questions.

Circles

The Basic Elements of a Circle

A circle is a set of points that are all the same distance from a central point. By definition, every circle has a center. Although the center is not itself a point on the circle, it is nevertheless an important component of the circle. The **radius** of a circle is defined as the distance between the center of the circle and a point on the circle. The first thing to know about radii is that *any* line segment connecting the center of the circle (usually labeled *O*) and *any* point on the circle is a radius (usually labeled *r*). All radii in the same circle have the same length.

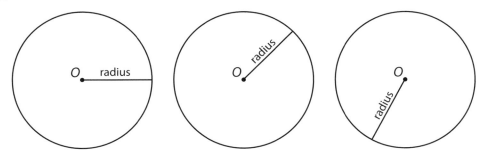

We'll discuss the other basic elements by dealing with a particular circle. Our circle will have a radius of 7, and we'll see what else we can figure out about the circle based on that one measurement. As you'll see, we'll be able to figure out quite a lot.

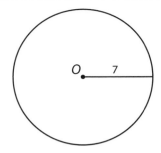

Once we know the radius, the next easiest piece to figure out is the **diameter.** The diameter passes through the center of a circle and connects 2 opposite points on the circle.

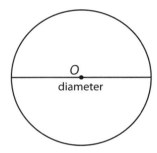

One way of thinking about the diameter (usually referred to as *d*) is that it is 2 radii laid end to end. The diameter will always be exactly twice the length of the radius. This relationship can be expressed as $d = 2r$. That means that our circle with radius 7 has a diameter of 14.

Now it's time for our next important measurement—the **circumference.** Circumference (usually referred to as *C*) is a measure of the distance around a circle. One way to think about circumference is that it's the perimeter of a circle.

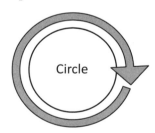

As it happens, there is a consistent relationship between the circumference and the diameter of any circle. If you were to divide the circumference by the diameter, you would always get the same number—3.14... (the number is actually a non-repeating decimal, so it's usually rounded to the hundredths place). You may be more familiar with this number as the greek letter π (pi). To recap:

$$\frac{\text{circumference}}{\text{diameter}} = \pi. \text{ Or } \pi d = C.$$

In our circle with a diameter of 14, the circumference is $\pi(14) = 14\pi$. The vast majority of questions that involve circles and π will use the greek letter and a decimal approximation.

Suppose a question about our circle with radius 7 asked for the circumference. The correct answer would read 14π, and not 43.96 (which is 14×3.14). It's worth mentioning that another very common way of expressing the circumference is that twice the radius times π also equals C, because the diameter is twice the radius. This relationship is commonly expressed as $C = 2\pi r$. As you prepare for the GMAT, you should be comfortable with using either equation.

There is one more element of a circle that you'll need to be familiar with, and that is **area.** The area (usually referred to as A) is the space inside the circle.

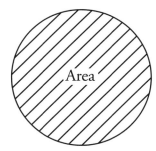

Once again, it turns out that there is a consistent relationship between the area of a circle and its diameter (and radius). If you know the radius of the circle, then the formula for the area is $A = \pi r^2$. For our circle of radius 7, the area is $\pi(7)^2 = 49\pi$. To recap, once we know the radius, we are able to determine the diameter, the circumference, and the area.

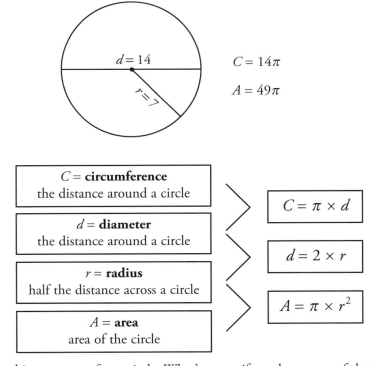

These relationships are true of any circle. What's more, if you know *any* of these values, you can determine the rest. In fact, the ability to use one element of a circle to determine another is one of the most important skills for answering questions about circles.

To demonstrate, we'll work through another circle, but this time we know that the area of the circle is 36π. Well, we know the formula for the area, so let's start by plugging this value into the formula.

$$36\pi = \pi r^2$$

Now we can solve for the radius by isolating r.

$36\pi = \pi r^2$	Divide by π
$36 = r^2$	Take the square root of both sides
$6 = r$	

Now that we know the radius, we can simply multiply it by 2 to get the diameter, so our diameter is 12. Finally, to find the circumference, simply multiply the diameter by π, which gives us a circumference of 12π.

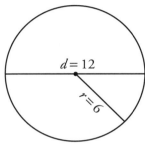

Check Your Skills

1. The radius of a circle is 7. What is the area?
2. The circumference of a circle is 17π. What is the diameter?
3. The area of a circle is 25π. What is the circumference?

Answers can be found on page 287.

Sectors

Let's continue working with our circle that has an area of 36π. But now, let's cut it in half and make it a semicircle. Any time you have a fractional portion of a circle, it's known as a **sector**.

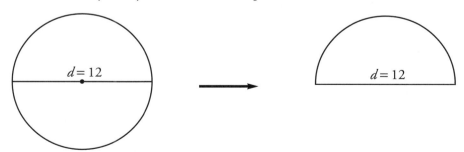

What effect does cutting the circle in half have on the basic elements of the circle? The diameter stays the same, as does the radius. But what happened to the area and the circumference? They're also cut in half. So the area of the semicircle is 18π and the circumference is 6π. When dealing with sectors, we call the portion of the circumference that remains the **arc length.** So the arc length of this sector is 6π.

In fact, this rule applies even more generally to circles. If, instead of cutting the circle in half, we had cut it into 1/4's, each piece of the circle would have 1/4 the area of the entire circle and 1/4 the circumference.

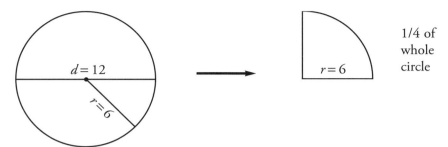

1/4 of whole circle

Now, on the GMAT, you're unlikely to be told that you have 1/4th of a circle. There is one more basic element of circles that becomes relevant when you are dealing with sectors, and that is the **central angle.** The central angle of a sector is the degree measure between the two radii. Take a look at the quarter circle. Normally, there are 360° in a full circle. What is the degree measure of the angle between the 2 radii? The same thing that happens to area and circumference happens to the central angle. It is now 1/4th of 360°, which is 90°.

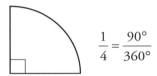

$$\frac{1}{4} = \frac{90°}{360°}$$

Let's see how we can use the central angle to determine sector area and arc length. For our next example, we will still use the circle with area 36π, but now the sector will have a central angle of 60°.

We need to figure out what fractional amount of the circle remains if the central angle is 60°. If 360° is the whole amount, and 60° is the part, then 60/360 is the fraction we're looking for. 60/360 reduces to 1/6. That means a sector with a central angle of 60° is 1/6th of the entire circle. If that's the case, then the sector area is 1/6 × (Area of circle) and arc length is 1/6 × (Circumference of circle). So:

Sector Area = 1/6 × (36π) = 6π

Arc Length = 1/6 × (12π) = 2π

$$\frac{1}{6} = \frac{60°}{360°} = \frac{\text{Sector Area}}{\text{Circle Area}} = \frac{\text{Arc Length}}{\text{Circumference}}$$

In our last example, we used the central angle to find what fractional amount of the circle the sector was. But any of the three properties of a sector, namely central angle, arc length and area, could be used.

Let's look at an example.

> A sector has a radius of 9 and an area of 27π. What is the central angle of the sector?

We still need to determine what fractional amount of the circle the sector is. This time, however, we have to use the area to figure that out. We know the area of the sector, so if we can figure out the area of the whole circle, we can figure out what fractional amount the sector is.

We know the radius is 9, so we can calculate the area of the whole circle. Area = πr^2, so Area = $\pi(9)^2 = 81\pi$. $\dfrac{27\pi}{81\pi} = \dfrac{1}{3}$, so the sector is 1/3 of the circle. The full circle has a central angle of 360, so we can multiply that by 1/3. $1/3 \times 360 = 120$, so the central angle of the sector is 120°.

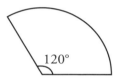

$$\frac{1}{3} = \frac{120°}{360°} = \frac{27\pi \ \text{(sector area)}}{81\pi \ \text{(circle area)}}$$

Let's recap what we know about sectors. Every question about sectors involves determining what fraction of the circle the sector is. That means that every question about sectors will provide you with enough info to calculate one of the following fractions:

$$\frac{\text{central angle}}{360} \qquad \frac{\text{sector area}}{\text{circle area}} \qquad \frac{\text{arc length}}{\text{circumference}}$$

Once you know any of those fractions, you know them all, and you can find the value of any piece of the sector or the original circle.

Check Your Skills

4. A sector has a central angle of 270° and a radius of 2. What is the area of the sector?
5. A sector has an arc length of 4π and a radius of 3. What is the central angle of the sector?
6. A sector has an area of 40π and a radius of 10. What is the arc length of the sector?

Answers can be found on page 287.

Triangles

The Basic Properties of a Triangle

Triangles show up all over the GMAT. You'll often find them hiding in problems that seem to be about rectangles or other shapes. Of the basic shapes, triangles are perhaps the most challenging to master. One reason is that several properties of triangles are tested.

Let's start with some general comments on triangles:

The sum of any two side lengths of a triangle will always be greater than the third side length. This is because the shortest distance between two points is a straight line. At the same time, the third side length will always be greater than the difference of the other two side lengths. The pictures below illustrate these two points.

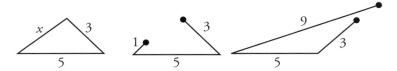

What is the largest number x could be? What's the smallest? Could it be 9? 1?

> x must be less than $3 + 5 = 8$
> x must be greater than $5 - 3 = 2$
> $2 < x < 8$

Check Your Skills

7. Two sides of a triangle have lengths 5 and 19. Can the third side have a length of 13?
8. Two sides of a triangle have lengths 8 and 17. What is the range of possible values of the length of the third side?

Answers can be found on page 287.

The internal angles of a triangle must add up to 180°. This rule can sometimes allow us to make inferences about angles of unknown size. It means that if we know the measures of 2 angles in the triangle, we can determine the measure of the third angle. Take a look at this triangle:

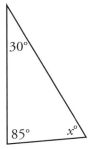

> **Time Saving Tip:** You can ignore the degree sign (°) when performing these calculations.

The 3 internal angles must add up to 180°, so we know that $30 + 85 + x = 180$. Solving for x tells us that $x = 65$. So the third angle is 65°. The GMAT can also test your knowledge of this rule in more complicated ways. Take a look at this triangle:

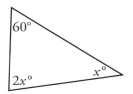

In this situation, we only know one of the angles. The other 2 are given in terms of x. Even though we only know one angle, we can still determine the other 2. Again, we know that the 3 angles will add up to 180. So $60 + x + 2x = 180$. That means that $3x = 120$. So $x = 40$. Thus the angle labeled $x°$ has a measure of 40° and the angle labeled $2x°$ has a measure of 80°.

The GMAT will not always draw triangles to scale, so don't try to guess angles from the picture, which could be distorted. Instead, solve for angles mathematically.

Check Your Skills
Find the missing angle(s).

9.

10.

11.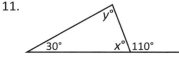

Answers can be found on pages 287–288.

Internal angles of a triangle are important on the GMAT for another reason. Sides correspond to their opposite angles. This means that the longest side is opposite the largest angle, and the smallest side is opposite the smallest angle. Think about an alligator opening its mouth, bigger and bigger… as the angle between its upper and lower jaws increases, the distance between the front teeth on the bottom and top jaws would get longer and longer.

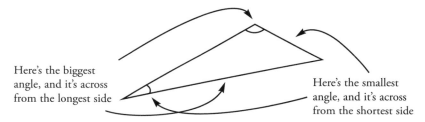

Here's the biggest angle, and it's across from the longest side

Here's the smallest angle, and it's across from the shortest side

One important thing to remember about this relationship is that it works both ways. If we know the sides of the triangle, we can make inferences about the angles. If we know the angles, we can make inferences about the sides.

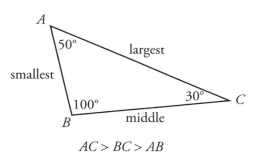

$AC > BC > AB$

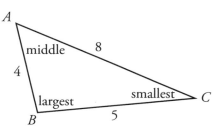

$\angle ABC > \angle BAC > \angle ACB$

Things get interesting when a triangle has sides that are the same length or angles that have the same measure. We can classify triangles by the number of equal sides that they have.

- A triangle that has 2 equal angles and 2 equal sides (opposite the equal angles) is an **isosceles triangle.**

- A triangle that has 3 equal angles (all 60°) and 3 equal sides is an **equilateral triangle.**

Once again, it is important to remember that this relationship between equal angles and equal sides works in both directions. Take a look at these isosceles triangles, and think about what additional information we can infer from them.

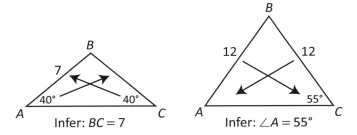

The GMAT loves isosceles triangles and uses them in a variety of ways. The following is a more challenging application of the equal sides/equal angles rule.

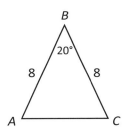

Take a look at the triangle and see what other information you can fill in. Specifically, do you know the degree measure of either *BAC* or *BCA*?

Because side *AB* is the same length as side *BC*, we know that *BAC* has the same degree measure as *BCA*. For convenience we could label each of those angles as $x°$ on our diagram.

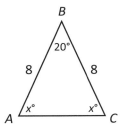

We also know that the 3 internal angles will add up to 180. So $20 + x + x = 180$. $2x = 160$, and $x = 80$. So *BAC* and *BCA* each equal 80°. We can't find the side length *AC* without more advanced math, but the GMAT wouldn't ask you for this side length for that very reason.

Check Your Skills

Find the value of *x*.

12.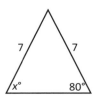

13.

14.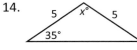

Answers can be found on pages 288 – 289.

Perimeter and Area

The **perimeter** of a triangle is the sum of the lengths of all 3 sides.

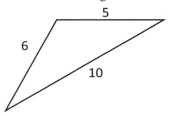

In this triangle, the perimeter is 5 + 6 + 10 = 21. This is a relatively simple property of a triangle, so often it will be used in combination with another property. Try this next problem. What is the perimeter of triangle *PQR*?

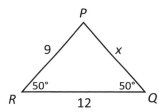

To solve for the perimeter, we will need to determine the value of *x*. Because angles *PQR* and *PRQ* are both 50°, we know that their opposite sides will have equal lengths. That means sides *PR* and *PQ* must have equal lengths, so we can infer that side *PQ* has a length of 9. The perimeter of triangle *PQR* is 9 + 9 + 12 = 30.

Check Your Skills

What is the perimeter of each triangle?

15.

16.

Answers can be found on page 289.

Note: Figures not drawn to scale. You need to be ready to solve geometry problems without depending on exactly accurate figures.

The final property of a triangle we will discuss is area. You may be familiar with the equation Area = 1/2 (base) × (height). One very important thing to understand about the area of a triangle (and area in general) is the relationship between the base and the height. The base and the height MUST be perpendicular to each other. In a triangle, one side of the triangle is the base, and the height is formed by dropping a line from the third point of the triangle straight down towards the base, so that it forms a 90° angle with the base. The small square located where the height and base meet (in the figure below) is a very common symbol used to denote a right angle.

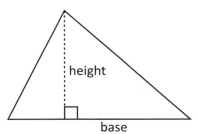

An additional challenge on the GMAT is that problems will ask you about familiar shapes but present them to you in orientations you are unused to. Even the area of a triangle is affected. Most people generally think of the base of the triangle as the bottom side of the triangle, but in reality, any side of the triangle could act as a base. In fact, depending on the orientation of the triangle, there may not actually be a bottom side. The three triangles below are all the same triangle, but in each one we have made a different side the base, and drawn in the corresponding height.

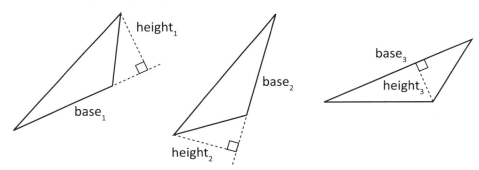

As it turns out, not only can any side be the base, but the height doesn't even need to appear in the triangle! The only thing that matters is that the base and the height are perpendicular to each other.

Check Your Skills

What are the areas of the following triangles?

17.   18.

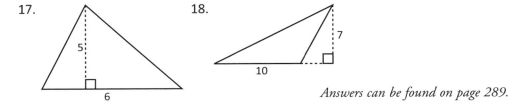

Answers can be found on page 289.

Right Triangles

There is one more class of triangle that is very common on the GMAT: the **right triangle.** A right triangle is any triangle in which one of the angles is a right triangle. The reason they are so important will become more clear as we attempt to answer the next question.

What is the perimeter of triangle *ABC*?

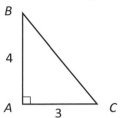

> **Safety Tip:** There is more advanced math called trigonometry that deals with triangle sides and angles. No question on the GMAT will require trigonometry in order to arrive at an answer.

Normally we would be unable to answer this question. We only have two sides of the triangle, but we need all three sides to calculate the perimeter.

The reason we can answer this question is that right triangles have an additional property that the GMAT likes to make use of: there is a consistent relationship among the lengths of its sides. This relationship is known as the **Pythagorean Theorem.** For *any* right triangle, the relationship is $a^2 + b^2 = c^2$, where *a* and *b* are the lengths of the sides touching the right angle, also known as **legs,** and *c* is the length of the side opposite the right angle, also known as the **hypotenuse.**

In the above triangle, sides *AB* and *AC* are *a* and *b* (it doesn't matter which is which) and side *BC* is *c*. So $(3)^2 + (4)^2 = (BC)^2$. $9 + 16 = (BC)^2$, so $25 = (BC)^2$, and the length of side *BC* is 5. Our triangle really looks like this:

> **Safety Tip:** In Geometry, lengths *must* be positive, so you can ignore any negative solutions in equations with multiple solutions.

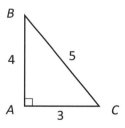

Finally, the perimeter = 3 + 4 + 5 = 12.

Pythagorean Triplets

As mentioned above, right triangles show up in many problems on the GMAT, and many of these problems require the Pythagorean Theorem. But there is a shortcut that we can use in many situations to make the calculations easier.

The GMAT favors a certain subset of right triangles in which all three sides have lengths that are integer values. The triangle we saw above was an example of that. The lengths of the sides were 3, 4 and 5—all integers. This group of side lengths is a **Pythagorean triplet**—a 3–4–5 triangle. Although there is an infinite number of Pythagorean triplets, a few are likely to appear on the test and should be memorized. For each triplet, the first two numbers are the lengths of the sides that touch the right angle, and the third (and largest) number is the length of the hypotenuse. They are:

> **Nerd Note:** In 1637, a famous mathematician named Fermat claimed he had devised a proof that, while there are an infinite number of integer solutions for $a^2 + b^2 = c^2$, there are no integer solutions for $a^3 + b^3 = c^3$ or similar higher order equations, although he never wrote it down. It took until 1995 (358 years later!) for another mathematician to finally devise a general proof.

3–4–5	5–12–13	8–15–17	6–8–10	10–24–26
			(this is 3–4–5 doubled)	(this is 5–12–13 doubled)

Let's look at a practice question to see how memorizing these triplets can save us time on the GMAT.

What is the area of triangle *DEF*?

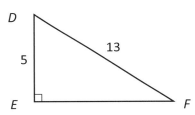

What do we need in order to find the area of triangle *DEF*? Like any triangle, the formula is area = 1/2 (base) × (height), so we need a base and a height. This is a right triangle, so sides *DE* and *EF* are perpendicular to each other, which means that if we can figure out the length of side *EF*, we can calculate the area.

The question then becomes, how do we find the length of side *EF*? First, realize that we can *always* find the length of the third side of a right triangle if we know the lengths of the other two sides. That's because we know the Pythagorean Theorem. In this case, the formula would look like this: $(DE)^2 + (EF)^2 = (DF)^2$. We know the lengths of two of those sides, so we could rewrite the equation as $(5)^2 + (EF)^2 = (13)^2$. Solving this equation, we get $25 + (EF)^2 = 169$, so $(EF)^2 = 144$, which means $EF = 12$. But these calculations are unnecessary; once you see a right triangle in which one of the legs has a length of 5 and the hypotenuse has a length of 13, you should recognize the Pythagorean triplet. The length of the other leg must be 12.

However you find the length of side *EF*, our triangle now looks like this:

Manhattan **GMAT** Prep

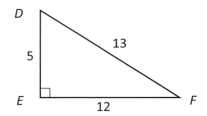

Now we have what we need to find the area of triangle *DEF*. Area = ¹/₂(12) × (5) = ¹/₂(60) = 30. Note that in a right triangle, you can consider one leg the base and the other leg the height.

Check Your Skills

What is the length of the third side of the triangle? For #21, find the area.

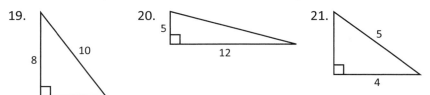

Answers can be found on pages 289–290.

Quadrilaterals

A quadrilateral is any figure with 4 sides. The GMAT largely deals with one class of quadrilaterals known as **parallelograms.** A parallelogram is any 4 sided figure in which the opposite sides are parallel and equal and opposite angles are equal. This is an example of a parallelogram.

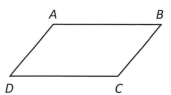

In this figure, sides *AB* and *CD* are parallel and have equal lengths, sides *AD* and *BC* are parallel and equal length, angles *ADC* and *ABC* are equal and angles *DAB* and *DCB* are equal.

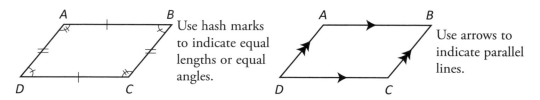

An additional property of any parallelogram is that the diagonal will divide the parallelogram into 2 equal triangles.

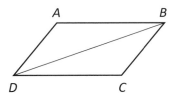 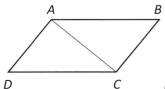 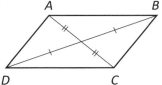

Triangle *ABD* = Triangle *BCD*   Triangle *ADC* = Triangle *ABC*   The diagonals also cut
each other in half (bisect
each other)

For any parallelogram, the perimeter is the sum of the lengths of all the sides and the area is equal to (base) × (height). With parallelograms, as with triangles, it is important to remember that the base and the height MUST be perpendicular to one another.

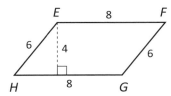

In this parallelogram, what is the perimeter, and what is the area? The perimeter is the sum of the sides, so it's 6 + 8 + 6 + 8 = 28. Alternatively, you can use one of the properties of parallelograms to calculate the perimeter in a different way. We know that parallelograms have 2 sets of equal sides. In this parallelogram, two of the sides have a length of 6 and 2 of the sides have a length of 8. So the perimeter equals 2 × 6 + 2 × 8. We can factor out a 2, and say that perimeter = 2 × (6 + 8) = 28.

To calculate the area, we need a base and a height. It might be tempting to say that the area is 6 × 8 = 48. But the two sides of this parallelogram are not perpendicular to each other. The dotted line drawn into the figure, however, is perpendicular to side *HG*. The area of parallelogram *EFGH* is 8 × 4 = 32.

Check Your Skills

22. What is the perimeter of the parallelogram?

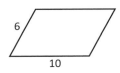

23. What is the area of the parallelogram?

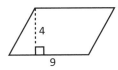

Answers can be found on page 290.

*Manhattan*GMAT*Prep

Rectangles

Rectangles are a specific type of parallelogram. Rectangles have all the same properties of parallelograms, with one additional property—all 4 internal angles of a rectangle are right angles. Additionally, with rectangles, we refer to one pair of sides as the length and one pair of sides as the width.

> **Safety Tip:** In many problems, the "length" and "width" are interchangeable. When you draw diagrams, just make sure that opposite sides have equal lengths.

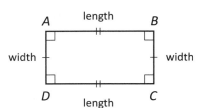

The formula for the perimeter of a rectangle is the same as for the perimeter of a parallelogram —either sum the lengths of the 4 sides or add the length and the width and multiply by 2.

The formula for the area of a rectangle is also the same as for the area of a parallelogram, but for any rectangle, the length and width are by definition perpendicular to each other, so you don't need a separate height. For this reason, the area of a rectangle is commonly expressed as (length) × (width).

Let's practice. For the following rectangle, find the perimeter and the area.

Let's start with the perimeter. Again, we can either fill in the missing sides and add them all up, or recognize that we have two sides with a length of 5 and two sides with a length of 7. Therefore, perimeter = 2 × (5 + 7), which equals 24. Alternatively, 5 + 5 + 7 + 7 also equals 24.

Now to find the area. The formula for area is (length) × (width). For the purposes of finding the area, it is irrelevant which side is the length and which side is the width. If we make *AD* the length and *DC* the width, then the area = (5) × (7) = 35. If, instead, we make *DC* the length and *AD* the width, then we have area = (7) × (5) = 35. The only thing that matters is that we choose two sides that are perpendicular to each other.

Check Your Skills

Find the area and perimeter of each rectangle.

24.
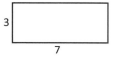

25.
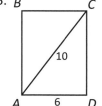

Answers can be found on pages 290–291.

Squares

One particular type of rectangle warrants mention—a square. A square is a rectangle in which all 4 sides are equal. Everything that is true of rectangles is true of squares as well. What this means is that knowing only one side of a square is enough to determine the perimeter and area of a square.

For instance, if we have a square, and we know that the length of one of its sides is 3, we know that all 4 sides have a length of 3.

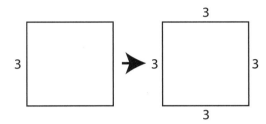

The perimeter of the square is $3 + 3 + 3 + 3$, which equals 12. Alternatively, once you know the length of one side of a square, you can multiply that length by 4 to find the perimeter. $3 \times 4 = 12$.

To find the area, we use the same formula as for a rectangle—Area = length × width. But, because the shape is a square, we know that the length and the width are equal. Therefore, we can say that the area of a square is Area = (side)^2. In this case, Area = $(3)^2 = 9$.

Using Equations to Solve Geometry Problems

Now that we know the various properties of shapes, such as perimeter and area, we need to know how to use these properties to answer Geometry questions on the GMAT. Let's do the following problem together.

> Rectangles *ABCD* and *EFGH*, shown below, have equal areas. The length of side *AB* is 5. What is the length of diagonal *AC*?

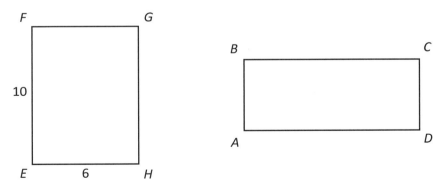

The first step in any geometry question involving shapes is to draw your own copies of the shapes on your note paper and fill in everything you know. In this problem in particular, you would want to redraw both rectangles and add to your picture the information that side *AB* has a length of 5. Also, make note of what you're looking for—in this case we want the length of diagonal *AC*. So your new figures would look like this:

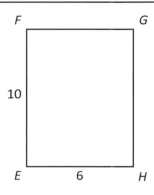

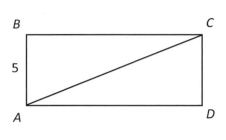

Now that we have redrawn our figures and filled in all the given information, it's time to begin answering the question. Realize that many geometry questions are similar to the word problems discussed in Chapter 3. Both types of problems provide us with information that describes relationships that can be expressed mathematically. The only difference is that sometimes this information is stated in words, and sometimes it's presented visually.

So now the question becomes—has the question provided us any information that can be expressed mathematically? In other words, can we create equations? Well, they did tell us one thing that we can use—the two rectangles have equal areas. So we can say that $Area_{ABCD} = Area_{EFGH}$. But we can do better than that. The formula for area of a rectangle is Area = (length) × (width). So our equation can be rewritten as $(length_{ABCD}) \times (width_{ABCD}) = (length_{EFGH}) \times (width_{EFGH})$.

The length and width of rectangle *EFGH* are 6 and 10 (it doesn't matter which is which) and the length of *AB* is 5. So our equation becomes $(5) \times (width_{ABCD}) = (6) \times (10)$. So $(5) \times (width_{ABCD}) = 60$, which means that the width of rectangle *ABCD* equals 12.

Any time you learn a new piece of information (in this case the width of rectangle *ABCD*) you should put that information into your picture. So our picture of rectangle *ABCD* now looks like this:

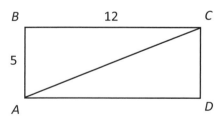

To recap what we've done so far, we started this problem by redrawing the shapes described in the question and filling in all the information (such as side lengths, angles, etc.) that we knew, and made note of the value the question was asking us for. Just as the first steps for solving word problems are to identify unknowns, create variables, and write down givens, the first step for geometry problems is to **draw or redraw figures and fill in all given information.** Of course, we should also confirm what we're being asked!

Next we made use of additional information provided in the question. The question stated that the two rectangles had equal areas. We created an equation to express this relationship, and then plugged in the values we knew (length and width of rectangle *EFGH* and length of rectangle *ABCD*) and solved for the width of rectangle *ABCD*. This process was identical to the process used to solve word problems—we **identified relationships and created equations.** After that, we **solved the equations for the missing value** (in this case, the width of *ABCD*).

In some ways, all we have done so far is set up the problem. In fact, aside from noting that we need to find the length of diagonal *AC*, nothing we have done so far seems to have directly helped us actually solve for that value. The result of the work we've done to this point is to find that the width of rectangle *ABCD* is 12.

So why did we bother solving for the width of rectangle *ABCD* when we didn't even know why we would need it? The answer is that there is a very good chance that we will need that value in order to answer the question. On the vast majority of GMAT problems, two general principles hold: 1) intermediate steps are required to solve for the value you want and 2) the GMAT does not provide extra information.

There was no way initially to find the length of diagonal *AC*. We simply did not have enough information. They did, however, provide us enough information to find the width of rectangle *ABCD*. More often than not, if you have enough information to solve for a value, you need that value to answer the question.

So the question now becomes, what can we do now that we know the width of *ABCD* that we couldn't do before? To answer that, let's take another look at the value we're looking for: the length of *AC*.

As mentioned earlier, an important part of problem solving is to identify relationships. We already identified the relationship mentioned in the question—that both rectangles have equal areas. But for many geometry problems there are additional relationships that aren't as obvious.

The key to this problem is to recognize that *AC* is not only the diagonal of rectangle *ABCD*, but is also the hypotenuse of a right triangle. We know this because one property of rectangles is that all four interior angles are right angles.

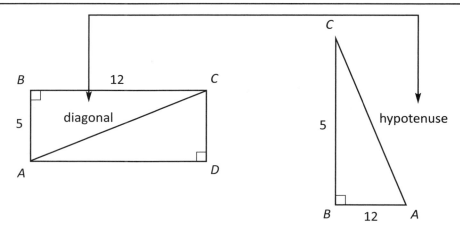

Now that we know *AC* is the hypotenuse of a right triangle, we can use the Pythagorean Theorem to find the length of the hypotenuse using the two side lengths.

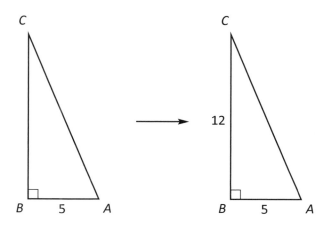

Sides *BC* and *AB* are the legs of the triangle, and *AC* is the hypotenuse, so:

$(BC)^2 + (AB)^2 = (AC)^2$
$(12)^2 + (5)^2 = (AC)^2$
$144 + 25 = (AC)^2$
$169 = (AC)^2$
$13 = AC$

Alternatively, you can avoid that work by recognizing that this triangle is one of the Pythagorean triplets: a 5–12–13 triangle. Either way, the answer to the question is *AC* = 13.

Let's recap what we did in the last portion of this question. The process that allowed us to solve for the width of *ABCD* was based on information explicitly presented to us in the question. To proceed from there, however, required a different sort of process. The key insight was that the diagonal of rectangle *ABCD* was also the hypotenuse of right triangle *ABC*. Additionally, we needed to know that, in order to find the length of *AC*, we needed the lengths of the other two sides of the triangle. The last part of this problem required us to **make inferences from the figures.** Sometimes these inferences require you to make a jump from one shape to another through a common element. For instance, we needed to see *AC* as both a diagonal of a rectangle and as a hypotenuse of a right triangle. Here *AC* was the common element in both a rectangle and a right triangle. Other times, these inferences make you think about what information you would need in order to find another value.

In a moment, we'll go through another sample problem, but before we do, let's revisit the important steps to answering geometry problems.

Recap:

Step 1: **Draw or redraw figures and fill in all given information.**
        Fill in all known angles and lengths and make note of any equal sides or angles.

Step 2: **Identify relationships and create equations.**
        Often these relationships will be explicitly stated in the question.

Step 3: **Solve the equations for the missing value.**
        If you can solve for a value, you will often need that value to answer the question.

Step 4: **Make inferences from the figures.**
        You will often need to make use of relationships that are not explicitly stated.

Now that we've got the basic process down, let's do another problem. Try it on your own first, then we'll walk through it together.

> Rectangle *PQRS* is inscribed in Circle *O* pictured below. The center of Circle *O* is also the center of Rectangle *PQRS*. If the circumference of Circle *O* is 5π, what is the area of Rectangle *PQRS*?

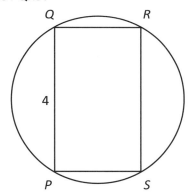

The first thing you should have done is **redraw the figure** on whatever note paper you are using and **fill in all the given information.** The question didn't explicitly give us the value of any side lengths or angles, but it did say that *PQRS* is a rectangle. That means all 4 internal angles are right angles. So when you redraw the figure, it might look like this.

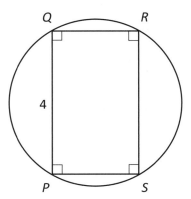

Now it's time to **identify relationships and create equations.** The question stated that the circumference of Circle O is 5π, and we know the formula for circumference. Circumference equals $2\pi r$, so $5\pi = 2\pi r$. Now that we know the circumference, there's only one unknown (r), so we should **solve the equation for the missing value** and find the radius, which turns out to be 2.5. We also know that $d = 2r$, so the diameter of Circle O is 5.

As with the previous problem, we are now left with the question—why did we find the radius and diameter? We were able to solve for them, which is a very good clue that we need one of them to answer the question. Now is the time to **make inferences from the figures.**

Ultimately, this question is asking for the area of rectangle $PQRS$. What information do we need to find that value? We have the length of QP, which means that if we can find the length of either QR or PS, we can find the area of the rectangle. So we need to somehow find a connection between the rectangle and the radius or diameter. Let's put a diameter into the circle.

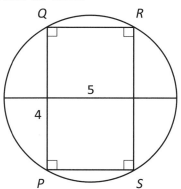

That didn't really seem to help much, because we still have no way to make the connection between the diameter and the rectangle. It's important to remember, though, that *any* line that passes through the center is a diameter. What if we drew the diameter so that it passed through the center but touched the circle at points P and R? We know that the line connecting points P and R will be a diameter because we know that the center of the circle is also the center of the rectangle. Our circle now looks like this:

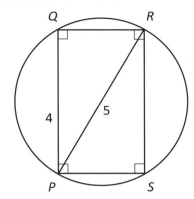

What was the advantage of drawing the diameter so that it connected points *P* and *R*? Now the diameter of the circle is also the diagonal of the rectangle. The circle and the rectangle have a common element.

Where do we go from here? We still need the length of either *QR* or *PS*. Do we have a way to get either one of those values? As a matter of fact, we do. *PQR* is a right triangle. It's not oriented the way we are used to seeing it, but all the important elements are there. It's a triangle, and one of its internal angles is a right angle. Additionally, we know the lengths of 2 of the sides: *QP* and *PR*. That means we can use the Pythagorean Theorem to find the length of the third side: *QR*.

$$(QR)^2 + (QP)^2 = (PR)^2$$
$$(QR)^2 + (4)^2 = (5)^2$$
$$(QR)^2 + 16 = 25$$
$$(QR)^2 = 9$$
$$QR = 3$$

Alternatively, we could have recognized the Pythagorean triplet—triangle *PQR* is a 3–4–5 triangle. Either way we arrive at the conclusion that the length of *QR* is 3. Our circle now looks like this:

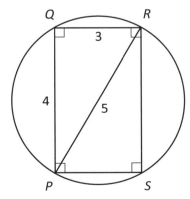

Now we have what we need to find the area of rectangle *PQRS*. Area = (length) × (width) = (4) × (3) = 12. So the answer to the question is 12.

What did we need to do in order to arrive at that answer? For starters, we needed to make sure that we had an accurate figure to work with, and that we populated that figure with all the information that had been given to us. Next we had to realize that knowing the circumference of the circle allowed us to find the diameter of the circle.

After that came what is often the most difficult part of the process—we had to make inferences based on the figure. The key insight in this problem was that we could draw a diameter in our figure that could also act as the diagonal of the rectangle. As if that wasn't difficult enough, we then had to recognize that *PQR* was a right triangle, even though it was rotated in a way that made it difficult to see. It is these kinds of insights that are going to be crucial to success on the GMAT—recognizing shapes when they're presented in an unfamiliar format and finding connections between different shapes.

Check Your Skills

26. In rectangle *ABCD*, the distance from *A* to *C* is 10. What is the area of the circle inside the rectangle, if this circle touches both *AD* and *BC*? (This is known as an inscribed circle).

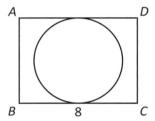

The answer can be found on pages 291–292.

The Number Line—Redux

Before we discuss the coordinate plane, let's review the number line.

The Number Line

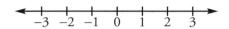

The number line is a ruler or measuring stick that goes as far as we want in both directions. With the number line, we can say where something is with a single number. In other words, we can link a position with a number.

Position	Number	Number Line
"Two units right of zero"	2	
"One and a half units left of zero"	−1.5	

We use both positive and negative numbers, because we want to indicate positions both left and right of zero.

You might be wondering "The position of what?" The answer is, a **point**, which is just a dot. When we are dealing with the number line, a point and a number mean the same thing.

If you show me where the point is on the number line, I can tell you the number.

→ *the point is at −2*

If you tell me the number, I can show you where the point is on the number line.

the point is at 0 →

This works even if we only have partial information about our point. If you tell me *something* about where the point is, I can tell you *something* about the number, and vice-versa.

For instance, if I say that the number is positive, then I know that the point lies somewhere to the right of 0 on the number line. Even though I don't know the exact location of the point, I do know a range of potential values.

The number is positive.
In other words, the number is greater than (>) 0.

This also works in reverse. If I see a range of potential positions on a number line, I can tell you what that range is for the number.

 The number is less than (<) 0.

Everything we've done so far should be familiar. We discussed the number line and inequalities in the last chapter. But now let's make things more complicated. What if we want to be able to locate a point that's not on a straight line, but on a page?

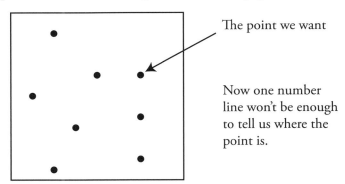

The point we want

Now one number line won't be enough to tell us where the point is.

Let's begin by inserting our number line into the picture. This will help us determine how far to the right or left of 0 our point is.

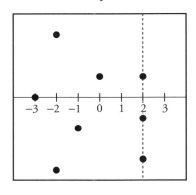

The point is two units to the right of zero.

But all three points that touch the dotted line are two units to the right of zero. We don't have enough information to determine the unique location of our point.

In order to know the location of our point, we also need to know how far up or down the dotted line we need to go. To determine how far up or down we need to go, we're going to need another number line. This number line, however, is going to be vertical. Using this vertical number line, we will be able to measure how far above or below 0 a point is.

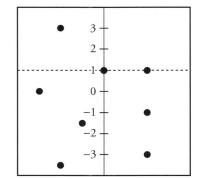

The point is one unit above zero.

Notice that this number line by itself also does not provide enough information to determine the unique location of the point.

But, if we combine the information from the two number lines, we can determine both how far left or right *and* how far up or down the point is.

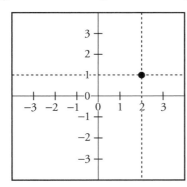

The point is 2 units to the right of 0.

AND

The point is 1 unit above 0.

Now we have a unique description of the point's position. There is only one point on the page that is BOTH 2 units to the right of 0 AND 1 unit above 0. So, on a page, we need two numbers to indicate position.

Just like with the number line, information can travel in either direction. If I tell you where the point is located with the two numbers, you can place that point on the page.

The point is 3 units to the left of 0.

AND

The point is 2 unit below 0.

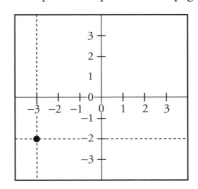

If, on the other hand, we see a point on the page, we can identify its location and extract the two numbers.

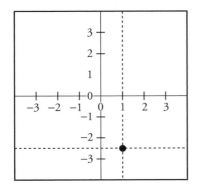

The point is 1 units to the right of 0.

AND

The point is 2.5 units below 0.

Now that we have two pieces of information for each point, we need to keep straight which number is which. In other words, we need to know which number gives the left-right position and which number gives the up-down position.

To indicate the difference, we use some technical terms:

The **x-coordinate** is the left right-number.

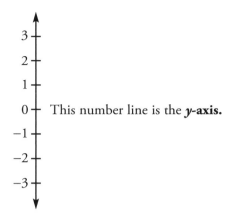

This number line is the **x-axis.**

    Numbers to the right of 0 are positive.
    Numbers to the left of 0 are negative.

The **y-coordinate** is the up-down number.

    Numbers above 0 are positive.
    Numbers below 0 are negative.

This number line is the **y-axis.**

Now, when describing the location of a point, we can use the technical terms.

The x-coordinate of the point is 1 and the y-coordinate of the point is 0.

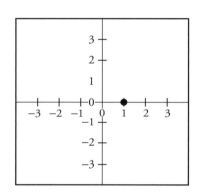

We can condense this down and say that, for this point, $x = 1$ and $y = 0$. In fact, we can go even further. We can say that the point is at $(1, 0)$. This shorthand always has the same basic layout. The first number in the parentheses is the x-coordinate, and the second number is the y-coordinate. One easy way to remember this is that x comes before y in the alphabet.

The point is at (−3, −1)

OR

The point has an *x*-coordinate of −3 and a *y*-coordinate of −1.

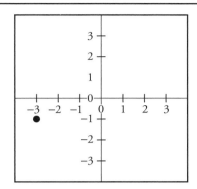

Nerd Note: The point on the plane (0, 0) is known as the **origin**.

Now we have a fully functioning **coordinate plane:** an *x*-axis and a *y*-axis drawn on a page. The coordinate plane allows us to determine the unique position of any point on a **plane** (essentially, a really big and flat sheet of paper).

And in case you were ever curious about what **one-dimensional** and **two-dimensional** mean, now you know. A line is one dimensional, because you only need *one* number to identify a point's location. A plane is two-dimensional because you need *two* numbers to identify a point's location.

Check Your Skills

27. Draw a coordinate plane and plot the following points:

    1. (3, 1)   2. (−2, 3.5)   3. (0, −4.5)   4. (1, 0)

28. Which point on the coordinate plane below is indicated by the following coordinates?

    1. (2, -1)   2. (−1.5, −3)   3. (−1, 2)   4. (3, 2)

Answers can be found on page 292.

Knowing Just One Coordinate

As we've just seen, we need to know both the *x*-coordinate and the *y*-coordinate to plot a point exactly on the coordinate plane. If we only know one coordinate, we can't tell precisely where the point is, but we can narrow down the possibilities.

Consider this situation. Let's say that this is all we know: the point is 4 units to the right of 0.

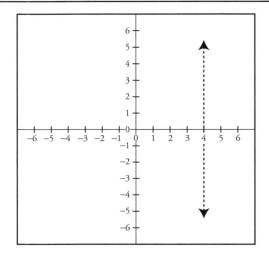

As we saw earlier, any point along the vertical dotted line is 4 units to the right of 0. In other words, every point on the dotted line has an *x*-coordinate of 4. We could shorten that and say $x = 4$. We don't know anything about the *y*-coordinate, which could be any number. All the points along the dotted line have different *y*-coordinates but the same *x*-coordinate, which equals 4.

So, if we know that $x = 4$, then our point can be anywhere along a vertical line that crosses the *x*-axis at (4, 0). Let's try with another example.

If we know that $x = -3$...

Then we know

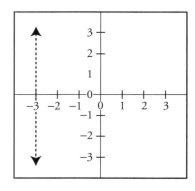

Every point on the dotted line has an *x*-coordinate of −3.

Points on the dotted line include (−3, 1), (−3, −7), (−3, 100) and so on. In general, if we know the *x*-coordinate of a point and not the *y*-coordinate, then all we can say about the point is that it lies on a vertical line.

The *x*-coordinate still indicates left-right position. If we fix that position but not the up-down position, then the point can only move up and down—forming a vertical line.

Now imagine that all we know is the *y*-coordinate of a number. Let's say we know that $y = -2$. How could we represent this on the coordinate plane? In other words, what are all the points for which $y = -2$?

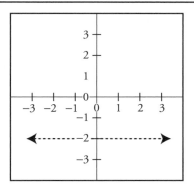

Every point 2 units below 0 fits this condition. These points form a horizontal line. We don't know anything about the *x*-coordinate, which could be any number. All the points along the horizontal dotted line have different *x*-coordinates but the same *y*-coordinate, which equals −2. For instance, $(-3, -2)$, $(-2, -2)$, $(50, -2)$ are all on the line.

Let's try another example. If we know that $y = 1$…

Then we know

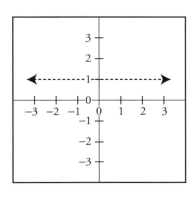

Every point on the dotted line has an *y*-coordinate of 1.

If we know the *y*-coordinate but not the *x*-coordinate, then we know the point lies somewhere on a horizontal line.

Check Your Skills

Draw a coordinate plane and plot the following lines.

29. $x = 6$
30. $y = -2$
31. $x = 0$

Answers can be found on pages 292–293.

Knowing Ranges

Now let's provide even less information. Instead of knowing the actual *x*-coordinate, let's see what happens if all we know is a range of possible values for *x*. What do we do if all we know is that $x > 0$? To answer that, let's return to the number line for a moment. As we saw earlier, if $x > 0$, then the target is anywhere to the right of 0.

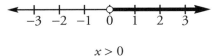

$x > 0$

Now let's look at the coordinate plane. All we know is that x is greater than 0. And we don't know *anything* about y, which could be any number.

How do we show all the possible points? We can shade in part of the coordinate plane: the part to the right of 0.

If we know that $x > 0$...

Then we know

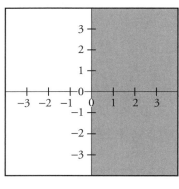

Every point in the shaded region has an x-coordinate greater than 0.

Now let's say that all we know is $y < 0$. Then we can shade in the bottom half of the coordinate plane—where the y-coordinate is less than 0. The x-coordinate can be anything.

If we know that $y < 0$...

Then we know

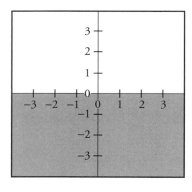

Every point in the shaded region has a y-coordinate less than 0.

Finally, if we know information about both x and y, then we can narrow down the shaded region.

If we know that $x > 0$ AND $y < 0$...

Then we know

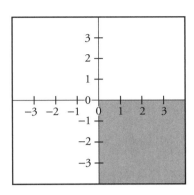

The only place where x is greater than 0 AND y is less than 0 is the bottom right quarter of the plane. So we know that the point lies somewhere in the bottom right quarter of the coordinate plane.

The four quarters of the coordinate plane are called **quadrants.** Each quadrant corresponds to a different combination of signs of x and y. The quadrants are always numbered as shown below, starting on the top right and going counter-clockwise.

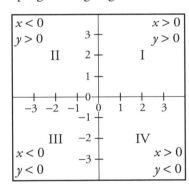

Nerd Note: The axes themselves do not lie in any quadrant. They lie between the quadrants.

Check Your Skills

32. Which quadrant do the following points lie in?
    1. $(1, -2)$ 2. $(-4.6, 7)$ 3. $(-1, -2.5)$ 4. $(3, 3)$
33. Which quadrant or quadrants are indicated by the following?
    1. $x < 0, y > 0$ 2. $x < 0, y < 0$ 3. $y > 0$ 4. $x < 0$

Answers can be found on page 293.

Reading a Graph

If we see a point on a coordinate plane, we can read off its coordinates as follows. To find an x-coordinate, drop an imaginary line down to the x-axis and read off the number.

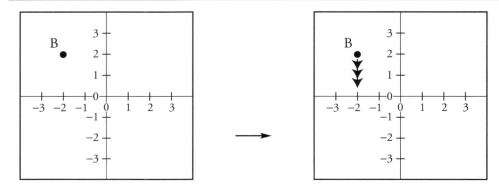

> **Safety Tip:** If the point is below the *x*-axis, then you'll need to draw a line up to the *x*-axis.

The line hit the *x*-axis at −2, which means the *x*-coordinate of our point is −2. Now, to find the *y*-coordinate, we employ a similar technique, only now we draw a horizontal line instead of a vertical line.

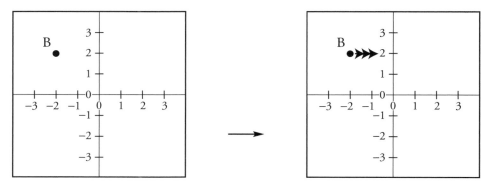

Our line touched the *y*-axis at 2, which means the *y*-coordinate of our point is 2. Thus, the coordinates of point B are (−2, 2).

Now suppose that we know the target is on a slanted line in the plane. We can read coordinates off of this slanted line. Try this problem on your own first.

> On the line shown, what is the *y* coordinate of the point that has an *x*-coordinate of −4?

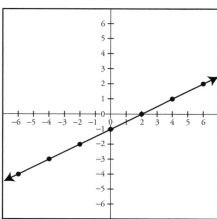

To answer this question, think about reading the coordinates of a point. We went from the point to the axes. Here, we will go from the axis that we know (here, the *x*-axis) to the line that contains the point, and then to the *y*-axis (the axis we don't know).

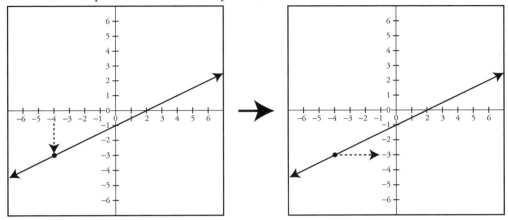

So the point on the line that has an *x*-coordinate of −4 has a *y*-coordinate of −3.

This method of locating points applies equally well to any shape or curve you may encounter on a coordinate plane. Try this next problem.

On the curve shown, what is the value of *y* when *x* = 2?

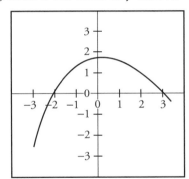

Once again, we know the *x*-coordinate, so we draw a line from the *x*-axis (where we know the coordinate) to the curve, and then draw a line to the *y*-axis.

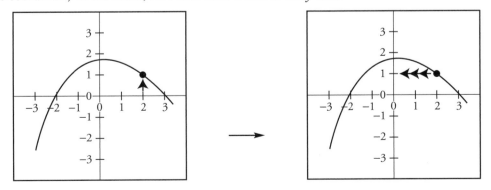

On the curve shown, the point that has an *x*-coordinate of 2 has a *y* coordinate of 1.

*Manhattan*GMAT*Prep
the new standard

Note that the GMAT will mathematically define each line or curve, so you will never be forced to guess visually where a point falls. This discussion is meant to convey how to use any graphical representation.

Check Your Skills

34. On the following graph, what is the y-coordinate of the point on the line that has an x-coordinate of −3?

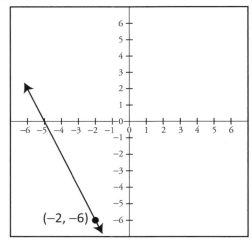

The answer can be found on page 294.

Plotting a Relationship

The most frequent use of the coordinate plane is to display a relationship between x and y. Often, this relationship is expressed this way: if you tell me x, I can tell you y.

As an equation, this sort of relationship looks like this:

y = some expression involving x Another way of saying this is we have y "in terms of" x

Examples: $y = 2x + 1$ If you plug a number in for x in any of these
            $y = x^2 - 3x + 2$ equations, you can calculate a value for y.

$$y = \frac{x}{x+2}$$

Let's take $y = 2x + 1$. We can generate a set of y's by plugging in various values of x. Start by making a table.

x	$y = 2x + 1$
−1	$y = 2(-1) + 1 = -1$
0	$y = 2(0) + 1 = 1$
1	$y = 2(1) + 1 = 3$
2	$y = 2(2) + 1 = 5$

> **Safety Tip:** We can use literally any value of x to find a corresponding value of y. x can be an integer, a fraction, a decimal, etc.

Now that we have some values, let's see what we can do with them. We can say that when x equals 0, y equals 1. These two values form a pair. We express this connection by plotting the point (0, 1) on the coordinate plane. Similarly, we can plot all the other points that represent an x-y pair from our table:

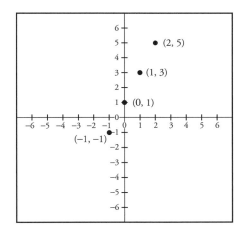

You might notice that these points seem to lie on a straight line. You're right—they do. In fact, any point that we can generate using the relationship $y = 2x + 1$ will also lie on the line.

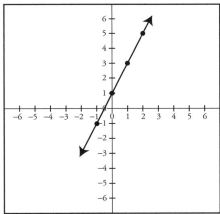

This line is the graphical representation of $y = 2x + 1$

So now we can talk about equations in visual terms. In fact, that's what lines and curves on the coordinate plane are—they represent all the x-y pairs that make an equation true. Take a look at the following example:

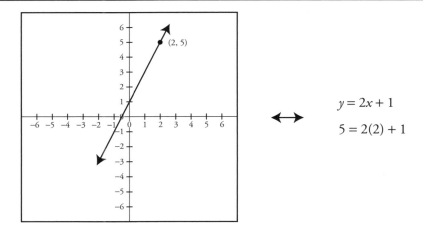

$$y = 2x + 1$$
$$5 = 2(2) + 1$$

The point (2, 5) lies on the line $y = 2x + 1$ ⟷   If we plug in 2 for x in $y = 2x + 1$, we get 5 for y

We can even speak more generally, using variables.

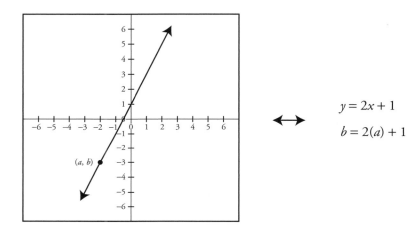

$$y = 2x + 1$$
$$b = 2(a) + 1$$

The point (a, b) lies on the line $y = 2x + 1$ ⟷   If we plug in a for x in $y = 2x + 1$, we get b for y

Check Your Skills

35. True or False? The point (9, 21) is on the line $y = 2x + 1$
36. True or False? The point (4, 14) is on the curve $y = x^2 - 2$

Answers can be found on page 294.

Lines in the Plane

The relationship $y = 2x + 1$ formed a line in the coordinate plane, as we saw. We can actually generalize this relationship. *Any* relationship of the following form represents a line:

    $y = mx + b$ m and b represent numbers (positive or negative)

For instance, in the equation $y = 2x + 1$, we can see that m = 2 and b = 1.

Lines   Not Lines

$y = 3x - 2$ m = 3, b = −2 $y = x^2$

$y = -x + 4$ m = −1, b = 4 $y = \dfrac{1}{x}$

These are called linear equations.   These equations are not linear.

> **Safety Tip:** In *every* linear equation, both x and y will be raised to the first power.

The numbers m and b have special meanings when we are dealing with linear equations. m = **slope.** This tells you how steep the line is and whether the line is rising or falling.

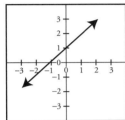
Positive Slope
$m > 0$

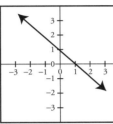
Negative Slope
$m < 0$

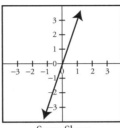
Steep Slope
$m > 1$

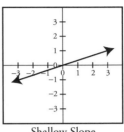
Shallow Slope
$0 < m < 1$

b = **y-intercept.** This tells you where the line crosses the y-axis. Any line or curve crosses the y-axis when $x = 0$. To find the y-intercept, plus in 0 for x into the equation.

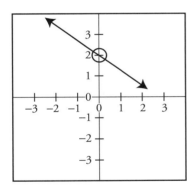

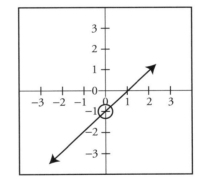

By recognizing linear equations and identifying m and b, we can plot a line more quickly than by plotting several points on the line.

Check Your Skills

What are the slope and y-intercept of the following lines?

37. $y = 3x + 4$
38. $2y = 5x - 12$

Answers can be found on page 294.

Now the question becomes, how do we use m and b to sketch a line? Let's plot the line $y = \tfrac{1}{2}x - 2$.

The easiest way to begin graphing a line is to begin with the y-intercept. We know that the line crosses the y-axis at $y = -2$, so let's begin by plotting that point on our coordinate plane.

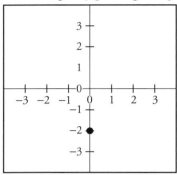

Now we need to figure out how to use slope in order to finish drawing our line. Every slope, whether an integer or a fraction, should be thought of as a fraction. In this equation, our m is 1/2. Let's look at the parts of the fraction and see what they can tell us about our slope.

$$\frac{1}{2} \;\rightarrow\; \frac{\text{Numerator}}{\text{Denominator}} \;\rightarrow\; \frac{\text{Rise}}{\text{Run}} \;\rightarrow\; \frac{\text{Change in } y}{\text{Change in } x}$$

The numerator of our fraction tells us how many units we want to move in the y direction—in other words, how far up or down we want to move. The denominator tells us how many units we want to move in the x direction—in other words, how far left or right we want to move. For this particular equation, the slope is 1/2, which means we want to move up 1 unit and right 2 units.

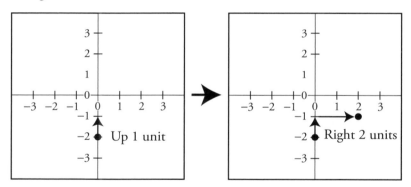

After we went up 1 unit and right 2 units, we ended up at the point $(2, -1)$. What that means is that the point $(2, -1)$ is also a solution to the equation $y = \frac{1}{2}x - 2$. In fact, we can plug in the x value and solve for y to check that we did this correctly.

$$y = \frac{1}{2}x - 2 \;\rightarrow\; y = \frac{1}{2}(2) - 2 \;\rightarrow\; y = 1 - 2 \rightarrow\; y = -1$$

What this means is that we can use the slope to generate points and draw our line. If we go up another 1 unit and right another 2 units, we will end up with another point that appears on the line. Although we could keep doing this indefinitely, in reality, with only 2 points we can figure out what our line looks like. Now all we need to do is draw the line that connects the 2 points we have, and we're done.

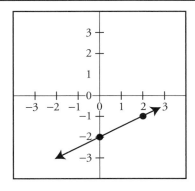

$y = {}^1/_2 x - 2$

That means that this line is the graphical representation of $y = {}^1/_2 x - 2$.

Let's try another one. Graph the equation $y = (^{-3}/_2)x + 4$.

Once again, the best way to start is to plot the *y*-intercept. In this equation, b = 4, so we know the line crosses the *y*-axis at the point (0, 4)

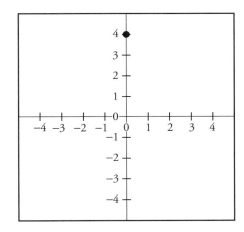

Now we can use the slope to find a second point. This time, the slope is −3/2, which is a negative slope. While positive slopes go up and to the right, negative slopes go down and to the right. Now, to find the next point, we need to go *down* 3 units and right 2 units.

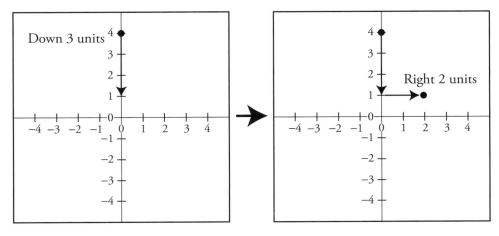

That means that (2, 1) is another point on the line. Now that we have 2 points, we can draw our line.

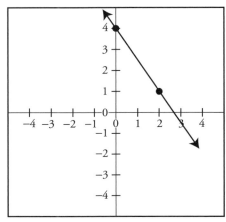

$$y = (^{-3}/_2)x + 4$$

Check Your Skills

39. Draw a coordinate plane and graph the line $y = 2x - 4$. Identify the slope and the y-intercept.

The answer can be found on page 294.

Check Your Skills Answers

1. The formula for area is $A = \pi r^2$. The radius is 7, so Area $= \pi(7)2 = 49\pi$.

2. Circumference of a circle is either $C = 2\pi r$ or $C = \pi d$. The question asks for the diameter, so we'll use the latter formula. $17\pi = \pi d$. Divide by π, and we get $17 = d$. The diameter is 17.

3. The link between area and circumference of a circle is that they are both defined in terms of the radius. Area of a circle is $A = \pi r^2$, so we can use the area of the circle to find the radius. $25\pi = \pi r^2$, so $r = 5$. If the radius equals 5, then the circumference is $C = 2\pi(5)$, which equals 10π. The circumference is 10π.

4. If the central angle of the sector is 270°, then it is 3/4 of the full circle, because $\dfrac{270°}{360°} = \dfrac{3}{4}$.

If the radius is 2, then the area of the full circle is $\pi(2)2$, which equals 4π. If the area of the full circle is 4π, then the area of the sector will be $3/4 \times 4\pi$, which equals 3π.

5. To find the central angle, we first need to figure out what fraction of the circle the sector is. We can do that by finding the circumference of the full circle. The radius is 3, so the circumference of the circle is $2\pi(3) = 6\pi$. That means the sector is 2/3 of the circle, because $\dfrac{4\pi}{6\pi} = \dfrac{2}{3}$. That means the central angle of the sector is $2/3 \times 360°$, which equals 240°.

6. We can begin by finding the area of the whole circle. The radius of the circle is 10, so the area is $\pi(10)2$, which equals 100π. That means the sector is 2/5 of the circle, because $\dfrac{40\pi}{100\pi} = \dfrac{4}{10} = \dfrac{2}{5}$. We can find the circumference of the whole circle using $C = 2\pi r$. The circumference equals 20π. $2/5 \times 20\pi = 8\pi$. The arc length of the sector is 8π.

7. If the two known sides of the triangle are 5 and 19, then the third side of the triangle cannot have a length of 13, because that would violate the rule that any two sides of a triangle must add up to greater than the third side. $5 + 13 = 18$, and $18 < 19$.

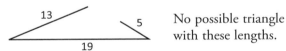

No possible triangle with these lengths.

8. If the two known sides of the triangle are 8 and 17, then the third side must be less than the sum of the other 2 sides. $8 + 17 = 25$, so the third side must be less than 25. The third side must also be greater than the difference of the other two sides. $17 - 8 = 9$, so the third side must be greater than 9. That means that $9 <$ third side < 25

9. The internal angles of a triangle must add up to 180°, so we know that $40 + 75 + x = 180$. Solving for x gives us $x = 65°$.

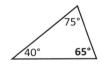

10. The 3 internal angles of the triangle must add up to 180°, so $50 + x + x = 180$. That means that $2x = 130$, and $x = 65$.

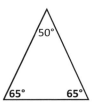

11. In order to determine the missing angles of the triangle, we need to do a little work with the picture. We can figure out the value of x, because straight lines have a degree measure of 180, so $110 + x = 180$, which means $x = 70$.

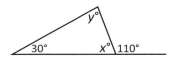

That means our picture looks like this:

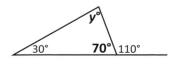

Now we can find y, because $30 + 70 + y = 180$. Solving for y gives us $y = 80$.

12. In this triangle, two sides have the same length, which means this triangle is isosceles. We also know that the two angles opposite the two equal sides will also be equal. That means that x must be 80.

13. In this triangle, two angles are equal, which means this triangle is isosceles. We also know that the two sides opposite the equal angles must also be equal, so x must equal 4.

14. This triangle is isosceles, because two sides have the same length. That means that the angles opposite the equal sides must also be equal.

That means our triangle really looks like this:

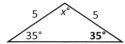

Now we can find x, because we know $35 + 35 + x = 180$. Solving for x gives us $x = 110$.

15.

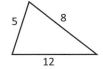

To find the perimeter of the triangle, we add up all three sides. $5 + 8 + 12 = 25$, so the perimeter is 25.

16. To find the perimeter of the triangle, we need the lengths of all three sides. This is an isosceles triangle, because two angles are equal. That means that the sides opposite the equal angles must also be equal. So our triangle looks like this:

So the perimeter is $6 + 6 + 4$, which equals 16. The perimeter is 16.

17. The area of a triangle is $\frac{1}{2}b \times h$. In the triangle shown, the base is 6 and the height is 5. So the area is $\frac{1}{2}(6) \times 5$, which equals 15.

18. In this triangle, the base is 10 and the height is 7. Remember that the height must be perpendicular to the base—it doesn't need to lie within the triangle. So the area is $\frac{1}{2}(10) \times 7$, which equals 35. The area of the triangle is 35.

19. This is a right triangle, so we can use the Pythagorean Theorem to solve for the length of the third side. The hypotenuse is the side with length 10, so the formula is $(8)^2 + b^2 = (10)^2$. $64 + b^2 = 100$. $b^2 = 36$, which means $b = 6$. So the third side of the triangle has a length of 6. Alternatively, you could recognize that this triangle is one of the Pythagorean triplets—a 6–8–10 triangle, which is just a doubled 3–4–5 triangle.

20. This is a right triangle, so we can use the Pythagorean Theorem to solve for the length of the third side. The hypotenuse is the unknown side, so the formula is $(5)^2 + (12)^2 = c^2$. $25 + 144 = c^2$. $c^2 = 169$, which means $c = 13$. So the third side of the triangle has a length of 13. Alternatively, you could recognize that this triangle is one of the Pythagorean triplets—a 5–12–13 triangle.

21. This is a right triangle, so we can use the Pythagorean Theorem to solve for the third side, or alternatively recognize that this is a 3–4–5 triangle. Either way, the result is the same: The length of the third side is 3.

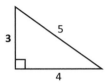

Now we can find the are of the triangle. Area of a triangle is $\frac{1}{2}b \times h$, so the area of this triangle is $\frac{1}{2}(3) \times (4)$, which equals 6. The area of the triangle is 6.

22. In parallelograms, opposite sides have equal lengths, so we know that two of the sides of the parallelogram have a length of 6 and two sides have a length of 10.

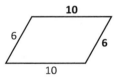

So the perimeter is $6 + 10 + 6 + 10$, which equals 32.

23. Area of a parallelogram is $b \times h$. In this parallelogram, the base is 9 and the height is 4, so the area is $(9) \times (4)$, which equals 36. The area of the parallelogram is 36.

24. In rectangles, opposite sides have equal lengths, so our rectangle looks like this:

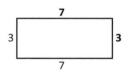

So the perimeter is $3 + 7 + 3 + 7$, which equals 20. The area of a rectangle is $b \times h$, so the area is $(7) \times (3)$, which equals 21. So the perimeter is 20, and the area is 21.

25. To find the area and perimeter of the rectangle, we need to know the length of either side *AB* or side *CD*. The diagonal of the rectangle creates a right triangle, so we can use the Pythagorean Theorem to find the length of side *CD*. Alternatively, we can recognize that triangle *ACD* is a 6–8–10 triangle, and thus the length of side *CD* is 8. Either way, our rectangle now looks like this:

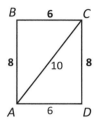

So the perimeter of the rectangle is 6 + 8 + 6 + 8, which equals 28. The area is (6) × (8), which equals 48. So the perimeter is 28 and the area is 48.

26. Redraw the diagram *without* the circle, so you can focus on the rectangle. Add in the diagonal *AC*, since we're given its length.

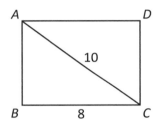

Now we look at right triangle *ABC*. *AC* functions not only as the diagonal of rectangle *ABCD* but also as the hypotenuse of right triangle *ABC*. So now we find the third side of triangle *ABC*, either using the Pythagorean Theorem or recognizing a Pythagorean triplet (6–8–10).

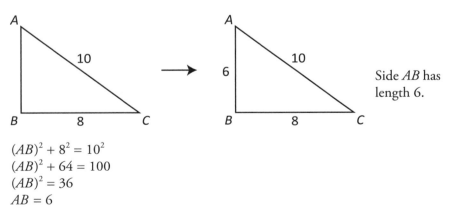

$(AB)^2 + 8^2 = 10^2$
$(AB)^2 + 64 = 100$
$(AB)^2 = 36$
$AB = 6$

Now, we redraw the diagram *with* the circle but without the diagonal, since we've gotten what we needed from that: the other side of the rectangle.

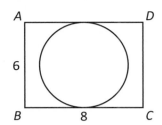

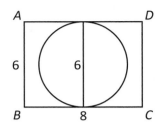

Since the circle touches both *AD* and *BC*, we know that its diameter must be 6.

Finally, we find the radius and compute the area:

$$d = 6 = 2r \qquad \text{Area} = \pi r^2$$
$$3 = r \qquad\qquad = \pi 3^2$$
$$\qquad\qquad\qquad \text{Area} = 9\pi$$

27.

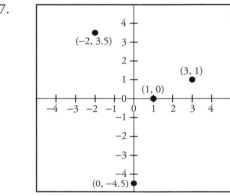

28.   1. (2, −1): **E**
      2. (−1.5, −3): **C**
      3. (−1, 2): **B**
      4. (3, 2): **D**

29.

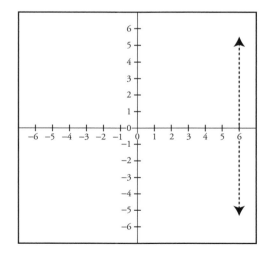

$x = 6$

30.

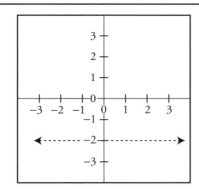

$y = -2$

31.

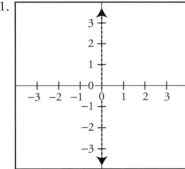

$x = 0$ is the y-axis.

32.   1. $(1, -2)$ is in Quadrant IV
2. $(-4.6, 7)$ is in Quadrant II
3. $(-1, -2.5)$ is in Quadrant III
4. $(3, 3)$ is in Quadrant I

$x < 0$ $y > 0$		$x > 0$ $y > 0$
II		I

33.   1. $x < 0$, $y > 0$ indicates Quadrant II
2. $x < 0$, $y < 0$ indicates Quadrant III
3. $y > 0$ indicates Quadrants I and II
4. $x < 0$ indicates Quadrants II and III

34. The point on the line with $x = -3$ has a y-coordinate of -4.

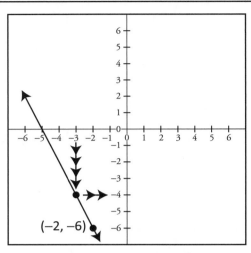

35. False. The relationship is $y = 2x + 1$, and the point we are testing is (9, 21). So we plug in 9 for x and see if we get 21 for y. $y = 2(9) + 1 = 19$. The point (9, 21) does not lie on the line.

36. True. The relationship is $y = x^2 - 2$, and the point we are testing is (4, 14). So we plug in 4 for x and see if we get 14 for y. $y = (4)2 - 2 = 14$. The point (4, 14) lies on the curve.

37. The equation $y = 3x + 4$ is already in $y = mx + b$ form, so we can directly find the slope and y-intercept. The slope is 3, and the y-intercept is 4.

38. To find the slope and y-intercept of a line, we need the equation to be in $y = mx + b$ form. We need to divide our original equation by 2 to make that happen. So $2y = 5x - 12$ becomes $y = 2.5x - 6$. So the slope is 2.5 (or 5/2) and the y-intercept is -6.

39.

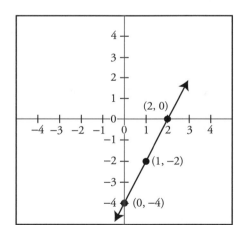

$y = 2x - 4$

slope $= 2$

y-intercept $= -4$

Geometry Drill Sets

DRILL SET 1:

Drill 1

1. The radius of a circle is 4. What is its area?
2. The diameter of a circle is 7. What is its circumference?
3. The radius of a circle is 3. What is its circumference?
4. The area of a circle is 36π. What is its radius?
5. The circumference of a circle is 18π. What is its area?

Drill 2

1. The area of a circle is 100π. What is its circumference?
2. The diameter of a circle is 16. Calculate its radius, circumference, and area.
3. Which circle has a larger area? Circle *A* has a circumference of 6π and Circle *B* has an area of 8π.
4. Which has a larger area? Circle *C* has a diameter of 10 and Circle *D* has a circumference of 12π.
5. A circle initially has an area of 4π. If the radius is doubled, how many times greater is the new area than the original area?

Drill 3

1. A sector has a central angle of 90°. If the sector has a radius of 8, what is the area of the sector?
2. A sector has a central angle of 30°. If the sector has a radius of 6, what is the arc length of the sector?
3. A sector has an arc length of 7π and a diameter of 14. What is the central angle of the sector?
4. A sector has a central angle of 270°. If the sector has a radius of 4, what is the area of the sector?
5. A sector has an area of 24π and a radius of 12. What is the central angle of the sector?

Drill 4

1. The area of a sector is 1/10th the area of the full circle. What is the central angle of the sector?
2. What is the perimeter of a sector with a radius of 5 and a central angle of 72°?
3. A sector has a radius of 8 and an area of 8π. What is the arc length of the sector?
4. A sector has an arc length of $\pi/2$ and a central angle of 45°. What is the radius of the sector?
5. Which of the following two sectors has a larger area? Sector *A* has a radius of 4 and a central angle of 90°. Sector *B* has a radius of 6 and a central angle of 45°.

DRILL SET 2:

Drill 1

1. A triangle has two sides with lengths of 5 and 11, respectively. What is the range of values for the length of the third side?

2. In a right triangle, the length of one of the legs is 3 and the length of the hypotenuse is 5. What is the length of the other leg?

3. What is the area of Triangle *DEF*?

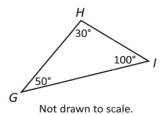

4. Which side of Triangle *GHI* has the longest length?

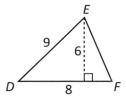

Not drawn to scale.

5. What is the value of *x*?

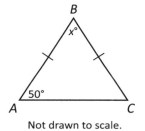

Not drawn to scale.

Drill 2

1. Two sides of a triangle have lengths 4 and 8. Which of the following are possible side lengths of the third side? (More than one may apply)

     a. 2   b. 4   c. 6   d. 8

2. *DFG* is a straight line. What is the value of *x*?

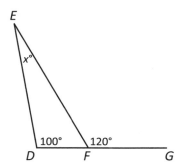

*ManhattanGMAT*Prep
the new standard

3. Isosceles triangle *ABC* has two sides with lengths 3 and 9. What is the length of the third side?

4. Which of the following could be the length of side *AB*, if $x < y < z$?

   a. 6   b. 10   c. 14

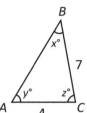

5. What is the area of right triangle *ABC*?

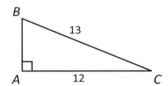

Drill 3
1. What is the perimeter of triangle *ABC*?

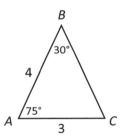

2. The area of right triangle *ABC* is 15. What is the length of hypotenuse *BC*?

3. What is the length of side *HI*?

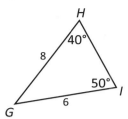

   Not drawn to scale.

4. Which triangle has the greatest perimeter?

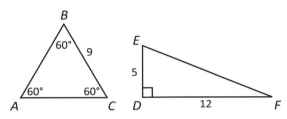

5. *WZ* has a length of 3 and *ZX* has a length of 6. What is the area of Triangle *XYZ*?

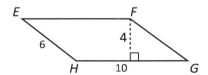

DRILL SET 3

Drill 1:

1. What is the perimeter of parallelogram *ABCD*?

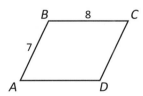

2. What is the area of parallelogram *EFGH*?

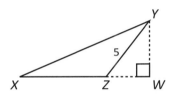

3. The two parallelograms pictured below have the same perimeter. What is the length of side *EH*?

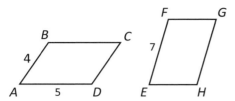

4. In Parallelogram *ABCD*, Triangle *ABC* has an area of 12. What is the area of Triangle *ACD*?

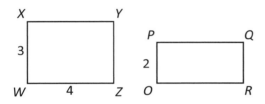

5. Rectangle *WXYZ* and Rectangle *OPQR* have equal areas. What is the length of side *PQ*?

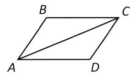

Drill 2
1. What is the area of Rectangle *ABCD*?

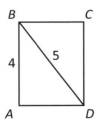

2. In Rectangle *ABCD*, the area of Triangle *ABC* is 30. What is the length of diagonal *AC*?

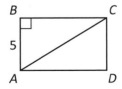

3. Rectangles *ABCD* and *EFGH* have equal areas. What is the length of side *FG*?

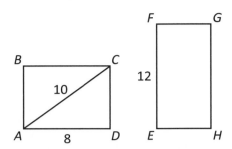

4. A rectangle has a perimeter of 10 and an area of 6. What are the length and width of the rectangle?

5. Triangle *XYZ* and Rectangle *JKLM* have equal areas. What is the perimeter of Rectangle *JKLM*?

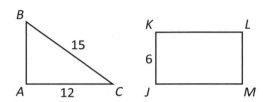

Drill 3

1. What is the perimeter of a square with an area of 25?

2. A rectangle and a square have the same area. The square has a perimeter of 32 and the rectangle has a length of 4. What is the width of the rectangle?

3. A circle is inscribed inside a square, so that the circle touches all four sides of the square. The length of one of the sides of the square is 9. What is the area of the circle?

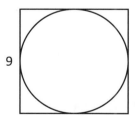

*Manhattan*GMAT*Prep
the new standard

4. Square *ABCD* has an area of 49. What is the length of diagonal *AC*?

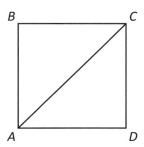

5. Right Triangle ABC and Rectangle *EFGH* have the same perimeter. What is the value of *x*?

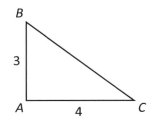

DRILL SET 4:

Drill 1

1. Draw a coordinate plane and plot the following points:

     1. (2, 3)   2. (−2, −1)   3. (−5, −6)   4. (4, −2.5)

2. What are the *x*- and *y*-coordinates of the following points?

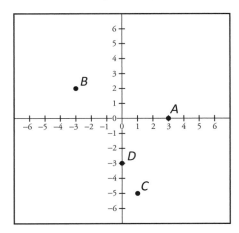

3. What is the *y*-coordinate of the point on the line that has an *x*-coordinate of 3?

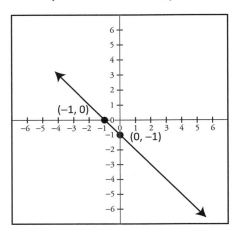

4. What is the *x*-coordinate of the point on the line that has a *y*-coordinate of −4?

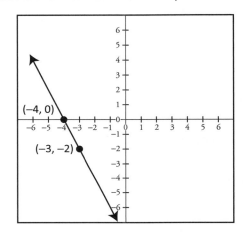

5. Does the point (3, −2) lie on the line $y = 2x − 8$?

Drill 2
1. Does the point (−3, 0) lie on the curve $y = x^2 − 3$?
2. For the line $y = 4x + 2$, what is the *y*-coordinate when $x = 3$?
3. What is the *y*-intercept of the line $y = −2x − 7$?
4. Graph the line $y = \frac{1}{3}x − 4$.
5. Graph the line $\frac{1}{2}y = −\frac{1}{2}x + 1$.

Drill Set Answers

<u>DRILL SET 1:</u>

Set 1, Drill 1

1.   The radius of a circle is 4. What is its area?

Area of a circle is πr^2, so the area of the circle is $\pi(4)^2$, which equals 16π.

2.   The diameter of a circle is 7. What is its circumference?

Circumference of a circle is $2\pi r$, or πd. We have the diameter, so the circumference equals $\pi(7)$, which equals 7π.

3.   The radius of a circle is 3. What is its circumference?

Circumference of a circle is $2\pi r$, or πd. We have the radius, so circumference equals $2\pi(3)$, which equals 6π.

4.   The area of a circle is 36π. What is its radius?

Area of a circle is πr^2, so $36\pi = \pi r^2$. We need to solve for r. Divide both sides by π, so $36 = r^2$. Take the square root of both sides, and $6 = r$. We can ignore the negative solution because distances cannot be negative.

5.   The circumference of a circle is 18π. What is its area?

The connection between circumference and area is radius. We can use the circumference to solve for the radius. $18\pi = 2\pi r$, which means that $9 = r$. That means that Area = $\pi(9)^2$, which equals 81π.

Set 1, Drill 2

1.   The area of a circle is 100π. What is its circumference?

The connection between circumference and area is radius. $100\pi = \pi r^2$, and solving for r gives us $r = 10$. That means that Circumference = $2\pi(10)$, which equals 20π.

2.   The diameter of a circle is 16. Calculate its radius, circumference, and area.

$d = 2r$, so $16 = 2r$. Radius = 8. Circumference = $2\pi r$, so Circumference = $2\pi(8) = 16\pi$. Area = πr^2, so Area = $\pi(8)^2 = 64\pi$.

3.   Which circle has a larger area? Circle A has a circumference of 6π and Circle B has an area of 8π.

To figure out which circle has a larger area, we need to find the area of Circle A. If we know the circumference, then $6\pi = 2\pi r$, which means $r = 3$. If $r = 3$, then Area = $\pi(3)^2 = 9\pi$. $9\pi > 8\pi$, so Circle A has a larger area.

4.   Which has a larger area? Circle C has a diameter of 10 and Circle D has a circumference of 12π.

We need to find the area of both circles. Let's start with Circle C. If the diameter of Circle C is 10, then the radius is 5. That means that Area $= \pi(5)^2 = 25\pi$.

If the circumference of Circle D is 12π, the $12\pi = 2\pi r$. $r = 6$. If $r = 6$, then Area $= \pi(6)^2 = 36\pi$. $36\pi > 25\pi$, so Circle D has the larger area.

5.   A circle initially has an area of 4π. If the radius is doubled, how many times greater is the new area than the original area?

To begin, we need to find the original radius of the circle. $4\pi = \pi r^2$, so $r = 2$. If we double the radius, the new radius is 4. A circle with a radius of 4 has an area of 16π. 16π is 4 times 4π, so the new area is 4 times the original area.

Set 1, Drill 3

1.   A sector has a central angle of 90°. If the sector has a radius of 8, what is the area of the sector?

If the sector has a central angle of 90°, then the sector is 1/4 of the circle, because $\dfrac{90}{360} = \dfrac{1}{4}$. To find the area of the sector, we need to find the area of the whole circle first. The radius is 8, which means the area is $\pi(8)^2 = 64\pi$. $1/4 \times 64\pi = 16\pi$. The area of the sector is 16π.

2.   A sector has a central angle of 30°. If the sector has a radius of 6, what is the arc length of the sector?

If the sector has a central angle of 30°, then it is 1/12th of the circle, because $\dfrac{30}{360} = \dfrac{1}{12}$. To find the arc length of the sector, we need to know the circumference of the entire circle. The radius of the circle is 6, so the circumference is $2\pi(6) = 12\pi$. That means that the arc length of the sector is $1/12 \times 12\pi = \pi$.

3.   A sector has an arc length of 7π and a diameter of 14. What is the central angle of the sector?

To find the central angle of the sector, we first need to find what fraction of the full circle the sector is. We have the arc length, so if we can find the circumference of the circle, we can figure out what fraction of the circle the sector is. The diameter is 14, so the circumference is $\pi(14) = 14\pi$. $\dfrac{7\pi}{14\pi} = \dfrac{1}{2}$. So the sector is 1/2 the full circle. That means that the central angle of the sector is $1/2 \times 360° = 180°$. So the central angle is 180°.

4.   A sector has a central angle of 270°. If the sector has a radius of 4, what is the area of the sector?

The sector is 3/4 of the circle, because $\dfrac{270°}{360°} = \dfrac{3}{4}$. To find the area of the sector, we need the area of the whole circle. The radius of the circle is 4, so the area is $\pi(4)^2 = 16\pi$. That means the area of the circle is $3/4 \times 16\pi = 12\pi$.

5.   A sector has an area of 24π and a radius of 12. What is the central angle of the sector?

      We first need to find the area of the whole circle. The radius is 12, which means the area is $\pi(12)^2 = 144\pi$. $\dfrac{24\pi}{144\pi} = \dfrac{1}{6}$, so the sector is 1/6th of the entire circle. That means that the central angle is 1/6th of 360. $1/6 \times 360 = 60$, so the central angle is 60°.

Set 1, Drill 4

1.   The area of a sector is 1/10th the area of the full circle. What is the central angle of the sector?

      If the area of the sector is 1/10th of the area of the full circle, then the central angle will be 1/10th of the degree measure of the full circle. $1/10 \times 360 = 36$, so the central angle of the sector is 36°.

2.   What is the perimeter of a sector with a radius of 5 and a central angle of 72°?

      To find the perimeter of a sector, we need to know the radius of the circle and the arc length of the sector.

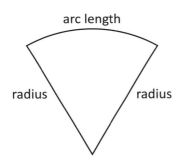

      We know the radius is 5, so now we need to find the arc length. Let's begin by determining what fraction of the circle the sector is. The central angle of the sector is 72°, so the sector is 1/5th of the circle, because $\dfrac{72}{360} = \dfrac{1}{5}$. Now we need to find the circumference. The radius is 5, so the circumference of the circle is $2\pi(5) = 10\pi$. The arc length of the sector is 1/5th the circumference. $1/5 \times 10\pi = 2\pi$. So now our sector looks like this. The perimeter of the sector is $10 + 2\pi$.

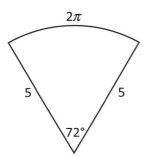

3. A sector has a radius of 8 and an area of 8π. What is the arc length of the sector?

    We first need to find what fraction of the circle the sector is. We can do this by comparing areas. The radius of the circle is 8, so the area of the circle is $\pi(8)^2 = 64\pi$. That means the sector is 1/8th of the circle, because $\dfrac{8\pi}{64\pi} = \dfrac{1}{8}$. If we want to find the arc length of the sector, we need to know the circumference. The radius is 8, so the circumference is $2\pi(8) = 16\pi$. The sector is 1/8th of the circle, so the arc length will be 1/8th of the circumference. $1/8 \times 16\pi = 2\pi$. The arc length of the sector is 2π.

4. A sector has an arc length of $\pi/2$ and a central angle of 45°. What is the radius of the sector?

    If the sector has a central angle of 45°, then the sector is 1/8th of the circle, because $\dfrac{45}{360} = \dfrac{1}{8}$. If the sector is 1/8th of the circle, then that means the arc length of the sector is 1/8th of the circumference of the circle. That means that $\pi/2$ is 1/8th of the circumference. If we designate x as the circumference of the circle, then we can say that $\dfrac{\pi}{2} = \dfrac{1}{8}x$. Multiply both sides by 8, and we get $4\pi = x$. That means the circumference is 4π. We know the formula for circumference, so we know that $4\pi = 2\pi r$. Divide both sides by 2π and we get $r = 2$. The radius of the sector is 2.

5. Which of the following two sectors has a larger area? Sector A has a radius of 4 and a central angle of 90°. Sector B has a radius of 6 and a central angle of 45°.

    We need to find the area of each circle. Sector A is 1/4th of the circle, because $\dfrac{90}{360} = \dfrac{1}{4}$. The radius is 4, so the area of the circle is $\pi(4)^2 = 16\pi$. That means the area of Sector A is 1/4th of 16π. $1/4 \times 16\pi = 4\pi$, so the area of Sector A is 4π.

    Sector B is 1/8th of the circle, because $\dfrac{45}{360} = \dfrac{1}{8}$. The radius of Sector B is 8, so the area of the full circle is $\pi(6)^2 = 36\pi$. Sector B is 1/8th of the circle, so the area of Sector B is $1/8 \times 36\pi = 4.5\pi$. The area of Sector B is 4.5π.

    $4.5\pi > 4\pi$, so the area of Sector B is greater than the area of Sector A.

DRILL SET 2:

Set 2, Drill 1

1. A triangle has two sides with lengths of 5 and 11, respectively. What is the range of values for the length of the third side?

    The lengths of any two sides of a triangle must add up to greater than the length of the third side. The third side must be less than $5 + 11 = 16$. It must also be greater than $11 - 5 = 6$. Therefore, $6 <$ third side < 16.

*Manhattan*GMAT Prep
the new standard

2.   In a right triangle, the length of one of the legs is 3 and the length of the hypotenuse is 5. What is the length of the other leg?

If you know the lengths of two sides of a right triangle, you can use the Pythagorean Theorem to solve for the length of the third side. Remember that the hypotenuse must be the side labeled c in the equation $a^2 + b^2 = c^2$. That means that $(3)^2 + (b)^2 = (5)^2$. $9 + b^2 = 25$. $b^2 = 16$, so $b = 4$.

Alternatively, you can recognize the Pythagorean triplet. This is a 3–4–5 triangle.

3.   What is the area of Triangle *DEF*?

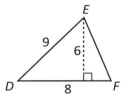

The area of a triangle is ¹/₂ base × height. Remember that the base and the height must be perpendicular to each other. That means that in Triangle *DEF*, side *DF* can act as the base, and the line dropping straight down from point *E* to touch side *DF* at a right angle can act as the base. Therefore Area = ¹/₂ (8) × (6) = 24.

4.   Which side of Triangle *GHI* has the longest length?

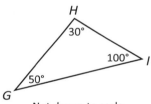

Not drawn to scale.

Although *GI* looks like the longest side, remember that you can't trust what the picture looks like when the question states the picture is not drawn to scale. In any triangle, the longest side will be opposite the larger angle. Angle *GIH* is the largest angle in the triangle, and side *GH* is thus the longest side.

5.   What is the value of *x*?

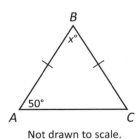

Not drawn to scale.

If you know the other 2 angles in a triangle, then you can find the third, because all 3 angles must add up to 180. In Triangle *ABC*, sides *AB* and *BC* are equal. That means their opposite angles are also equal. That means that angle *ACB* is also 50°.

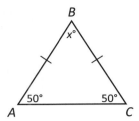

Now that we know the other 2 angles, we can find angle *x*. We know that 50 + 50 + *x* = 180, so *x* = 80.

Set 2, Drill 2

1.   Two sides of a triangle have lengths 4 and 8. Which of the following are possible side lengths of the third side? (More than one may apply)

a. 2   b. 4   c. 6   d. 8

The lengths of any two sides of a triangle must add up to greater than the length of the third side. The third side must be less than 4 + 8 = 12 and greater than 8 − 4 = 4. So 4 < third side < 12. Only choices c. and d. are in that range.

2.   *DFG* is a straight line. What is the value of *x*?

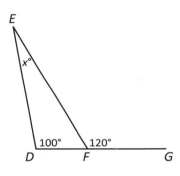

To find the value of *x*, we need to find the degree measures of the other two angles in Triangle *DEF*. We can make use of the fact that *DFG* is a straight line. Straight lines have a degree measure of 180, so angle *DFE* + 120 = 180, which means angle *DFE* = 60.

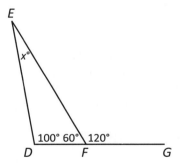

Now we can solve for *x*, because 100 + 60 + *x* = 180. Solving for *x*, we get *x* = 20.

3.   Isosceles triangle *ABC* has two sides with lengths 3 and 9. What is the length of the third side?

It may at first appear like we don't have enough information to answer this question. If all we know is that the triangle is isosceles, then all we know is that two sides have equal length, which means the third side has a length of either 3 or 9.

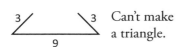

But if the third side were 3, then the lengths of two of the sides would not add up to greater than the length of the third side, because 3 + 3 is not greater than 9.

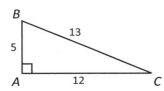

3 / \ 3   Can't make
     9   a triangle.

3 |‾‾‾9‾‾‾>   Can make a
     9   triangle.

That means that the length of the third side must be 9.

4. Which of the following could be the length of side *AB*, if $x < y < z$?

    a. 6   b. 10   c. 14

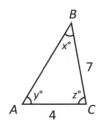

There are two properties of a triangle at play here. The lengths of any two sides of a triangle must add up to greater than the length of the third side. Also, longer sides must be opposite larger angles. Answer choice a. is out because side *AB* is opposite the largest angle, so side *AB* must have a length greater than 7. Answer choice c. is out, because 4 + 7 = 11, so the third side has to be less than 11. The only remaining possibility is b. 10.

5. What is the area of right triangle *ABC*?

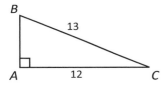

To find the area, we need a base and a height. If we can find the length of side *AB*, then *AB* can be the height and *AC* can be the base, because the two sides are perpendicular to each other.

We can use the Pythagorean Theorem to find the length of side *AB*. $(a)^2 + (12)^2 = (13)^2$. $a^2 + 144 = 169$. $a^2 = 25$. $a = 5$. Alternatively, we could recognize that the triangle is a Pythagorean triplet 5–12–13.

Now that we know the length of side *AB* we can find the area. Area = $^1/_2(12) \times (5) = 30$.

B
    13
5
  ⌐
A   12   *C*

Set 2, Drill 3

1.   What is the perimeter of triangle *ABC*?

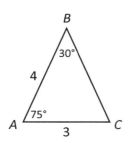

To find the perimeter of Triangle *ABC*, we need the lengths of all 3 sides. There is no immediately obvious way to find the length of side *BC*, so let's see what inferences we can make from the information the question gave us.

We know the degree measures of two of the angles in Triangle *ABC*, so we can find the degree measure of the third. We'll label the third angle *x*. We know that $30 + 75 + x = 180$. Solving for *x* we find that *x* = 75.

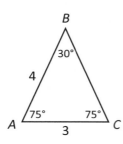

Angle *BAC* and angle *BCA* are both 75, which means Triangle *ABC* is an isosceles triangle. If those two angles are equal, we know that their opposite sides are also equal. Side *AB* has a length of 4, so we know that *BC* also has a length of 4.

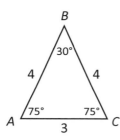

To find the perimeter, we add up the lengths of the three sides. $4 + 4 + 3 = 11$.

2.   The area of right triangle *ABC* is 15. What is the length of hypotenuse *BC*?

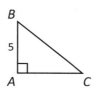

To find the length of the hypotenuse, we need the lengths of the other two sides. Then we can use the Pythagorean Theorem to find the length of the hypotenuse. We can use the area formula to find the length of *AC*. Area = $\frac{1}{2}$ base × height, and we know the area and the height. So $15 = \frac{1}{2}$ (base) × (5). When we solve this equation, we find that the base = 6.

Now we can use the Pythagorean Theorem. $(5)^2 + (6)^2 = c^2$. $25 + 36 = c^2$. $61 = c^2$. $\sqrt{61} = c$. Since 61 is not a perfect square, we know that *c* will be a decimal. 61 is also prime, so we cannot simplify $\sqrt{61}$ any further. (It will be a little less than $\sqrt{64} = 8$.)

*Manhattan*GMAT*Prep
the new standard

3.   What is the length of side *HI*?

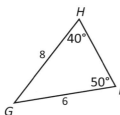

Not drawn to scale.

There is no immediately obvious way to find the length of side *HI*, so let's see what we can infer from the picture. We know two of the angles of Triangle *GHI*, so we can find the third. We'll label the third angle *x*. $40 + 50 + x = 180$. That means $x = 90$. So really our triangle looks like this:

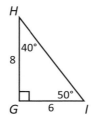

You should definitely redraw once you discover the triangle is a right triangle!

Now that we know Triangle *GHI* is a right triangle, we can use the Pythagorean Theorem to find the length of *HI*. *HI* is the hypotenuse, so $(6)^2 + (8)^2 = c^2$. $36 + 64 = c^2$. $100 = c^2$. $10 = c$. The length of *HI* is 10.

Alternatively, we could have recognized the Pythagorean triplet. Triangle *GHI* is a 6–8–10 triangle.

4.   Which triangle has the greater perimeter?

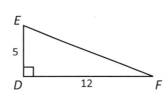

To determine which triangle has the greater perimeter, we need to know the side lengths of all three sides of both triangles. Let's begin with Triangle *ABC*.

There's no immediate way to find the lengths of the missing sides, so let's start by seeing what we can infer from the picture. We know two of the angles, so we can find the third. We'll label the unknown angle *x*. $60 + 60 + x = 180$. $x = 60$.

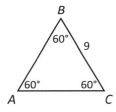

All three angles in Triangle *ABC* are 60°. If all three angles are equal, that means all three sides are equal in this equilateral triangle. So every side of Triangle *ABC* has a length of 9. That means the perimeter = $9 + 9 + 9 = 27$.

Now let's look at Triangle *DEF*. Triangle *DEF* is a right triangle, so we can use the Pythagorean Theorem to find the length of side *EF*. *EF* is the hypotenuse, so $(5)^2 + (12)^2 = c^2$. $25 + 144 = c^2$. $169 = c^2$. $13 = c$. That means the perimeter is $5 + 12 + 13 = 30$. Alternatively, 5–12–13 is a Pythagorean triplet.

$30 > 27$, so Triangle *DEF* has a greater perimeter than Triangle *ABC*.

the new standard

5.   *WZ* has a length of 3 and *ZX* has a length of 6. What is the area of Triangle *XYZ*?

Let's start by filling in everything we know about Triangle *XYZ*.

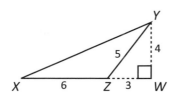

To find the area of Triangle *XYZ*, we need a base and a height. If Side *XZ* is a base, then *YW* can act as a height. We can find the length of *YW* because Triangle *ZYW* is a right triangle, and we know the lengths of two of the sides. *YZ* is the hypotenuse, so $(a)^2 + (3)^2 = (5)^2$. $a^2 + 9 = 25$. $a^2 = 16$. $a = 4$.

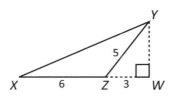

Alternatively, we could recognize the Pythagorean triplet: *ZYW* is a 3–4–5 triangle.

Now we know that the area of Triangle *XYZ* is $\frac{1}{2}b \times h = \frac{1}{2}(6) \times (4) = 12$.

DRILL SET 3:

Set 3, Drill 1

1.   What is the perimeter of parallelogram *ABCD*?

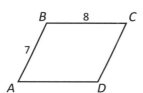

Opposite sides of a parallelogram are equal, so we know that side *CD* has a length of 7 and side *AD* has a length of 8. So the perimeter is $7 + 8 + 7 + 8 = 30$.

Alternatively, the perimeter is $2 \times (7 + 8) = 30$. We can say this because we know that 2 sides have a length of 7 and 2 sides have a length of 8.

2.   What is the area of parallelogram *EFGH*?

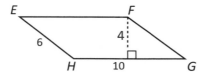

The area of a parallelogram is base × height. In this parallelogram, the base is 10 and the height is 4 (remember, base and height need to be perpendicular). So the area is $10 \times 4 = 40$.

3.   The two parallelograms pictured below have the same perimeter. What is the length of side *EH*?

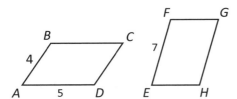

First we can find the perimeter of Parallelogram *ABCD*. We know that 2 sides have a length of 4, and 2 sides have a length of 5. The perimeter is $2 \times (4 + 5) = 18$. That means Parallelogram *EFGH* also has a perimeter of 18. We know side *GH* also has a length of 7. We don't know the lengths of the other 2 sides, but we know they have the same length, so for now let's say the length of each side is *x*. Our parallelogram now looks like this:

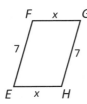

So we know that $7 + x + 7 + x = 18$ → $2x + 14 = 18$ → $2x = 4$ → $x = 2$

The length of side *EH* is 2.

4.   In Parallelogram *ABCD*, Triangle *ABC* has an area of 12. What is the area of Triangle *ACD*?

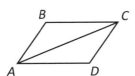

One property that is true of any parallelogram is that the diagonal will split the parallelogram into two equal triangles. If Triangle *ABC* has an area of 12, then Triangle *ACD* must also have an area of 12.

5.   Rectangle *WXYZ* and Rectangle *OPQR* have equal areas. What is the length of side *PQ*?

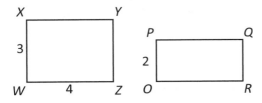

We can start by finding the area of Rectangle *WXYZ*. Area of a rectangle is length × width, so the area of Rectangle *WXYZ* is $3 \times 4 = 12$. So Rectangle *OPQR* also has an area of 12. We know the length of side *OP*, so that is the width of Rectangle *OPQR*. So now we know the area, and we know the width, so we can solve for the length. $l \times 2 = 12 \rightarrow l = 6$. The length of side *PQ* is 6.

Set 3, Drill 2

1.   What is the area of Rectangle *ABCD*?

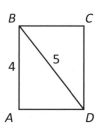

To find the area of Rectangle *ABCD*, we need to know the length of *AD* or *BC*. In a rectangle, every internal angle is 90 degrees, so Triangle *ABD* is actually a right triangle. That means we can use the Pythagorean Theorem to find the length of side *AD*. Actually, this right triangle is one of the Pythagorean Triplets—a 3–4–5 triangle. The length of side *AD* is 3. That means the area of Rectangle *ABCD* is $3 \times 4 = 12$.

2.   In Rectangle *ABCD*, the area of Triangle *ABC* is 30. What is the length of diagonal *AC*?

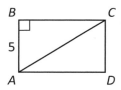

We know the area of Triangle *ABC* and the length of side *AB*. Because side *BC* is perpendicular to side *AB*, we can use those as the base and height of Triangle *ABC*. So we know that $\frac{1}{2}(5) \times (BC) = 30$. That means the length of side *BC* is 12.

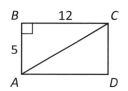

Now we can use the Pythagorean Theorem to find the length of diagonal *AC*, which is the hypotenuse of right triangle *ABC*. We can also recognize that this is a Pythagorean Triplet—a 5–12–13 triangle. The length of diagonal *AC* is 13.

3.   Rectangles *ABCD* and *EFGH* have equal areas. What is the length of side *FG*?

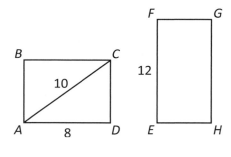

The first thing to notice in this problem is that we can find the length of side *CD*. Triangle *ACD* is a right triangle, and we know the lengths of two of the sides. We can either use the Pythagorean Theorem or recognize that this is one of our Pythagorean Triplets—a 6–8–10 triangle. The length of side *CD* is 6. Now we can find the area of Rectangle *ABCD*. Side *AD* is the length and side *CD* is the width. $8 \times 6 = 48$.

That means that the area of Rectangle *EFGH* is also 48. We can use the area and the length of side *EF* to solve for the length of side *FG*. $12 \times (FG) = 48$. The length of side *FG* is 4.

4.   A rectangle has a perimeter of 10 and an area of 6. What are the length and width of the rectangle?

In order to answer this question, let's begin by drawing a rectangle. In this rectangle, we'll make one pair of equal sides have a length of x, and the other pair of equal sides has a length of y.

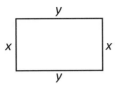

Using the lengths x and y, we know the perimeter of the rectangle is $2x + 2y$. So we know that:

    $2x + 2y = 10$ This can be simplified to $\boldsymbol{x + y = 5}$.

We also know the area of the rectangle is $xy = 6$.

    $\boldsymbol{xy = 6}$ Area of the rectangle $= l \times w = 6$

Now we can use substitution to solve for the values of our variables. In the first equation, we can isolate x.

    $x = 5 - y$

Substitute $(5 - y)$ for x in the second equation.

    $(5 - y)y = 6$
    $5y - y^2 = 6$ This is a quadratic, so we need to get everything on one side.
    $y^2 - 5y + 6 = 0$ Now we can factor the equation.
    $(y - 3)(y - 2) = 0$

                 So $y = 2$ or 3.

When we plug in these values to solve for x, we find something a little unusual. When $y = 2$, $x = 3$. When $y = 3$, $x = 2$. What that means is that either the length is 2 and the width is 3, or the length is 3 and the width is 2. Both of these rectangles are identical, so we have our answer.

5.   Triangle *XYZ* and Rectangle *JKLM* have equal areas. What is the perimeter of Rectangle *JKLM*?

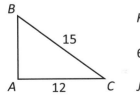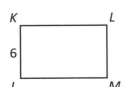

If we can find the length of side *AB*, then we can find the area of Triangle *ABC*. We can use the Pythagorean Theorem to find the length of side *AB*. $(12)^2 + (AB)^2 = (15)^2$ → $144 + AB^2 = 225$ → $AB^2 = 81$ → $AB = 9$. (A 9–12–15 triangle is a 3–4–5 triangle, with all the measurements tripled.)

Now that we know *AB*, we can find the area of Triangle *ABC*. It's $^1/_2(12) \times 9 = 54$.

That means that Rectangle *JKLM* also has an area of 54. We have one side of the rectangle, so we can solve for the other. $6 \times (JM) = 54$. So the length of side *JM* is 9. That means that the perimeter is $2 \times (6 + 9) = 30$.

Set 3, Drill 3

1.   What is the perimeter of a square with an area of 25?

     A square has four equal sides, so the area of a square is the length of one side squared. That means the lengths of the sides of the square are 5. If each of the four sides has a length of 5, then the perimeter is $4 \times (5) = 20$.

2.   A rectangle and a square have the same area. The square has a perimeter of 32 and the rectangle has a length of 4. What is the width of the rectangle?

     We should start by drawing the shapes that they describe.

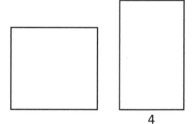

The square has four equal sides, so that means that the perimeter is 4 times the length of one side. If we designate the length of the sides of the square *s*, then the perimeter is $4s = 32$. That means that *s* is 8. Now that we know the length of the sides, we can figure out the area of the square. Area $= 8^2$. So the area of the square is 64.

     That means that the area of the rectangle is also 64. We know the length of the rectangle is 4, so we can solve for the width. $4 \times (width) = 64$. The width is 16.

3.   A circle is inscribed inside a square, so that the circle touches all four sides of the square. The length of one of the sides of the square is 9. What is the area of the circle?

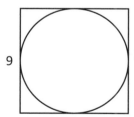

We need to find a common link between the square and the circle, so that we can find the area of the circle. We know that the length of the sides of the square is 9. We can draw a new line in our figure that has the same length as the sides AND is the diameter of the circle.

*Manhattan*GMAT*Prep
the new standard

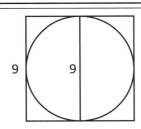

That means that the diameter of the circle is 9. If the diameter is 9, then the radius is 4.5. That means the area of the circle is $\pi(4.5)^2$, which equals 20.25π.

4.   Square *ABCD* has an area of 49. What is the length of diagonal *AC*?

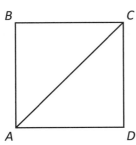

If the square has an area of 49, then (side)^2 = 49. That means that the length of the sides of the square is 7. So our square looks like this:

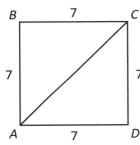

Now we can use the Pythagorean Theorem to find the length of diagonal *AC*, which is also the hypotenuse of Triangle *ACD*. $7^2 + 7^2 = (AC)^2$ → $98 = (AC)^2$ → $\sqrt{98} = AC$. But this can be simplified. $AC = \sqrt{2 \times 49} = \sqrt{2 \times 7 \times 7} = 7\sqrt{2}$.

5.   Right Triangle *ABC* and Rectangle *EFGH* have the same perimeter. What is the value of *x*?

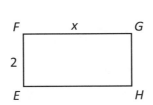

Triangle *ABC* is a right triangle, so we can find the length of hypotenuse *BC*. This is a 3–4–5 triangle, so the length of side *BC* is 5. That means the perimeter of Triangle *ABC* is 3 + 4 + 5 = 12.

That means the perimeter of Rectangle *EFGH* is also 12. That means that $2 \times (2 + x)$ = 12. So 4 + 2x = 12 → 2x = 8 → x = 4.

<u>DRILL SET 4:</u>

Set 4, Drill 1

1.   Draw a coordinate plane and plot the following points:
        1. (2, 3)   2. (−2, −1)   3. (−5, −6)   4. (4, −2.5)

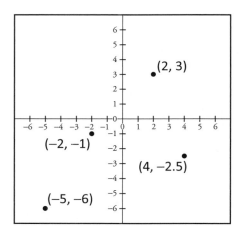

2.   *A*: (3, 0)   *B*: (−3, 2)   *C*: (1, −5)   *D*: (0, −3)

3.   The *y*-coordinate of the point on the line that has an *x*-coordinate of 3 is −4. The point is (3, −4). If you want, you can determine that the line has a slope of −1 from the two labeled points that the line intercepts, (−1, 0) and (0, −1).

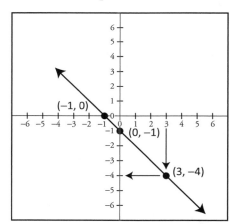

4. The *x*-coordinate of the point on the line that has a *y*-coordinate of −4 is −2. The point is (−2, −4). If you want, you can determine that the line has a slope of −2 from the two labeled points that the line intercepts, (−4, 0) and (−3, −2).

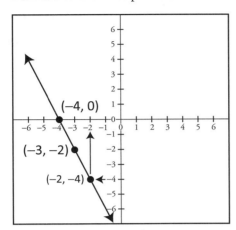

5. For the point (3, −2) to lie on the line $y = 2x − 8$, *y* needs to equal −2 when we plug in 3 for *x*.

$y = 2(3) − 8$
$y = 6 − 8 = −2$
y does equal −2 when *x* equals 3, so the point does lie on the line.

Set 4, Drill 2

1. For the point (−3, 0) to lie on the curve $y = x^2 − 3$, *y* needs to equal 0 when we plug in −3 for *x*.

$y = (−3)^2 − 3$
$y = 9 − 3 = 6$
y does not equal 0 when *x* equals −3, so the point does not lie on the curve.

2. To find the *y*-coordinate, we need to plug in 3 for *x* and solve for *y*.

$y = 4(3) + 2$
$y = 12 + 2 = 14$
The *y*-coordinate is 14. The point is (3, 14).

3. The equation of the line is already in $y = mx + b$ form, and b stands for the *y*-intercept, so we just need to look at the equation to find the *y*-intercept. The equation is $y = −2x − 7$. That means the *y*-intercept is −7. The point is (0, −7).

4.   Graph the line $y = \frac{1}{3}x - 4$

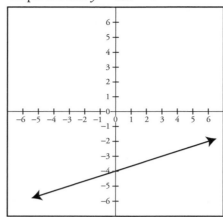

The slope (m) is 1/3, so the line slopes gently up to the right, rising only 1 unit for every 3 units of run.

The y-intercept (b) is −4, so the line crosses the y-axis at (0, −4).

5.   Graph the line $\frac{1}{2}y = -\frac{1}{2}x + 1$.

Before we can graph the line, we need to put the equation into $y = mx + b$ form. Multiply both sides by 2.

$y = -x + 2$

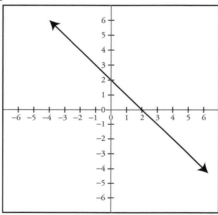

The slope (m) is −1, so the line drops to the right, falling 1 unit for every unit of run.

The y-intercept is 2, so the line crosses the y-axis at (0, 2).

Glossary

absolute value: The distance from zero on the number line for a particular term. E.g. the absolute value of −7 is 7 (written |−7|).

arc length: A section of a circle's circumference.

area: The space enclosed by a given closed shape on a plane; the formula depends on the specific shape. E.g. the area of a rectangle equals *length × width*.

axis: one of the two number lines (*x*-axis or *y*-axis) used to indicate position on a coordinate plane.

base: In the expression b^n, the variable b represents the base. This is the number that we multiply by itself n times. Also can refer to the horizontal side of a triangle.

center (circle): The point from which any point on a circle's radius is equidistant.

central angle: The angle created by any two radii.

circle: A set of points in a plane that are equidistant from a fixed center point.

circumference: The measure of the perimeter of a circle. The circumference of a circle can be found with this formula: $C = 2\pi r$, where C is the circumference and r is the radius.

coefficient: A number being multiplied by a variable. In the equation $y = 2x + 5$, the coefficient of the x term is 2.

common denominator: When adding or subtracting fractions, we first must find a common denominator, generally the smallest common multiple of both numbers.

Example:

> Given (3/5) + (1/2), the two denominators are 5 and 2. The smallest multiple that works for both numbers is 10. The common denominator, therefore, is 10.

composite number: Any number that has more than 2 factors.

constant: A number that doesn't change, in an equation or expression. We may not know its value, but it's "constant" in contrast to a variable, which varies. In the equation $y = 3x + 2$, 3 and 2 are constants. In the equation $y = mx + b$, m and b are constants (just unknown).

coordinate plane: Consists of a horizontal axis (typically labeled "*x*") and a vertical axis (typically labeled "*y*"), crossing at the number zero on both axes.

decimal: numbers that fall in between integers. A decimal can express a part–to–whole relationship, just as a percent or fraction can.

Example:

> 1.2 is a decimal. The integers 1 and 2 are not decimals. An integer written as 1.0, however, is considered a decimal. The decimal 0.2 is equivalent to 20% or to 2/10 (= 1/5).

denominator: The bottom of a fraction. In the fraction (7/2), 2 is the denominator.

diameter: A line segment that passes through the center of a circle and whose endpoints lie on the circle.

difference: When one number is subtracted from another, the difference is what is left over. The difference of 7 and 5 is 2, because $7 - 5 = 2$.

digit: The ten numbers 0, 1, 2, 3, 4, 5, 6, 7, 8, and 9. Used in combination to represent other numbers (e.g., 12 or 0.38).

distributed form: Presenting an expression as a sum or difference. In distributed form, terms are added or subtracted. $x^2 - 1$ is in distributed form, as is $x^2 + 2x + 1$. In contrast, $(x + 1)(x - 1)$ is not in distributed form; it is in factored form.

divisible: If an integer x divided by another number y yields an integer, then x is said to be divisible by y.

Example:

> 12 divided by 3 yields the integer 4. Therefore, 12 is divisible by 3. 12 divided by 5 does not yield an integer. Therefore, 12 is not divisible by 5.

divisor: The part of a division operation that comes after the division sign. In the operation $22 \div 4$ (or 22/4), 4 is the divisor. Divisor is also a synonym for factor. See: factor

equation: A combination of mathematical expressions and symbols that contains an equals sign. $3 + 7 = 10$ is an equation, as is $x + y = 3$. An equation makes a statement: left side equals right side

equilateral triangle: A triangle in which all three angles are equal; in addition, all three sides are of equal length.

even: An integer is even if it is divisible by 2. 14 is even because 14/2 = an integer (7).

exponent: In the expression b^n, the variable n represents the exponent. The exponent indicates how many times to multiple the base, b, by itself. For example, $4^3 = 4 \times 4 \times 4$, or 4 multiplied by itself three times.

expression: A combination of numbers and mathematical symbols that does not contain an equals sign. xy is an expression, as is $x + 3$. An expression represents a quantity.

factored form: Presenting an expression as a product. In factored form, expressions are multiplied together. The expression $(x + 1)(x - 1)$ is in factored form: $(x + 1)$ and $(x - 1)$ are the factors. In contrast, $x^2 - 1$ is not in factored form; it is in distributed form.

factor: Positive integers that divide evenly into an integer. Factors are equal to or smaller than the integer in question. 12 is a factor of 12, as are 1, 2, 3, 4, and 6.

factor foundation rule: If a is a factor of b, and b is a factor of c, then a is also a factor of c. For example, 2 is a factor of 10. 10 is a factor of 60. Therefore, 2 is also a factor of 60.

factor tree: Use the "factor tree" to break any number down into its prime factors. For example:

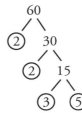

FOIL: First, Outside, Inside, Last; an acronym to remember the method for converting from factored to distributed form in a quadratic equation or expression. $(x + 2)(x - 3)$ is a quadratic expression in factored form. Multiply the First, Outside, Inside, and Last terms to get the distributed form. $x \times x = x^2$, $x \times -3 = -3x$, $x \times 2 = 2x$, and $2 \times -3 = -6$. The full distributed form is $x^2 - 3x + 2x - 6$. This can be simplified to $x^2 - x - 6$.

fraction: A way to express numbers that fall in between integers (though integers can also be expressed in fractional form). A fraction expresses a part-to-whole relationship in terms of a numerator (the part) and a denominator (the whole). (E.g. 3/4 is a fraction.)

hypotenuse: The longest side of a right triangle. The hypotenuse is opposite the right angle.

improper fraction: Fractions that are greater than 1. An improper can also be written as a mixed number. (7/2) is an improper fraction. This can also be written as a mixed number: $3^1/_2$.

inequality: A comparison of quantities that have different values. There are four ways to express inequalities: less than (<), less than or equal to ($\leq$), greater than (>), or greater than or equal to ($\geq$). Can be manipulated in the same way as equations with one exception: when multiplying or dividing by a negative number, the inequality sign flips.

integers: Numbers, such as -1, 0, 1, 2, and 3, that have no fractional part. Integers include the counting numbers (1, 2, 3, …), their negative counterparts (-1, -2, -3, …), and 0.

interior angles: The angles that appear in the interior of a closed shape.

isosceles triangle: A triangle in which two of the three angles are equal; in addition, the sides opposite the two angles are equal in length.

line: A set of points that extend infinitely in one direction without curving. On the GMAT, lines are by definition perfectly straight.

line segment: A continuous, finite section of a line. The sides of a triangle or of a rectangle are line segments.

linear equation: An equation that does not contain exponents or multiple variables multiplied together. $x + y = 3$ is a linear equation; $xy = 3$ and $y = x^2$ are not. When plotted on a coordinate plane, linear equations create lines.

mixed number: An integer combined with a proper fraction. A mixed number can also be written as an improper fraction. $3^1/_2$ is a mixed number. This can also be written as an improper fraction: (7/2).

multiple: Multiples are integers formed by multiplying some integer by any other integer. 12 is a multiple of 12 (12×1), as are 24 ($= 12 \times 2$), 36 ($= 12 \times 3$), 48 ($= 12 \times 4$), and 60 ($= 12 \times 5$). (Negative multiples are possible in mathematics but are not typically tested on the GMAT.)

negative: Any number to the left of zero on a number line; can be integer or non-integer.

negative exponent: Any exponent less than zero. To find a value for a term with a negative exponent, put the term containing the exponent in the denominator of a fraction and make the exponent positive. $4^{-2} = 1/4^2$. $1/3^{-2} = 1/(1/3)^2 = 3^2 = 9$.

number line: A picture of a straight line that represents all the numbers from negative infinity to infinity.

numerator: The top of a fraction. In the fraction, $(7/2)$, 7 is the numerator.

odd: An odd integer is not divisible by 2. 15 is not even because 15/2 is not an integer (7.5).

order of operations: The order in which mathematical operations must be carried out in order to simplify an expression. (See PEMDAS)

the origin: The coordinate pair $(0,0)$ represents the origin of a coordinate plane.

parallelogram: A four-sided closed shape composed of straight lines in which the opposite sides are equal and the opposite angles are equal.

PEMDAS: An acronym that stands for Parentheses, Exponents, Multiplication, Division, Addition, Subtraction, used to remember the order of operations.

percent: Literally, "per one hundred"; expresses a special part-to-whole relationship between a number (the part) and one hundred (the whole). A special type of fraction or decimal that involves the number 100. (E.g. 50% = 50 out of 100.)

perimeter: In a polygon, the sum of the lengths of the sides.

perpendicular: Lines that intersect at a 90° angle.

plane: A flat, two-dimensional surface that extends infinitely in every direction.

point: An object that exists in a single location on the coordinate plane. Each point has a unique x-coordinate and y-coordinate that together describe its location. (E.g. $(1, -2)$ is a point.

polygon: A two-dimensional, closed shape made of line segments. For example, a triangle is a polygon, as is a rectangle. A circle is a closed shape, but it is not a polygon because it does not contain line segments.

positive: Any number to the right of zero on a number line; can be integer or non-integer.

prime factorization: A number expressed as a product of prime numbers. For example, the prime factorization of 60 is $2 \times 2 \times 3 \times 5$.

prime number: A positive integer with exactly two factors: 1 and itself. The number 1 does not qualify as prime because it has only one factor, not two. The number 2 is the smallest prime number; it is also the only even prime number. The numbers 2, 3, 5, 7, 11, 13 etc. are prime.

product: The end result when two numbers are multiplied together. (E.g. the product of 4 and 5 is 20.

Pythagorean Theorem: A formula used to calculate the sides of a right triangle. $a^2 + b^2 = c^2$, where a and b are the lengths of the two legs of the triangle and c is the length of the hypotenuse of the triangle.

Pythagorean triplet: A set of 3 numbers that describe the lengths of the 3 sides of a right triangle in which all 3 sides have integer lengths. Common Pythagorean triplets are 3–4–5, 6–8–10 and 5–12–13.

quadrant: One quarter of the coordinate plane. Bounded on two sides by the x- and y-axes.

quadratic expression: An expression including a variable raised to the second power (and no higher powers). Commonly of the form $ax^2 + bx + c$, where a, b, and c are constants.

quotient: The result of dividing one number by another. The quotient of $10 \div 5$ is 2.

radius: A line segment that connects the center of a circle with any point on that circle's circumference. Plural: radii.

reciprocal: The product of a number and its reciprocal is always 1. To get the reciprocal of an integer, put that integer on the denominator of a fraction with numerator 1. The reciprocal of 3 is (1/3). To get the reciprocal of a fraction, switch the numerator and the denominator. The reciprocal of (2/3) is (3/2).

rectangle: A four-sided closed shape in which all of the angles equal 90° and in which the opposite sides are equal. Rectangles are also parallelograms.

right triangle: A triangle that includes a 90°, or right, angle.

root: The opposite of an exponent (in a sense). The square root of 16 (written $\sqrt{16}$) is the number (or numbers) that, when multiplied by itself, will yield 16. In this case, both 4 and −4 would multiply to 16 mathematically. However, when the GMAT provides the root sign for an even root, such as a square root, then the only accepted answer is the positive root, 4. That is, $\sqrt{16} = 4$, NOT +4 or −4. In contrast, the equation $x^2 = 16$ has TWO solutions, +4 and −4.

sector: A "wedge" of the circle, composed of two radii and the arc connecting those two radii.

simplify: Reduce numerators and denominators to the smallest form by taking out common factors. Dividing the numerator and denominator by the same number does not change the value of the fraction.

Example:

Given (21/6), we can simplify by dividing both the numerator and the denominator by 3. The simplified fraction is (7/2).

slope: "Rise over run," or the distance the line runs vertically divided by the distance the line runs horizontally. The slope of any given line is constant over the length of that line.

square: A four-sided closed shape in which all of the angles equal 90° and all of the sides are equal. Squares are also rectangles and parallelograms.

sum: The result when two numbers are added together. The sum of 4 and 7 is 11.

term: Parts within an expression or equation that are separated by either a plus sign or a minus sign. (E.g. in the expression $x + 3$, "x" and "3" are each separate terms.)

triangle: A three-sided closed shape composed of straight lines; the interior angles add up to 180°.

two-dimensional: A shape containing a length and a width.

variable: Letter used as a substitute for an unknown value, or number. Common letters for variables are x, y, z and t. In contrast to a constant, we generally think of a variable as a value that can *change* (hence the term variable). In the equation $y = 3x + 2$, both y and x are variables.

x-axis: A horizontal number line that indicates left–right position on a coordinate plane.

x-coordinate: The number that indicates where a point lies along the x-axis. Always written first in parentheses. The x-coordinate of $(2, -1)$ is 2.

x-intercept: The point where a line crosses the x-axis (that is, when $y = 0$).

y-axis: A vertical number line that indicates up–down position on a coordinate plane.

y-coordinate: The number that indicates where a point lies along the y-axis. Always written second in parentheses. The y-coordinate of $(2, -1)$ is -1.

y-intercept: the point where a line crosses the y-axis (that is, when $x = 0$). In the equation of a line $y = mx + b$, the y-intercept equals b. Technically, the coordinates of the y-intercept are $(0, b)$.

Different Exam,
Same Standard of Excellence

From the teachers who created Manhattan GMAT, the Atlas LSAT Strategy Guides deliver the same standard of excellence to students to students studying for the LSAT.

Every Guide uses real LSAT questions and delves deeply into one section of the LSAT exam. Together, the Strategy Guides form the heart of our advanced, flexible curriculum, featuring techniques geared towards students aiming for top scores on the LSAT.

SAVE 10%
When you buy a Guide from
AtlasLSAT.com. Use code:
MGMAT10GUIDE

Focus and Breadth:

Atlas LSAT Guides can be stand-alone courses-in-a book, going far beyond a simple textbook.

Free LSAT Tutoring:

Receive a free hour of LSAT tutoring online!

Online Resources:

Access to a Proctor LSAT Video, study syllabus, a 3-hour LSAT Class, and more.

Student Testimonials

"The [Strategy Guides] were extremely helpful. Providing many different examples and different methods of approaching problems made the curricular materials an amazing help." – Atlas LSAT Online Student, 2009

"The Strategy Guides were excellent, so much better than any other books I've used. I liked that the material was so concise and allowed you to practice questions in detail." – Atlas LSAT Online Student, 2009